THE TAMING OF THE WEST
AGE OF THE
GUNFIGHTER

Colt Model 1851 revolvers, cased set,
possibly owned by Samuel Colt.

THE TAMING OF THE WEST
AGE OF THE
GUNFIGHTER

MEN AND WEAPONS ON THE FRONTIER 1840-1900
JOSEPH G. ROSA
WITH ARTIFACTS FROM THE GENE AUTRY WESTERN HERITAGE MUSEUM
AND THE BUFFALO BILL HISTORICAL CENTER

*Winchester Model 1873 with .44 caliber
cartridges; man's hat.*

SMITHMARK

A SALAMANDER BOOK

This edition published in 1993 by SMITHMARK Publishers,
a division of U.S. Media Holdings, Inc., 16 East 32nd Street, New York, NY 10016

7 9 8

SMITHMARK books are available for bulk purchase for sales promotion and premium use. For details write or call the manager of special sales, SMITHMARK Publishers, 16 East 32nd Street, New York, NY 10016: (212) 532-6600

All correspondence concerning the content of this volume should be addressed to Salamander Books Ltd, 129–137 York Way, London N7 9LG, England

Library of Congress Cataloging-in-Publication Data

Rosa, Joseph G.
    The taming of the West: age of the gunfighter: men and weapons on the frontier, 1840–1900 / Joseph G. Rosa.
       p.   cm.
    Includes bibliographical references.
    ISBN 0-8317-0381-4: $24.98
    1. Frontier and pioneer life — West (U.S.)   2. Outlaws — West
(U.S.) — History — 19th century.   3. West (U.S.) — History.   I. Title.
F596.R835   1993   93-13920
978 — dc20   CIP

CREDITS

Editor: Richard Collins   **Designer:** Mark Holt
Color photography: Don Eiler, Richmond, Virginia © Salamander Books Ltd   **Line artwork:** Kevin Jones Associates © Salamander Books Ltd
Maps: Janos Marffy © Salamander Books Ltd   **Filmset:** SX Composing DTP, England   **Color reproduction:** Scantrans PTE, Singapore
Printed in Italy

ACKNOWLEDGMENTS

Salamander Books are grateful to the Buffalo Bill Historical Center, Cody, Wyoming, and the Gene Autry Western Heritage Museum, Los Angeles, California, for giving permission to photograph artifacts from their extensive collections. (Separate acknowledgments to each museum accompany color spreads within the book.) The editor would particularly like to thank the following for their help and expertise.

In Cody:
Peter Hassrick (Director), Dr Paul Fees (Senior Curator), Howard Madaus (Curator, Cody Firearms Museum), Frances Clymer (Curatorial Assistant, Cody Firearms Museum), Connie Marie Vunk (Collections Manager), Devendra Shrikhande (Photographer), Susie Ludwig and Candy Whitt (Packers).

Howard Madaus selected all the pieces for inclusion in the BBHC spreads and supplied textual information.

In Los Angeles:
Mrs Joanne D. Hale (Chief Executive Officer and Director), James H. Nottage (Chief Curator), Mary Ellen Nottage (Collections Manager) and Jim Wilke (Assistant Curator).

James Nottage also selected all the pieces for inclusion in the Gene Autry Museum spreads and wrote the accompanying text.

The author and editor are grateful to the following for so readily sending photographs from their private collections for inclusion in this book: Robert G. McCubbin, Harry E. Chrisman, Fred E. Egloff, Thomas P. Sweeney, MD., and Jack DeMattos. Their contributions are noted in the picture credits. Chuck Parsons also offered helpful advice.

Bob and Terry Edgar, Old Trail Town, Cody, Wyoming, kindly allowed us to take photographs in Old Trail Town and these appear on pp. 70–71, 114–15 and on the endpapers. Bob Edgar also supplied the information for the text which accompanies the photographs.

Finally, special thanks to Don Eiler, who photographed all the color spreads in this book and drove thousands of miles to do so.

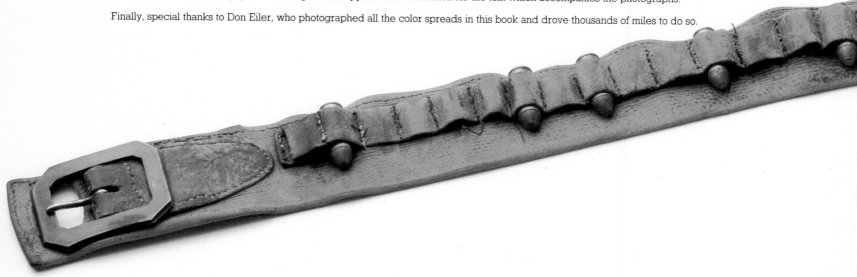

CONTENTS

Double-loop holster and belt; .45 caliber ammunition; Colt single-action Army revolver.

INTRODUCTION

The American gunfighter is unique. While it is true that he had his counterpart in Australia and South Africa during the period when both places experienced gold and diamond rushes, it was the American 'desperado' who attracted most attention. Australia's 'bush rangers' certainly emulated the Western gunfighter, and man for man was his equal, but thanks to William Frederick Cody, alias 'Buffalo Bill,' whose Wild West Show toured the world, the Indian and the cowboy captured the imagination of millions. And the cowboy's colorful dress, his pistols and daring horsemanship, quickly lent themselves to the emerging image of the gunfighter as a 'Knight Chivalric of the Plains'. However, the romantic concept of the gunfighter as a nineteenth-century knight errant has been questioned many times, for it creates an entirely false impression of the men who lived and died by the gun.

In this informal study, based upon contemporary and informed opinion, an attempt has been made to portray the gunfighter as he appeared to his contemporaries. Much of the present-day adulation heaped upon a number of noted individuals reflects a cinematic rather than an historical view. Some were admired for specific acts or because they fitted the public's idea of what a 'frontier desperado' or 'civilizer' should be. For beneath the heroic façade there lurked the stark fact that they were all killers, whether by choice or by provocation. And to suggest that they fought fair in the context of today's sense of fair play is erroneous. The business of survival meant getting the drop on an opponent, or disabling him in such a manner as to remove any further threat. This occasionally left the losers with severe gunshot wounds, gouged eyes, bitten ears, broken limbs or the additional indignity of a boot heel rammed into the face. Horrifying though that behavior may seem to modern audiences, it was an accepted hazard of frontier life.

The word 'gunfighter' can be traced back to 1874, but did not become common until the turn of the century. Most people, however, prefer the old-time description which graphically describes our subject – man-killers.

Joseph G. Rosa
Ruislip, Middlesex, England

Right: *Members of the 'Dodge City Peace Commission' pose in 1883.*

Below: *Frank Wesson's two-shot .22 caliber 'Vest Pocket' or 'Watch Fob' pistol.*

ONE

THE VIOLENT WEST

'. . . soon the cry "The Daltons! The Daltons!" echoed up and down the street. Armed citizens . . . were soon on hand, hiding themselves and laying in wait for the gang. Bob and Emmett successfully robbed the First National Bank, but when they rode to join their companions . . . they were met by a hail of bullets.'

Right: *Ed Dale, shot by one Howell, lies booted and dead in Morgan's place.*

Below: *A fine factory engraved Colt Model 1849 Pocket pistol, circa the early 1850s.*

THE GUNFIGHTER

The gunfighter is as much a part of American folklore as are the cowboy, the Indian and a host of other legendary characters whose exploits have enthralled a world-wide audience for generations. But unlike the majority of those folk heroes, the gunfighter evokes a sinister image; one that stirs emotions, arouses controversy and generates conflict. For many, he represents a knight errant fighting the dragon of crime and corruption; but to others he is the personification of evil; a character who, regardless of the circumstances, reacts to any situation with violence. In short, he is a professional killer both behind and in front of a badge.

Emphasis on the gunfighter's killer instinct has provoked some alarming reactions among today's pundits. Any civil unrest or violent behaviour involving firearms is seized upon by the media as a return to the 'Wild West' and its so-called lawlessness. But set against the harsh realities of the modern world with all its foibles and faults, such reasoning seems ironic and misplaced. Such cynicism is in stark contrast to the nineteenth-century view, when morality, religion and family, coupled with a sense of duty took precedence over the individual's civil rights. Most people at that time yearned for law and order, and those who transgressed soon learned that justice could be swift and terrible. Nowadays the emphasis is on the lawbreakers rather than the lawmakers, a view that is hard to discourage.

Such an extreme divergence of opinion is only fully appreciated when one remembers that America has been preoccupied with firearms since revolutionary times. The Constitution gave the individual the 'right to bear arms', which has been interpreted to mean to 'possess and to use them in defence of home, family and possessions'. Others claim that the right to bear arms really meant in defence of the Union in time of war or civil unrest. Either view is tacitly ignored by some members of the gun-owning fraternity who honestly believe that the possession of a firearm is their salvation against the criminal in a society that has overstretched police forces, and a judicial system that can sometimes take years to dispense justice.

Not surprisingly, a people's champion or a kind of Robin Hood in buckskins would have enormous appeal. And although the cowboy fits this image, it was the man who lived and died by the gun who exerted most influence. He can only be understood when one examines the circumstances that gave birth to the character we now call the gunfighter. The war with Mexico spawned him, and his adolescence witnessed the California gold rush and the Kansas–Missouri border wars of the middle and late 1850s. By the time of the Civil War, he had reached maturity and was prominent among the guerrillas on both sides. And his adult life was spent in the post-war cattle, rail and mining boom towns.

Right: *'The Admirable Outlaw' (oil on canvas), painted by N.C. Wyeth (1882–1945) in 1906, depicts a gentleman from south of the Rio Grande, and is typical of Wyeth's attention to detail.*

Above: *William 'Bill' Tilghman, an upright, honest and law-abiding individual who earned his reputation in the Kansas cow-towns such as Dodge City, and furthered it in early day Oklahoma Territory.*

Above: *Bat Masterson, who unequivocally stood on the side of right, dressed more in keeping with the latest business wear rather than his role as a gunfighter. Only in later life did Bat appear in 'casual dress'.*

Left: *Wild Bill Hickok, dressed for his appearance with Buffalo Bill Cody's theatrical troupe in 1873. Apart from his long hair, he looks a typical eastern dandy attired in the latest fashion.*

As a class, gunfighters did not conform to the stereotyped image of the motion picures. Generations of Western fans have seen them portrayed as cowboys, gamblers and occasionally in the guise of a frontier scout complete with buckskins. But the cowboy image dominates. From the earliest appearance of the Western film in 1903, the dress and manner of the gunfighter has been reflected in the image of the cowboy. The huge sombrero, neckerchief, double or single gunbelt, knee high boots (worn with pants tucked in or pulled down over them), and jingling spurs, all served to create a false image of the man behind the gun. In reality, most gunfighters dressed normally according to the current fashions of the time, and would probably be missed in a crowd. Only when they openly carried pistols would they command much attention. In fact, the editor of the Kansas City, Mo. *Journal* on 15 November 1881 made a point of describing the 'man-killer' or 'civilizer' that today we call the gunfighter:

The gentleman who has 'killed his man' is by no means a *rara avis* . . . He is met daily on Main street, and is the busiest of the busy throng. He may be seen on 'change, and in the congregations of the most aristocratic churches. He resides on 'Quality hill', or perhaps on the East Side . . . This ubiquitous individual may be seen almost anywhere. He may be found behind the bar in a Main street saloon; he may be seen by an admiring audience doing the pedestal clog at a variety theatre; his special forte may be driving a cab, or he may be behind the rosewood counters of a bank . . . He is usually quiet in demeanor, sober . . . [and] . . . he may take a drink occasionally, but seldom gets drunk . . . He is quiet – fatally quiet . . . Your gentleman who has dropped his man is, therefore, no uncommon individual . . .

The editor's graphic portrait of the typical gunfighter refutes the loud-mouthed, trouble-making 'shoot at anything that moves' Texas cowboy of the 1860s and early 1870s. Nevertheless, there were cowboy-gunfighters but they were the exception. For most of the men who lived and died by the gun were indeed a breed apart. Some were honest law-abiding individuals who became peace officers sworn to uphold the law. Others, equally honest but by no means as dedicated, took to the badge to avoid starvation or to fill in between other occupations. The likes of Bill Tilghman and Bat Masterson came within the first category, while Wild Bill Hickok and the Earp brothers were part of the second group. Few of these men were trained peace officers. They were motivated economically or politically rather than by any great sense of justice. Aligned against them were the likes of the James brothers, Billy the Kid and others for whom the gun symbolized power and the ease with which one could acquire wealth and instill fear in honest citizens whose only ambition was to survive in a very harsh environment.

Mid-nineteenth-century European views of the penchant for the pistol in certain parts of the United States make interesting reading. In England, for instance, the *Daily Telegraph* of 22 October 1869, remarked:

Duellists, travellers, and the rowdy bullies of the New World, enjoy the doubtful honour of having brought the pistol to its present sanguinary perfection. It is the weapon of the self-dependent man; and those who can find a 'final cause' of good rattlesnakes and poisonous drugs might cite a great many instances to prove that the pistol has furthered civilisation, and has been especially the arm of progress . . . Unhappily, the drunken bully and gambler of America and Mexico has found the six-shooter convenient, and carries it more regularly than his tooth-pick. Some day, we hope, the Government of The United States, remembering what Thucydides says about the barbarity of a people who 'wear iron', will make it a punishable offence to carry a 'Derringer' or a 'Colt'. But these blood-thirsty scoundrels complain of the revolver. It kills, but not immediately; its bullet is too small to paralyse; the victim dies by internal bleeding, but not before he has time to discharge his own battery. Hence those extraordinary encounters in the Western and Southern States, where a whole volley of shots is discharged before one of the wretched combatants succumbs.

This view neglected to examine (or perhaps was ignorant of) the West itself.

Above: *'I am a shootist,' declared Clay Allison in 1878; he meant 'gunfighter'. Feared killer that he was, this photograph, made in about 1868, is ironic – for Allison died in a wagon accident in 1887.*

Below: *'Holding up the Stage', by Edward Borein (1872–1945) is interesting for several reasons. Borein pays attention to detail in dress and the coach itself, and mules – rather than horses – hitched to it.*

The gunfighters, or perhaps their gunfights, loom large in America's folklore and remain the subject of debate a century or more since they last squeezed a trigger. Some died with their boots on and others in bed, but so fascinating is the subject that it has inspired a modern six-shooter cult that dwells primarily upon how fast on the draw certain individuals might have been rather than their accuracy and what first provoked them to kill.

The gunfighter arose out of the turbulent conditions that existed in the frontier West, when a man's best friend and hope of salvation was a gun, for there were many remote parts of states or territories where law and order was either over extended or unheard of. The classic gunfight of fact, fiction and the silver screen, which depicts two or more individuals facing each other down in a high noon duel, is now an accepted part of Western folklore. In reality, the gunfight was loosely based upon the old-time *code duello*, but it lacked the rules of the original and instead relied on the cold-blooded science of getting the drop on an opponent. The importance of the 'drop' was paramount. 'One must always have the drop on an antagonist,' noted the Topeka *Daily Commonwealth*, on 23 September 1871, 'or nothing more than an exercise of the vocal muscles ensues. The code of chivalry seems to be to fight only a smaller man who is unprepared and unsuspecting. Shoot him in the back, bite his ear or nose off as a memento, and your reputation as a fighting man is made . . .' Among men of reputation, however, such brawling was rare. A man's 'honor' was set above everything else. And it was a trait that can be traced right back to earlier times when duelists fought hand-to-hand encounters that would have appalled

Below: *An untitled painting (oil on canvas) by V.C. Forsythe (1885–1962). Depicting the drama of a night-time gunfight, it has a stark realism to it which is emphasized by the harsh moonlight that freezes the action. With* N.C. Wyeth, W.H.D. Koerner, Charles M. Russell, Frederic Remington and others who documented and interpreted the American West, Forsythe helped to shape our concepts of the meaning of the West.

some of the latter day six-shooter virtuosos who depended upon the drop and the killer instinct for survival.

Men have fought each other all through history, using rocks, clubs, and swords right down to firearms. The individual's preoccupation with personal supremacy has been motivated by debts of honor, sexual betrayal or public humiliation. In Europe, where dueling was considered the province of the aristocracy, young men were schooled in the art of fencing and knife-fighting. These weapons remained popular on the Continent until the nineteenth century; but in Great Britain, by the late eighteenth century, the dueling pistol was coming into its own. Some regarded dueling as a sport, others considered it a retrograde step in human relations and in England it was outlawed in the early years of the nineteenth century. Ireland, however, regarded the individual who would not fight a duel for his honor as a coward, and young men of breeding were expected to own a case of dueling pistols. Thus the Irish *code duello* formed the basis for similar rules and behavior in other English-speaking countries, notably America.

Dueling in the northern states was uncommon, whereas in the South, with its homegrown aristocracy based upon the European variety, it flourished. A man's honor or his wife's reputation meant everything to him and if it was necessary to carry weapons to protect or assert either he would do so. Many cited the famous English legal expert William Blackstone's definition of self-defense as 'the mutual and reciprocal defense of such as stand in the relations of husband and wife, parent and child, master and servant', which enabled him to 'repel force by force'. By the mid-1850s, however, with the arrival of the revolver, the old-fashioned rules of dueling disappeared. For every individual who relied upon his weapon for protection, there were many others who saw it as a means to an end. The day of the pistoleer had arrived.

History changes yet it remains the same. Despite revision and review old myths and fables concerning the American West and its gunfighters are perpetuated. While historians strive for the truth, they often find that people prefer legends. It is much more exciting to read that Billy the Kid killed twenty-one men – one for each year of his life – or that Wild Bill disposed of 'considerably over a hundred bad men', than to be told that the Kid killed perhaps six people, and Wild Bill's tally was closer to ten than 100. In each instance legend took care of the remainder and it is the legend that appeals to most people and not the facts.

In this book we intend to depict the gunfighter's role in society; its reaction to him; how he was accepted or rejected, rather than the time-warp image so beloved by film makers and novelists. For whatever one may think of the men who used firearms for good or evil, their exploits still fascinate and command a large following.

Although the heroic image of the gunfighter is not contemporary to his time, it is true that a man who could handle a pistol better than those who used one for gain or power was much in demand. But unlike his fictional counterpart, he was held responsible for his actions, if need be in a court of law.

THE BECKONING WEST

The frontier West in the early nineteenth century was unknown territory, a wilderness inhabited by nomadic tribes of Indians, vast herds of buffalo and other forms of wild life. It was widely believed that much of the land was a great desert and unfit for habitation. But following on from the early explorations of Lewis and Clark and later Pike, by the late 1840s there began a mass migration that was to turn that wilderness into a civilized country. In the process, however, many people perished; wars were fought and reputations made or lost. For it was also the age of the entrepre-neur, the visionary, the civilizer, and the man with the gun.

The most enduring part of the gunfighter legend is the belief that he played a part in civilizing the West; that his pistol pacified the lawless and strengthened the resolve of the law-abiding souls who sought to tame the wild land and provide a new life for themselves and their families. In fact, it was mass migration and not the individual with a gun who tamed the West. Perhaps the most important contribution was the railroad. As its silver rails spread like tentacles out across the country, in its wake came people anxious to settle somewhere on its route. And once the tracks moved on, in place of the chaos and confusion of tent cities that had housed hard-working, hard-drinking track-layers, graders and others bent upon pushing the rails West, sprang up permanent structures that became townships and cities.

As they advanced the railroads also posed their own problems, for the tracks frequently outpaced civilization. Most of the embryonic townships in their wake lacked government and witnessed bouts of lawlessness that deterred rather than encouraged would-be settlers. More hardy folk, however, were pre-pared to face up to the violence and fight for what they believed in. It was their self-reliance and spirit that conquered the frontier West.

THE VIOLENT WEST

The wilderness that was the West of the early 1840s soon became the focus of attention when mass migration overcame the many hazards that had deterred so many in the past. People moving west on foot, horseback or by wagon were prepared to face all manner of perils. Apart from Indians and wild animals, they also faced arid deserts and mountainous regions. But for the survivors, the rewards were worth the hardships.

The very nature of the country aided those anxious to avoid contact with civilization and its restrictions. For the honest citizen, however, the lack of law and order or communication was yet another of the hazards.

From the flat land of Kansas westward to the Rocky Mountains and then the Sierras, there sprang up a number of communities that existed primarily because of gold or silver deposits. Miners and speculators invaded the regions. On the plains where the flat grassland made travel easier, homesteaders soon located, especially in Kansas following its opening up as a territory in 1854. And it was Kansas that attracted the bulk of the cattle industry following the Civil War.

The West of the outlaw and vigilante was also changing. As communications improved across the country, the violent element began to retreat toward the more remote regions. The likes of Jesse James, Butch Cassidy and the Youngers learned the hard way that the West as they knew it was now becoming unsafe. The era of the guerrilla, the roadagent and the 'bad man' was fast coming to an end. Soon, there would be no place to hide. The James–Younger gang were broken at Northfield in 1876, and the Daltons at Coffeyville in 1892. As for Butch Cassidy, he and his friend Sundance were forced to quit the United States altogether. By the early 1900s, the wilderness that had been the violent West was tamed; but its legends and those that inspired them would live on.

JOHN X. BEIDLER
(1831–90)
Montana

JAMES DANIELS
(18??–1866)
Montana

TOM HORN
(1860–1903)
Wyoming

BUTCH CASSIDY
(1866–1911)
Utah, Colorado, Wyoming

VIGILANTE JUSTICE
Execution of Jose Forner on Russian Hill,
San Francisco, 10 December 1852

MONTANA

Helena

Alder Gulch • Virginia City   Hole-

Bannack

IDAHO   WYOMING

Union Pacific RR   Salt Lake City

UTAH

NEVADA   Circleville

Aurora

Bodie   Colorado R.

San Francisco   ARIZONA TERRITORY

CALIFORNIA

HARVEY LOGAN
(1865–1904)
Wyoming, Utah, Arizona

The West and its land were there for the taking. Yet it was no place for the weak, the timid or the hesitant. Rather, it was the individuals who grasped at the opportunities regardless of the odds. Of the thousands who invaded the region, no one will ever know how many failed to reach their goal. Perhaps understandably it is not the hard-working, dedicated farmer, homesteader or storekeeper that appeals to today's audiences and readers, but the outlaw, the scout, mountain man, cowboy and soldier. All of them exuded an aura of romanticism that inspires a mixture of adulation and nostalgia for an era that created legends.

The Easterner, living as so many of them did in overcrowded cities and ghettos, faced with a growing immigrant population that threatened his existence and employment prospects, yearned for the West where, if he believed the stories, there was greater freedom, more room to move around in, and a future. Only when they gave serious thought to the hazards to be faced did the less venturesome think twice about moving West. Westerners were people used to making on-the-spot decisions who were contemptuous of the Easterners' obsession with legal formalities, an attitude that in some areas still survives. The Westerners held similar views over law and

order. What suited the Easterner, used to courts and due process, meant little to a man in the wilds of Wyoming or the Great Plains who had stock rustled. If he could get his hands on the culprit he would deal with him himself, if need be kill to recover his property. This simplistic view was not in contempt of the law but because of the lack of it. Where no law existed, or it was too extended to rely upon, people tended to take care of their own problems. Cattle rustlers and horse-thieves risked being shot or hanged, while less dangerous or petty criminals might endure a severe thrashing. But whatever the crime, if caught, punishment (if not always justice) was swift. Time and the in-

JOHN BROWN
(1800–1859)
Kansas

JAMES H. LANE
(1814–66)
Mexico, Kansas

QUANTRILL'S GUERRILLAS
Kansas, Missouri

BILL ANDERSON
(1839–64)
Missouri, Kansas

JESSE JAMES
(1847–82)
Kansas, Missouri

BILL DOOLIN
(1858–96)
Kansas, Oklahoma

LUKE SHORT
(1854–93)
Kansas, Texas

COLE YOUNGER
(1844–1916)
Kansas, Missouri

THE DALTON GANG
(Bob 1868–92, Emmett 1871–1937, Grat 1865–92)
Oklahoma, Kansas

JOHN ARMSTRONG
(1850–1913)
Texas

JOHN WESLEY HARDIN
(1853–95)
Texas, Kansas

LAWMEN

Tools and emblems of office carried by those who enforced the law in the West varied in quality and formality. Accounts of San Francisco vigilantes suggest disorganized mobs and rampant ruffians, but these vigilantes were well organized and carried almost fraternal-like accessories. Some law agencies actually specified the use of uniforms, especially in cities. But usually, the Texas Ranger, sheriff or marshal chose weapons to suit individual taste.

Pistols carried by old-time gunfighters are prized. Bat Masterson faked notches in second-hand pistol butts to fool gullible collectors. Inscribed guns are also prized. The Navy pistol shown here (7) said to have once belonged to Wild Bill Hickok has an interesting history. In 1937 it was exhibited at the premier of Gary Cooper's film about Hickok, *The Plainsman*. At that time the backstrap inscription read 'J.B. Hickock 1869'. When it appeared again in 1975, the second 'c' had been skillfully removed.

1. San Francisco vigilante sword, silver plating, gold wash, precious stones, with the vigilante symbol of the 'all seeing eye' engraved on the scabbard.
2. Ivory club carried by one Samuel P. Hill in the San Francisco vigilantes, dated 1852.
3. Silver pocket watch carried by Bartholomew Williamson. The silver fob has the 'all seeing

eye' of the San Francisco vigilantes – a different kind of badge indicating membership in the group. (Items 1, 2 and 3 from the Collection of Greg Martin.)
4. This holster, belt and Colt revolver belonged to George Gardiner, sometime cowboy, Wild West performer and law officer in the 1890s and later.
5. Law badge worn by George Gardiner in

16

Sheridan, Wyoming.

6. Plain, finely lined holster with the initials 'JB' scratched on the back. Of the quality made by E.L. Gallatin in Cheyenne, Wyoming, the holster accompanies the Hickok Navy (7).

7. This factory engraved ivory Colt 1851 Navy bears Hickok's name on the backstrap. Serial No. 138813 chillingly reflects the 'Aces and Eights' of his last poker hand.

8. 'Aces and Eights' or 'The Dead Man's Hand' held by Hickok when he was murdered by Jack McCall in Deadwood.

9. Colt single-action Army .45 carried by Texas Ranger Tom Threepersons after the turn of the century.

10. Tom Threepersons' Texas Rangers badge.

11. Prohibition officer's badge, made from a silver dollar, and used by Tom Threepersons.

12. Sheriff's manual signed by successive sheriffs in Central City, Colorado, after 1882.

13. Reward notices for horse thieves.

14. Another source governing the activities of Colorado law officers – published Civil Procedure.

(Artifacts courtesy of Gene Autry Western Heritage Museum, Los Angeles, California.)

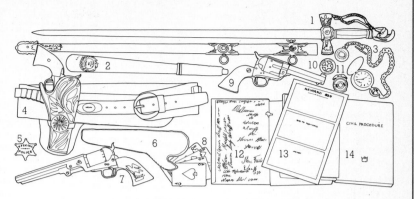

flux of more people, the establishment of local government, schools, churches and the essentials of civilization, eroded the need for expedient justice, and replaced it with both state and federal law.

A part of the frontier tradition was that the line between the outlaw and the lawman was thinly drawn; it was not unknown for a man to have a reputation on both sides. Indeed, some of the better known gunfighters had pasts which included court appearances or perhaps prison sentences. Yet a change of circumstances, a public need, and they were reinstated to society. Once they were no longer needed, and they were out of a job, there was the threat of being charged with vagrancy, 'for having no visible means of support'. Wild Bill Hickok suffered this indignity at Cheyenne in 1875 when he wandered in and out of the place for some months.

Perhaps the most prominent frontier tradition was that of the vigilante. No study of the era can ignore both the significance or the effect of those who followed this course. Two places in particular illustrate the power of the vigilante movement, for both exemplified the manifestation of 'people power' that followed the centuries old belief that if there was no law to take care of culprits, then they would. San Francisco, California, in the midst and wake of the gold rush formed a group of vigilantes that became world famous, while at Virginia City, Montana, the vigilantes proved that ordinary citizens could only take so much before retaliating against outlaw domination and terror.

California, following the discovery of gold in 1848, became the most popular place on earth. Thousands flocked there, and the population grew so much that the citizens petitioned the government for statehood. This was granted in 1850. But the huge influx of would-be miners, and the usual gamblers, prostitutes and 'speculators' presaged any but the most basic attempts at establishing law and order or local government. Although California had established law and order by 1851–2, with the aid of vigilantes who flourished despite complaints of a 'Reign of Terror' and talk of a 'Committee of Public Safety' reminiscent of the French Revolution, state laws made little impact upon the lawless element. The vastness of the country and lack of population in the more remote areas proved to be a haven for outlaws and desperadoes. However, when justice caught up with malefactors, it was swift.

In 1848 it was the small port of Yerba Buena, with a population of less than one thousand; but following the discovery of gold its name was changed to San Francisco, and it became the home of thousands of would-be goldseekers. Destroyed several times by fire, the young city nevertheless managed to improve with each new building, and by the mid-1850s the 'tent city' of the early days was largely constructed of bricks and mortar. By 1853, the 'Queen of the Pacific', as she was affectionately called, boasted a large number of hotels, churches,

Below: *This scene of placer mining, Columbia, Tuolumne County, California, depicts the Daley Claim, and is a good example of how limited machinery and muscle power were combined.*

Above: *This panoramic view of San Francisco is dated 1851, and graphically depicts the almost deserted look of the place and the ships – all abandoned by men in search of gold.*

schools, hospitals, banks and several fire companies, together with saloons, gambling halls and brothels. Access to the place was via the overland route from St Louis or via ship from eastern seaboard ports to the Isthmus of Panama (the canal had yet to be built), Nicaragua or 'round the Horn' at risk of violent seas and storms. Communication overland was slightly better after 1853 when a 200-mile telegraph link was installed between San Francisco and Marysville. This was later extended to Salt Lake City, Utah, and with the

arrival of Western Union in 1861, east was linked to west.

Back in the early 1850s, however, there were genuine fears that law and order would be slow to reach not only the 'diggings' but California in general. Consequently, the vigilantes were accepted as a necessary evil. A number of men were hanged, following a trial; the first of these was a man named Jenkins, a persistent criminal who hailed from Australia. Not surprisingly, a number of former convicts or men who had been transported to Australia from England for various crimes headed for California given the chance. The Americans named these characters 'Sydney Ducks' or 'Sydney Coves'. Some of them even established a 'Sydney Town' at Clark's Point on the outskirts of San Francisco. Although the vigi-

lantes, in hindsight, contributed much toward law and order, they were powerless to stop the increase in violence brought about by the use of firearms. For it was the revolver more than any other weapon that inspired the gunfighter; to the gun he owed his origin, his very *raison d'être*.

Although multi-barreled and revolving breech arms had been in existence for centuries, it was not until the early nineteenth century that they achieved any great success. In 1805, the Reverend Alexander John Forsyth

Below: *Wells Fargo stagecoaches meet the locomotives of the Central Pacific Railroad in 1867, then building east to meet the Union Pacific. The coaches had 1500 miles to go to reach Nebraska.*

of Belhelvie in Aberdeenshire, Scotland, was successful in utilizing fulminate of mercury in a new kind of ignition for firearms. He designed a pivoted magazine which contained small deposits of the fulminate which was ignited by the hammer of the weapon. This action sealed the escape of the flame, which in turn touched off the black powder in the breech and discharged the weapon. Later, the English artist Joshua Show is credited with producing the substance in paste form which was placed in minute steel cups, or cylinders. Later still, came the cone or nipple screwed to the breech on which a modified 'cap' made of copper and containing sufficient fulminate was placed. When struck by the hammer the flame flashed into the powder and discharged the arm. The percussion cap revolutionized firearms and by the 1830s percussion lock arms were rapidly superseding the older flintlocks. It was then that an enterprising young man from Hartford, Connecticut, came into his own.

Samuel Colt, the son of a successful merchant, did not claim to have invented the revolver but simply to have perfected a working, reliable investment. Following a number of setbacks and a lack of money, he eventually managed to get several prototype weapons made, and with money from his family, he sailed to England where he patented his invention in 1835. In February 1836, he also patented his arms in the United States. On 5 March, Colt signed contracts with some New York capitalists who formed the Patent Arms Manufacturing Company of Paterson, New Jersey, to produce his revolving breeched rifles and revolvers. Ironically, a day later, the Alamo fell to Santa Anna who was himself defeated shortly afterwards by General Sam Houston whose force of Texians' battle cry was 'Remember the Alamo!'

By the late 1830s Colt had sold a number of his revolving rifled muskets to the United States government, and the Republic of Texas purchased a number of pistols. By 1844, many of them had been issued to the Texas Rangers who used them to good effect against Comanche Indians. This was a turning point: where once the Indians had had the upper hand and were able to loose off a dozen arrows while the whites struggled to load their single shot arms, Colt's five-shot pistols were a distinct advantage. And in the hands of the Texas Rangers they proved to be formidable weapons.

SAM COLT'S REVOLVERS

Prior to the 1830s a practical and reliable repeating firearm was not available for hunters, soldiers, sportsmen or gunmen. Although 'repeating arms' had been known in various forms since the sixteenth century, they all lacked reliability. Collier's revolving flintlock pistols and longarms proved to be the first step toward 'revolving arms', but their ignition was a stumbling block. The invention of the percussion cap changed all that. And when Samuel Colt patented his revolver in 1835, he opened the floodgates to a whole new concept of firearms. Someone even remarked that 'God created man, but Sam Colt made them equal!' Others referred to 'Judge Colt and his jury of six'.

Colt's revolvers were much in demand both in the West and other parts of the country. And by the early 1850s he had established a factory in England. His mass production methods revolutionized gunmaking on both sides of the Atlantic and led to changes in other industries. His involvement with the Patent Arms Manufacturing Company, Paterson, New Jersey, which, with outside capital, manufactured his pistols and longarms, led to their adoption in Texas and some usage by the U.S. Army. When the Paterson venture failed, Colt, as mentioned elsewhere, secured government contracts in 1847 during the war with Mexico. He later set up a factory at Hartford, Connecticut, where he prospered and his arms were in demand world-wide.

1. Colt prototype revolver with folding bayonet, made by blacksmith John Pearson about 1834–5.
2. Colt first model ring lever revolving rifle, serial number 164, Paterson, New Jersey, about 1837.
3. 'Texas' Paterson Colt revolver, .36 caliber, about 1838–40.
4. Model 1839 Paterson revolving shotgun, serial number 138.
5. Cased Paterson belt model revolver with accessories, about 1838–40.
6. Soup tureen, about 1855, bearing Sam Colt's coat of arms.
7. Sam Colt's calling or business card, 1850s.
8. Silver cigar stand made for Sam Colt by New York silversmith William Adams, 1855.
9. Second Dragoon revolver in cutaway.
10. Engraved 1851 Navy revolver given to the Governor of Kansas at a time when violence characterized confrontations between pro- and anti-slavery forces.
11. Stock certificate for the Patent Arms Manufacturing Company.
12. Following the death of her husband, Mrs Colt celebrated her husband's life with publication of *Armsmear* (1866).

(Artifacts courtesy of Gene Autry Western Heritage Museum, Los Angeles, California.)

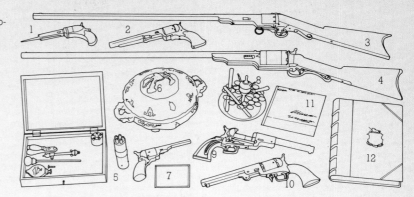

COLT PISTOLS ON THE PECOS

It seems fitting that the first civilian force to appreciate Colt's revolver should be the Texas Rangers. Formed originally in 1823 to provide some protection for outlying settlements against Indians in what was still Mexican territory, by the 1840s, when Texas was a republic, the 'Rangers' were already earning a tremendous reputation. They never had a uniform as such, and in the early days dressed casually. In appearance some resembled the 'desperadoes' that they fought. But they proved their worth up against hostile Comanches, whose own reputation as the finest light cavalry on the plains made them formidable opponents.

In his classic works *The Texas Rangers* and *The Great Plains* Walter Prescott Webb not only paid tribute to the work of these men, but pinpointed the moment when the revolver really came into its own. In 1839, the Texas government purchased 180 holster-size pistols from Colt. At that time 'holster' denoted weapons intended to be carried in 'saddle holsters' rather than on the belt. These five-shot .36 caliber 9-inch barreled pistols, together with 180 rifles, were intended for naval use. By 1840, however, many of these arms had been issued to the Rangers. It was an inspired decision; for perhaps the first time the mounted soldier or Ranger was a match for his Indian opponent. Armed with a bow that shot flint or steel-tipped arrows, and backed by a fourteen-foot lance, the Comanche was a daunting figure. But as was reported by the *Telegraph and Register* of 17 April 1844, a company of 'Western Rangers, under the command of the gallant Captain [Jack] Hays . . . are sent out by turns to scout the country in every direction. The men are well armed, and are probably the most happy, jovial and hearty set of men in all Texas.' One of those riders was Samuel Walker who was later to play an important part in redesigning Colt's pistol. In 1846, he described to Colt an incident that was publicised as far away as England:

> The pistols which you made for the Texas Navy have been in use by the Rangers for three years . . . In the Summer of 1844 Col. J. C. Hays with 15 men fought about 80 Camanche [*sic*] Indians, boldly attacking them upon their own ground, killing & wounding about half their number . . . Without your pistols we would not have had the confidence to have undertaken such daring adventures.

Such a reputation and in the hands of such renowned individuals as the Texas Rangers was music to Sam Colt's ears, but before he could make full use of such accolades he received a severe setback. The Patent Arms Manufacturing Company failed, due to a lack of government orders and certain defects in the arms themselves. Colt refused to give up, continuing his experiments with arms and other projects. Then, in 1846, the worsening relationship between the United States and Mexico came to a head. The Republic of Texas, which had been created following the defeat of Santa Anna, maintained a precarious amnesty with Mexico, but it was deemed only a matter of time before the two fought each

Above: *Samuel Colt (1814–62), from an oil painting by Charles Loring Elliott. Painted in 1865 at Mrs Colt's request, it was based upon existing photographs and is an excellent likeness. A man whose contribution to the 'winning' of the West is immeasurable, Colt has been described as 'charismatic, personable, a great showman, speculator . . . opportunist . . . ruthless but fair, demanding and getting what he wanted . . .'*

Above: *Arizona Ranger W.K. Farnsworth holds his 1895 Winchester carbine. Of particular note here is the double belt which has loops for both rifle and revolver ammunition.*

Right: *These tough looking Texas Rangers are dressed and armed in the accepted garb of the time. Clearly visible in this photograph are the ubiquitous Colt revolvers and Winchester rifles.*

other. A partial solution was reached in 1845 when, with mutual agreement, Texas was annexed by the United States. But on 8 May 1846, American and Mexican forces clashed in what is remembered as the Battle of Palo Alto, and they were at war. It lasted for two years before a peace treaty was signed in February 1848, at which time California became a territory of the United States.

In the opening months of the war, the few Paterson pistols in military hands proved themselves equal to the task, and demands for more 'revolvers' convinced the U.S. government that the arm was of practical value, but none was readily available. When Colt learned that Captain Samuel Walker, who had been newly commissioned into the United States Mounted Rifles Regiment, had publicly praised his pistols, he wrote to him pointing out that with a military contract he could produce revolvers for the war. He also asked the captain for an honest opinion of the Paterson pistol and his ideas for improvements. Colt also offered to supply 1,000 pistols for $25 each, reducing the cost with every thousand pistols

ordered. Walker, on orders from the Adjutant General's office, had been despatched to Fort McHenry to establish a recruiting base, so he was easily able to visit Colt. The pair met and thrashed out the faults in the existing design. On 7 December 1846, Walker managed to get an interview with President James K. Polk, who in turn introduced him to Secretary of War William L. Marcy. Marcy listened to Walker, who probably produced an existing Colt Paterson pistol, noting the proposed improvements. Despite objections from the Ordnance Department, Marcy approved a contract with Colt which was drawn up on 6 January 1847. Walker warned Sam that both their reputations were on the line and he had to meet his contractual obligations. Sam set to work and was able to persuade Eli Whitney, Jr., of New Haven, Connecticut, to manufacture the pistols on his behalf, and the Sheffield steelmakers, Naylor & Company, through their Boston agents, supplied the raw materials.

The pistol that was finally accepted was a massive thing. Weighing 4 pounds 9 ounces, it was a six-shot .44 caliber weapon with a 9-inch

barrel that could be loaded with up to 57 grains of black powder (40 grains was the recommended load) that could push a 140-grain lead ball at an estimated muzzle velocity of between 1300 to 1500 feet per second! A number of the pistols blew up through faults in manufacture, but they proved their worth in action, and in anticipation of more contracts Colt had Whitney manufacture a further 100 pistols for civilian use. Sadly, Walker, who had played a large part in the design and acceptance of the 'Colt–Walker' revolver, was last at a relatively early age, killed in action during the war.

One legacy of the Mexican War was the reaction of the Rangers and soldiers who had been armed with the new Colt revolvers. Some refused to surrender them, or claimed that they had been lost in action or simply blown up. Captain John Williams, writing in May 1848, from Vera Cruz, Mexico, advised Washington that only 191 of the 280 new pistols issued to the Texas Rangers under Colonel Jack Hays' command had been handed in. Of this number, only 82 were serviceable. Un-

PERCUSSION COLTS

Samuel Colt's idea of the revolver caught on quickly. Texans understood the value of the weapon and with the coming of the Mexican War one of them, Samuel Walker, helped to influence the government in ordering a newly designed .44 caliber monster. The Walker Colt and many of its successors (all of the latter made in Hartford, Connecticut) had images of dragoons fighting Indians on the cylinder. Sam Colt understood the value of his product to the Western market and he exploited this for all it was worth.

Until after the Civil War a variety of Colts in different sizes, calibers, and models were produced and widely used throughout the West. Along trails, in Western gold fields, gambling dens, and elsewhere there were other types of handguns, but none was ever as popular as the Colt. The .44 caliber Army and dragoon models served military and civilian needs alike. Premium prices were also paid in the West for the lighter .36 caliber models.

1. The massive Walker model revolver, .44 caliber, popular in the Mexican War. One of 100 civilian models which were made after the completion of the 1847 government contract.
2. First model Dragoon revolver, .44 caliber, made in 1848.
3. Model 1860 Colt Army revolver, .44 caliber, experimental model, serial number 4 with fluted cylinder.

Thousands saw use in the hands of civilians and Western cavalry in the 1860s and early 1870s.
4. Third model Dragoon revolver, with attachable shoulder stock, .44 caliber, carried by dragoon and cavalry troops in the pre-Civil War West.
5. Model 1851 Navy Model, .36 caliber, cutaway demonstration model.
6. Cased 1851 Navy, with London markings.

7. Model 1848 pocket revolver, known as the 'Baby Dragoon', light weight, easy to carry, and popular throughout the West.

8. Model 1849 pocket revolver, .31 caliber, five shot, cutaway demonstrator made in 1857.

9. Prototype of the 'Wells Fargo' model 1849 pocket revolver, serial number 1, caliber, .31, with separate loading tool – easily concealed, but all business.

10. Experimental pocket revolver, unfinished, in caliber .36.

11. Model 1862 pocket Navy revolver, made in 1863, stagecoach hold-up scene engraved on the cylinder.

12. 'Trapper's' model 1862 Police revolver, experimental prototype, without serial number.

13. Model 1862 Police revolver with accessories, inscribed 'H.A. Bridham/U.S.A.',

with rare casing in the form of a book.

14. Cased model 1855 side-hammer revolver with accessories, caliber .28, made in about 1856, the cylinder roll engraved with a scene of an Indian fight.

15. Standard model 1855 sidehammer revolver, cutaway demonstrator.

(Artifacts courtesy of Gene Autry Western Heritage Museum, Los Angeles, California.)

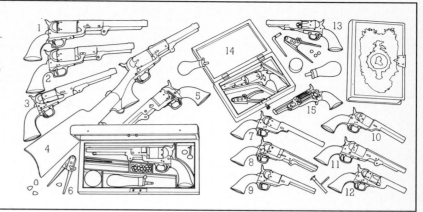

known to him, perhaps, some of the missing arms had fallen into Mexican hands. But the message was plain: the day of the pistol fighter had arrived.

Colt negotiated with Eli Whitney and purchased what remained of the pistol parts and machinery, and with the money received from his military contract he was able to set up a pistol manufactory at Hartford. Further government contracts followed, and in 1848 Colt redesigned the Walker pistol and produced the first of his 'Dragoon' or 'Holster' weapons now generally known as the 'Model of 1848'. The weight was reduced by 7 ounces, and the barrel shortened to 7½ inches. Several pocket pistols were also designed and produced, but it was the appearance in 1850 of a weapon tentatively called the 'New Ranger Size Pistol' that attracted most attention, for this pistol more than any other of its time inspired the reality and the myth of the gunfighter.

The new revolver was a six-shot .36 caliber weapon with a 7½ inch octagonal barrel, giving the pistol an overall length of 13 inches and a weight of 2 pounds 10 ounces. Around the cylinder was a die-rolled engraving depicting a battle between Texas and Mexican ships in 1843. The United States Board of Ordnance tested the new pistol and was impressed. On a single day's trial it was fired 1500 times, and cleaned only once. Penetration tests on pine boards were equally impressive. Loaded with 20 grains of powder (the chamber could accept 30 grains) and an 83-grain conical bullet, the bullets pierced six pine boards set one inch apart. Its accuracy was applauded, but the Board was more concerned with recoil, especially how it might affect a mounted horseman. Very shortly afterwards, the 'Ranger' title was dropped and substituted by 'Belt' or 'Navy' pistol, a factory definition. But the military and public preferred the 'Navy' tag by which it was to become immortalized.

The growth in the population of California and the increasing use of firearms aroused

much concern. By 1857, the *Chronicle*, according to *The Illustrated London News* of 15 September, was bemoaning the demoralizing effects caused by the 'universal and cowardly practise of carrying revolvers'. Personal disputes invariably led to shoot-outs, and the press paid much attention to the situation. Yet historians have tended to ignore the fact that California, Nevada and Montana were as violent and had their share of 'bad men' who were the equal of their better known mid-Western counterparts. The reason, of course, was a lack of publicity. Apart from William B. Secrest's *Dangerous Men: Gunfighters, Lawmen and Outlaws of Old California*; John Boessenecker's *Badge and Buckshot: Lawlessness in Old*

Below: *A typical freight wagon pauses outside one of Aurora's main buildings. Some idea of the size and weight of the wagon's load can be seen from the number of mules (twelve) harnessed to it.*

Above: *Bodie looks bleak but almost peaceful in this contemporary view, but the underlying violence of the place was not lost on resident or visitor alike. Gun ownership was essential in a place such as this.*

California, and *Gunfighters, Highwaymen & Vigilantes: Violence on the Frontier*, by Roger D. McGrath, little recent attention has been paid to the subject. McGrath, however, confines his subject to only two places: the gold and silver camps of Aurora and Bodie.

Contemporary reports of the San Francisco vigilantes caused some consternation, but Aurora and Bodie had similar organizations. The law being practically non-existent, the citizens provided their own (after a fashion) and soon emulated their San Francisco cousins by setting up lynch mobs or 'regulators' and 'committees of safety' which for the most part was the best that could be done. If nothing else, a number of murderers were 'jerked to

Jesus' in the approved manner, which convinced others of the error of their ways. Gangs of outlaws were common. Aurora boasted the John Daly gang, many of whom perished from lead poisoning or rope burns, and in their time ranked with the James brothers and the Daltons. One suspects, however, that Bodie's reputation at least was helped in later years by a story published in the Sacramento *Daily Bee* in 1880 entitled 'The Bad Man from Bodie'. But the eyes of the nation were fixed upon San Francisco in the early years, and by 1851, when the gold rush was at its height, a number of individuals were already making their mark within the city. Secrest recorded the exploits of several men who, for a variety of reasons, are now a part of California's folklore. Among them was Will Hicks Graham, a lawyer who had come to California in June 1850. He worked for Judge R. N. Morrison who was (so he and other clerks thought) unjustly criticised by the editor of the San Francisco *Herald*, William Walker, a noted duelist. Hot-headed action by the clerks led to Graham drawing the short straw and challenging Walker to a duel.

At that time, dueling was a popular means of settling disputes in California. Condemned by some but attended by the crowds, news of the challenge soon spread and on 12 January 1851 the pair met, watched by a vast crowd that included judges, policemen and other officials. The *Alta* noted that 'The weapons used were Colt's revolvers, and five [shots] were to be fired, unless one of the parties was hit before. Two shots were exchanged. At the first fire, Mr. Walker received his adversary's ball through the leg of his pantaloons, and at the second was shot through the fleshy part of the thigh. The wound was of a very trifling character.' Both men were ten paces apart. Walker conceded his opponent's victory and the affair closed. Graham was charged with aggravated assault and for engaging in an unlawful duel, but was later found not guilty. By which time, reported Secrest, he was involved in another

Above: *William Walker, the noted early California 'lawyer–duelist' and editor of the San Francisco* Herald. *Walker's 1850s-style dress is in sharp contrast to that of his latter-day rivals of the 1870s and later.*

duel when he learned that the love of his life was having an affair behind his back. Graham challenged his rival George Lemon to a duel, but Lemon was not anxious to swap lead. When they did eventually exchange shots, Graham missed with every one, and backing off, tripped and fell. Lemon then rushed up and shot him through the mouth, the bullet splitting his tongue and loosening several teeth before lodging in his throat. Amazingly,

Below: *A Bannack street scene in the 1860s. Depicted are a number of the buggy-type carriages that proved to be popular in most Western areas. Note the false-fronted buildings on the street.*

Graham recovered and again challenged Lemon. This time Lemon was seriously wounded and honor was satisfied. Graham survived a number of duels, served as a vigilante, and practised law. Yet he did not relish his reputation as a gunfighter. Such a reputation he thought was a curse and only encouraged every 'reckless fool who wants to get his name up as a desperado' to force one into a fight. For such an individual, his constitution was frail and he died in bed with his boots off in 1866.

Another of the lesser known California gunfighters was James ('Jim') McKinney, a badman who plagued the state in later years. Some recalled that when sober he was a fine man, but when drunk he was treacherous and deadly. A compulsive gambler he was involved in a number of shooting scrapes that brought him to the law's attention. He served some time in San Quentin Prison, from which place he was released in 1895. He was soon in trouble, and by 1900 was again on the wanted list. In 1901 he killed a man named Red Sears in a duel in Bakersfield, and in 1902 shot it out with the local law in Porterville after getting blind drunk in the Mint saloon in company with an equally obnoxious character named Scotty Calderwood, who owned a beer and eating establishment called Scotty's Chop House. McKinney shot Willis, the local marshal, in the mouth, and when a friend named Billy Lynn tried to intercede, Jim fired both barrels of a shotgun into his stomach. McKinney survived constant chases, and committed several more murders before being blasted to death by a shotgun held by the brother of a man he had just killed. So passed one of California's deadliest and feared old-time gunmen.

Montana's gold rush was overshadowed to some extent by that which took California by storm, but it was nonetheless as important. Gold deposits had been found as early as 1851, and again in 1858, but it was 1862 before the first big discovery was made at Bannack. This was followed on 26 May 1863 by a strike at

DERINGERS 1859–75

Between the late 1850s and the 1870s rimfire ammunition became available and 'deringer-type' single- or multi-barreled pistols were in great demand. In the 1870s single- and double-barreled versions proved popular. The carrying of such deadly weapons inspired much thought. Some relied upon boot tops, sleeve cuffs, waistbands, or even inside hats. Ladies of uneasy virtue even carried them in a form of 'crotch pouch'!

1. A Sharps & Co. .32 caliber four-barrel pocket pistol. By depressing the button at the front of the frame, with the pistol at half-cock, the barrel could be pushed forward to load or eject the cartridges.
2. A later version of the Sharps four-barrel model with a bird's head grip.
3. William Marston's three-shot pocket pistol.
4. Later version of the Marston pistol.
5. Remington's .41 'Double Derringer'. Made in .41 center- and rimfire.
6. Late Sharps four-barrel pocket pistol with bird's head grip.
7. Frank Wesson's two-shot pistol. Center 'barrel' sometimes contained a small 'dirk'.
8. .22 caliber long cased rimfire ammunition.
9. Two .32 caliber rounds.
10. Remington-Elliot .32 caliber rimfire four-barrel ring trigger deringer, sometimes called 'Pepperbox'.
11. Remington double deringer (s.n. 99745) shown opened.
12. A Sharps four-barrel pistol with checkered walnut stock.
13. Similar pistol but with gutta-percha grips.
14. Version of the Marston three-barrel pistol.
15. Eben T. Starr's four-barrel 'pepperboxes' were rivals to the Sharps version.
16. Remington's 'Saw Handle' deringer (c. 1865) was produced in rimfire calibers from .30 to .41.
17. David Williamson's .41 rimfire deringer was modeled upon Henry Deringer's original. Unique in having a percussion insert when fixed ammunition was not available.
18. Colt's first model deringer based upon National No. 1.
19. A left-hand view of a

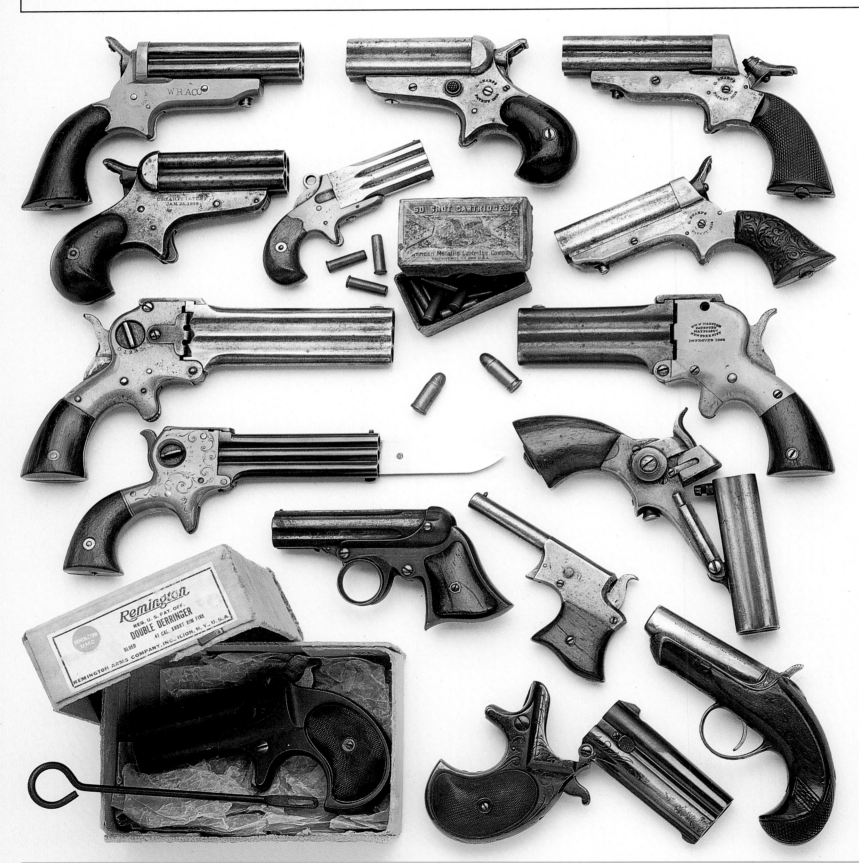

similar pistol.
20. Jacob Rupertus single-barreled pocket pistol.
21. Union single-shot deringer.
22. Rollin White pocket pistol with a unique swivel breech.
23. A J.T. Stafford single-shot .22 caliber pistol with original holster.
24. Colt's No. 3 deringer in .41 rimfire.
25. Dexter Smith patent single-shoot, .22 caliber breech-loading pistol.

26. Two .41 short rimfire cartridges.
27. Rupertus single-shot .38 caliber breech-loading pistol.
28. .32 rimfire cartridge.
29. F. Schoop patent two-shot 'harmonica' .30 caliber rimfire pocket pistol.
30. Merwin & Bray .30 cal. single-shot pistol.
31. American Arms Co.-Wheeler patent .32 caliber roll-over pocket pistol.
32. Dickinson .32 caliber

single-shot pistol. The ratchet is the extractor.
33. The Hammond Bulldog pistol.
34. Brown Manufacturing Co. 'Southerner' with a pivoting barrel.
35. Marlin Repeater cards, 'made by Miss Annie Oakley'.
36. Marlin's 'O.K.' Model deringer.

(Artifacts courtesy of Buffalo Bill Historical Center, Cody, Wyoming.)

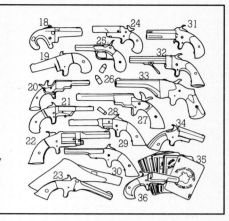

Above: *Hydraulic mining in the rubble-strewn landscape at Alder Gulch, Montana Territory, in 1860–71. By this time, much of the earlier pick and shovel work had been replaced by machinery.*

Below: *Virginia City, Montana, the scene of much violence, from a photograph made in the 1860s. The wooden buildings still dominate the town, some of them little more than cabins.*

Above: *Olaf Seltzer painted some of the most dramatic events in Montana history. His 1930s work depicts Robber's Rock, near Bannack, Montana, the reported rendezvous of the Plummer gang.*

Alder Gulch. The strike was made by one William Fairweather who was accompanied by six others. Once the news reached Bannack, hundreds and then thousands moved into the area, and within weeks Virginia City was teeming with would-be goldseekers and the fourteen mile long gulch would eventually yield more than $100 million in 'dust'. On 26 May 1864, exactly one year after the gold strike, Montana Territory was created. In July a further strike was made at the 'Last Chance Gulch' where Helena was established.

All manner of people arrived in the region: deserters from the Union or Confederate armies, speculators, gamblers, prostitutes, and a number of professional people, among them doctors, lawyers, newspapermen and a few priests. Rarest among them were genuine miners, but regardless of profession, most were prepared to dig and hoped to prosper. But inevitably, there also appeared numerous individuals whose exploits could at best be called colorful or at worse 'murderous'. These were professional thieves, roadagents and others devoted to the accumulation of wealth at someone else's expense.

The list of those associated with the lawless element is long and contains the names of individuals who are now immortalized in folklore. There was Henry Plummer, sheriff of Bannack, who was later discovered to be the leader of the roadagents: George Ives; Haze Lyons, Frank Parish; Boone Helm; George ('Club Foot') Lane and Jack Gallagher, among others. Of this motley crew, perhaps Plummer and Helm were the best known. Of Plummer, it was said that he spent much time perfecting his marksmanship, and according to Thomas Dimsdale, author of *The Vigilantes of Montana*,

Above: *John X. Beidler, the chief hangman of the Montana vigilantes, who 'jerked a number of noted bad men to Jesus' in the interests of law and order, if not in the name of justice.*

Above: *Seltzer's painting shows Montana vigilantes meeting to swear an oath to uphold some sense of law and order in the face of anarchy at the hands of the likes of Plummer and his roadagents.*

Above: *Captain James Williams, one of the mainstays of the Montana vigilante movement. People power counted for much in the early days when law and order was non-existent.*

he could draw 'his pistol and discharge the five loads in three seconds'. Modern fast draw fanatics might scoff at such a comment, but Dimsdale made it very clear that it was not just a case of drawing and pulling the trigger; Plummer also took aim. Sadly for Henry, his skill with a gun could not save him from the inevitable, for allied against him and his cronies were Captain James Williams and some very determined characters, among them Neil Howie and John Fetherstun, and the inimitable John X. Beidler, who acted as 'hangman' when the occasion demanded it. And among the so-called 'good bad men' who flocked to the

place was the notorious Joseph Alfred ('Jack') Slade who was, according to Mark Twain, 'more feared' in some parts than 'the Almighty'.

The murderous activities of Plummer and his gang eventually led to their deaths at the hands of the vigilantes with no remorse or regrets from any quarter, but in the case of Jack Slade it was different. He came from Illinois,

Below: *Olaf Seltzer's dramatic painting of the last living moments of George Ives, on 21 December 1863, at Nevada City, Madison County, Montana. Ives was soon followed by others of his ilk.*

had fought in the Mexican War and had achieved a good reputation as a line superintendent for Russell, Majors & Waddell. He was also regarded as one of the best shots on the plains, and was never loath to demonstrate his skill. Indeed, Mark Twain's description of his accuracy has both a touch of the humorous and the macabre:

> Slade was a matchless marksman with a Navy revolver. The legends say that one morning at Rocky Ridge, when he was feeling comfortable, he saw a man approaching who had offended him some days before – observe the fine memory he had for matters like that – and, 'Gentlemen,' said Slade, drawing, 'it is a good twenty-yard shot – I'll clip the third button on his coat!' Which he did. The bystanders all admired it. And they all attended the funeral too.

Slade's weakness was drink, and when liquored up he was dangerous. Having warned him several times of his behavior, the vigilantes finally called a halt and on 10 March 1864 they hanged him. His distraught wife rounded upon his slayers and berated them for not having the guts to shoot him rather than hang him like a dog. Indeed, some of those who had been involved were later reported to have wept openly as the box was kicked away and Slade choked to death. But right or wrong, legal or unlawful though the vigilante movement was, its role in containing violence prior to the establishment of courts and other due process cannot be ignored, for without such drastic action, there would have been only one alternative – anarchy.

BLEEDING KANSAS

If California and Montana exemplified the era of the vigilantes, then it was Kansas and Missouri that presaged the era of the guerrilla, whose penchant for the pistol was well known. On 30 May 1854, President Franklin Pierce signed the Kansas–Nebraska Act, opening up a territory some 200 miles long by 700 miles wide. Most of it was grassland inhabited by various Indian tribes and roaming herds of buffalo and other animals. The Act established the boundaries of Kansas on the west of the Missouri state line to the continental divide, and a part of the Rocky Mountains and present day eastern Colorado. The Act also provided for popular sovereignty, which meant that the people themselves would decide whether or not the territory would achieve statehood as a 'free' or 'slave' state.

The issue of slavery, that 'peculiar institution' that pervaded southern thoughts and actions, had long been a subject of debate. Under the Missouri Compromise of 1820, states were admitted to the Union on the basis that there should be an equal number of 'free' or 'slave' states in the Union. In simple terms, the 'Missouri Compromise' permitted slavery in that state, but she was forbidden to exclude free Negroes and mulattoes. West of the state, however, slavery was outlawed from all United States territories north of the 36° 30' parallel, Missouri's southern boundary. In 1850, California was admitted to the Union as a free state, which meant that the next admission – Kansas Territory – would be slave-owning. But since the Act allowed for a free vote, conflict was inevitable.

Once the Act became law, pro-slavery Missourians were poised to invade the territory and claim it for the South. In the meantime, the government had forcibly moved several Indian tribes further south to Indian Territory (present-day Oklahoma). It was now the calm before the storm.

The early months of 1854 proved to be quiet. Some Missourians crossed the border to establish pro-slavery towns, among them Leavenworth, Kickapoo and Atchison, while free staters set up places such as Topeka, which eventually become the state capital. Word filtered back East describing the lush grass and farming land awaiting settlement. Soon the trickle of immigrants became a flood.

The territory had six governors between 1854 and 1861, none of whom lasted long in office. Andrew Reeder, appointed in October 1854, set the first territorial election for 29 November 1854, which was a fiasco. Militant Missourians crossed the border and intimidated the electorate, forcing them to join the pro-slavery vote. The same thing happened at the next election on 30 March 1855. Patience was fast running out, and it was only a matter of time before there was violence.

It is traditional to assume that the free state element were the heroes and the pro-slavery Missourians the villains in the Kansas–Missouri disputes. But that is erroneous. A large number of the immigrants were God-fearing folk, anxious to settle in the territory and start a new life. Others, however, had different ideas. Politically as well as racially motivated, they sought power and prestige. And among them

Above: *John Brown, whose 'soul goes marching on'. Fanatic, madman, saint – many words can be found to describe this violent individual. But no one will ever forget John Brown of Kansas.*

Below: *General James H. Lane, the 'Grim Chieftain'; his 'Free State Army' played a major role in the Kansas–Missouri border wars. He committed suicide in July 1866 following a bout of depression.*

was the insane fanatic John Brown, whose abolitionist views were religiously motivated. On the Missouri side, a similar situation existed, for not every Missourian was a slave-owner. Many of them were more concerned with survival than slavery, and did not necessarily share the view of their vociferous neighbors that the Kansans were a bunch of 'Abolitionist nigger-stealers'.

In Washington, the government was seriously concerned at the developments in Kansas. Troops were despatched in an effort to cool tempers by keeping the warring factions apart. Then in June 1855 the free staters held a convention at Lawrence, repudiating bogus election results. Their aim was the abolition of slavery. Prominent among them, however, was James H. Lane, a former congressman from Indiana who had fought in the Mexican War, and who had come to Kansas in the belief that he could organize a Democratic party. When this was rejected, he changed sides and joined the free staters, becoming one of their best known leaders. It was James Lane's 'Free State Army' that pitted itself against the Missouri 'Border Ruffians'.

On 21 May 1856 the Border Ruffians attacked Lawrence. John Brown swore to avenge the attack and set off for Pottawatomie Creek where he knew a number of pro-slavery Missourians were camped. On the 24th, aided by four of his sons, he called at the homes of five men, dragged them out and murdered them in front of their families. The murders outraged the territory, and Brown was forced to flee. In May 1858, as a reprisal for the Pottawatomie raid, Missouri Border Ruffians murdered five free state men on the Marais des Cygnes.

Following the Brown outrage in 1856, additional troops were rushed to the area. Missourians, led by David R. Atchison, caught up with Brown and fought him, but he escaped. Federal troops then engaged the Missourians. Lane, anxious to join the fight was prevented from doing so by troops from Fort Leavenworth.

Daniel Woodson succeeded Governor Reeder as acting governor on 16 August 1855. Woodson, a pro-slavery man, organized companies of militia in the belief that the territory was in open rebellion. Wilson Shannon replaced him on 7 September, but the pair alternated as governor until 9 September 1856, when Governor John W. Geary was sworn in. Geary promptly disbanded the militia, but was unable to prevent Colonel James A. Harvey's company from fighting a minor engagement with the pro-slavery men at Hickory Point. Harvey had deserted his wife and family in Chicago to seek adventure in Kansas. Following the Hickory Point fight, a number of them were arrested by Federal troops and lodged in jail at Lecompton. Backed by Federal troops, Geary persuaded Atchison and his men to leave the territory.

The influx of people into the territory and the danger of attack proved to be a bonus for armsmakers and dealers in weapons. The Colt Navy, Dragoon and Pocket models were much in favor, but there was also a demand for rifles

Right: *This sketch of a Border Ruffian would also aptly describe the Civil War guerrilla – feather in cap; plain or fancy shirt; knee-boots complete with Bowie knife, and armed with two pistols.*

and carbines, the most popular arm being the Sharps. Christian Sharps, a native of New England, had worked at the government arsenal at Harpers Ferry and later set up on his own. His breech-loading pistols, rifles and carbines proved very popular, but it was the carbine that attracted most attention. In 1853 the British government purchased 6,000 of them. But the most famous or notorious model was the so-called 'Beecher's Bible' version. The Connecticut Kansas Colony, organized by a group of abolitionists in New England, among them the Reverend Henry Ward Beecher, shipped in a number of these weapons to the colony in boxes marked 'Bibles'. The colonists later built a church which they named the 'Beecher Bible and Rifle Church' which still stands. John Brown is also reported to have purchased two hundred Sharps carbines which were shipped to him in Kansas. Many of them were recovered following Brown's abortive raid on the Harpers Ferry arsenal, for which he was tried and hanged on 2 December 1859.

The individuals who formed part of the free state forces (or 'Jayhawkers' as some called them) were much on a par with their Missouri counterparts. The Pottawatomie and Marais des Cygnes massacres, horrible though they were, were minor events when compared to the antics of the guerrillas in Missouri, Arkansas and parts of Kansas in the Civil War.

Below: *In 1859, pro-slavery Missourians kidnapped Dr John Doy. Tried at St Joseph, he was found guilty of 'slave-stealing'. Jayhawker friends rescued him from jail, and were photographed with him at Lawrence.*

SHARPS RIFLES

Christian Sharps produced his first breech loading single-shot rifle in the late 1840s and by the mid-1850s had established himself as one of the premier American arms makers. His reputation was such that the British government purchased several thousand carbines for cavalry use, and by the late 1850s the weapon was a favorite on the frontier. As mentioned elsewhere, Sharps' 1853 Model carbine was shipped in Kansas Territory by the Reverend

Beecher and other abolitionists in crates marked 'Bibles'. They are now often referred to as 'Beecher's Bibles'.

By the time of the Civil War the Sharps rifles and carbines were much in demand, and Col. Hiram Berdan, chief of the celebrated 'Sharpshooters', used a number of the Model 1859 rifles, in .52 caliber, some with set triggers which enhanced accuracy. Following the war, Sharps, who had dissolved his own company in the early 1860s and then entered partnership with William Hankins,

manufacturing small four-barrel pistols, breech-loading rifles and carbines, parted from Hankins in 1866 and set up on his own again to produce small pistols and longarms.

After his death, the company began producing powerful rifles that bore his name, among them the celebrated .50 caliber buffalo rifle known as the 'Big Fifty'. The accuracy and stopping power of the large caliber Sharps rifles are legendary. At ranges of 1,000 yards they were reckoned to be deadly.

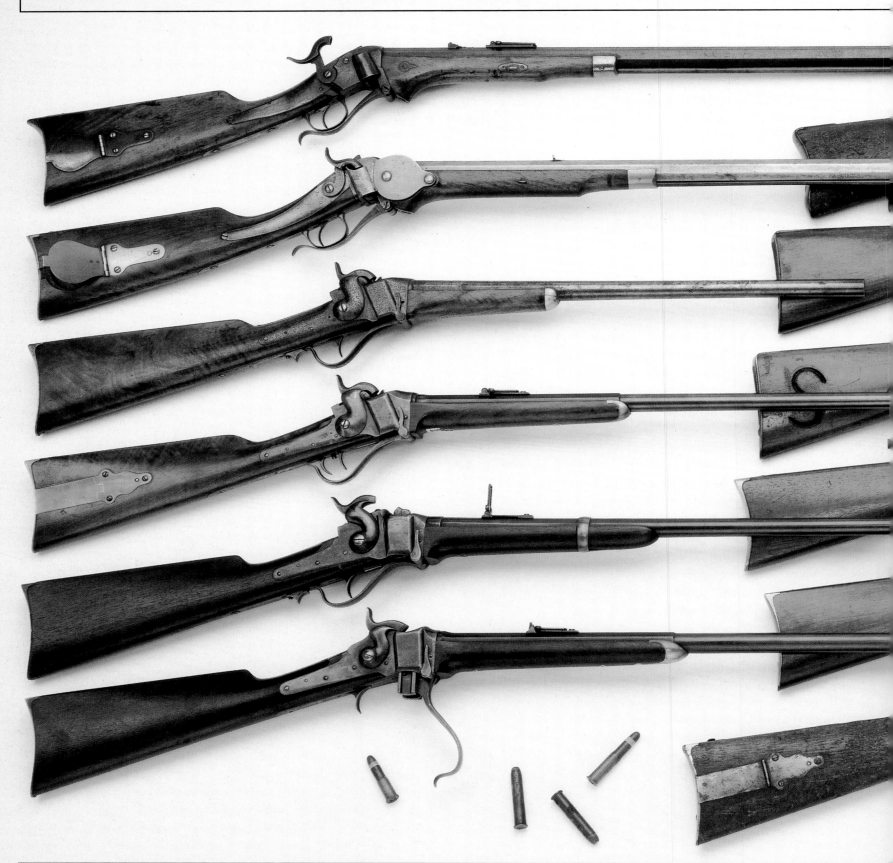

1. Sharps Model 1850 rifle complete with Maynard's tape primer.
2. Model 1849 with circular disk automatic capping device.
3. Sharps Model 1852 carbine in .52 caliber and slanting breech.
4. The rifle version complete' with set triggers for targets and hunting.
5. Sharps 1869 carbine, produced in calibers as large as .60.
6. Rifle version of the Model 1869.
7. A .40-50 caliber Sharps cartridge. Both the percussion and the rim- or centerfire versions could be loaded at speed.
8. .49-90 cartridge.
9. .44-70 cartridge.
10. This 1874 Sharps rifle has a repaired stock. Many rifles were prone to breakage at this point due to recoil.
11. Version of 1874 Model with blade foresight.
12. Fine Sharps in 'as new' condition.
13. This rifle has normal rear sights on the barrel and peep or adjustable sights on the stock.
14. Round-barreled Sharps rifles were uncommon.
15. Box of .40 caliber shells 1⅞ in. long.
16. New Model 1863 rifle.
17. Plains cartridge belt.

(Artifacts courtesy of Buffalo Bill Historical Center, Cody, Wyoming.)

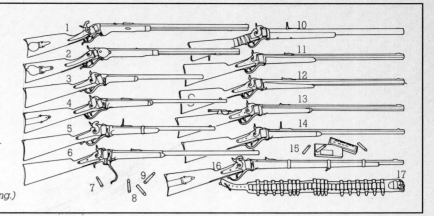

THE GUERRILLA WARS

History records that the American Civil War was fought for the most part in the eastern states, where victories, defeats and appalling casualties captured the interest of the world. But there was another war going on at the same time where murder and mayhem were constant companions. This took place in south-west Missouri, eastern Kansas and much of Arkansas. It was a guerrilla war where no quarter was given, none asked and those that survived it carried the scars for life.

When the Civil War erupted following the firing on Fort Sumter, there was a lull in the mid-western states while in the East men rushed to join the Union or Confederate cause. Kansas, which had been admitted to the Union in January 1861, was relatively quiet, but in Missouri, where the Union army had immediately gained control of St Louis, the railroads and other places where their military influence was felt, many of the inhabitants were pro-South. Most people considered the state to be a part of the Confederacy, and the suggestion that she had been 'invaded' encouraged resistance among much of the population. Several attempts had been made by the Confederacy to take over the state, but apart from a number of noted victories – Wilson's Creek in August 1861 and the occupation of Springfield – they had not been too successful. The Union regained Springfield and its forces continued to occupy important strategic places right through the war. Among the population were many thousands of young pro-Southern men whose families occupied homesteads behind Union lines, where they lived at peace with Unionists. Some of them slipped south and joined the Confederate army. Others, however, remained behind. This left a confusion of loyalties. Many of the Missourians, caught between both sides, tried to remain loyal to the

Above: *Captain John Jarrett, a former guerrilla and later member of Jesse James' gang. He was present when the James–Younger gang robbed the Russellville, Kentucky, bank on 21 March 1868.*

Above: *Noted guerrilla George Maddox, dressed in the approved fashion, also sports a pair of Remington's 1863 New Model Army pistols. The chambers of the left-hand pistol are clearly seen to be loaded and ready for action. Despite his dandified appearance, Maddox was a cold-blooded killer. Some historians have erroneously confused him with one Dick Maddox who also followed the 'black flag' of Quantrill.*

Union, resentful though they were of Federal intrusion. Some others thought that they could serve the South better by direct action, and many a former Border Ruffian simply changed tack and henceforth acquired a new name – guerrilla.

By the fall of 1861 there were a number of guerrillas operating in Missouri, foremost among them the infamous William Clarke Quantrill. His acts of terrorism in the name of the Confederacy aroused bitter hatred, even among some Southerners who felt that the wholesale destruction of persons and property was unjustified. And when, in August 1863, his band attacked Lawrence, Kansas, and murdered 150 civilian men and boys the Union was determined that he should be destroyed.

The earliest attempts to stop Quantrill were made in late 1861 or early 1862 with the formation of the equally infamous Kansas 'Red Legs' (so-called because of the red-dyed sheepskin toppings to their boots), formed from men of Colonel C. R. Jennison's 7th Kansas Regiment known as 'Jennison's Jayhawkers'. The 'Red Legs' survived until 1863, by which time they had degenerated into a band of thieves and murderers. They were disbanded and orders given that anyone seen wearing the familiar red boot topping would be shot on sight.

William ('Bloody Bill') Anderson, Quantrill's able lieutenant and eventual successor, vied with his chief to be even more vicious, and on several occasions proved it. He was eventually killed by Union troops (ironically, so was Quantrill himself, a month after the war ended). But others, many of them now lost to history, fought in the woods and forests of Missouri and Arkansas. In scenes reminiscent of Revolutionary France in the 1790s or Nazi-occupied Europe, no one was sure whether his neighbor might betray him, or if the late night visitor was a friend or foe. And worse, the arrival of a military detail in the uniform ex-

Above: *The aptly named 'Bloody Bill' Anderson was with Quantrill at the Lawrence, Kansas, massacre in 1863. Note the bullet holes in his forehead and cheek.*

pected sometimes turned out to be the enemy in disguise, who lost no time in looting and killing. Many a family was woken in the night, their menfolk dragged away, and their bodies found hanging or lying shot dead in the woods.

The sort of men who perpetrated these crimes claimed that they did it for 'the cause'. Even in old age, many of them skated around the atrocities and instead remembered only the excitement and the thrill of battle. And invariably they would bring out their prized Navy revolver which had been the principal weapon of the guerrilla on either side. Quantrill's men were reputed to have carried as many as eight such pistols spread around their belts or in saddle bags. Other weapons were

used, of course, and the Colt New Model Army of 1860, a .44 caliber weapon intended for cavalry use, proved very popular. It had been designed to replace the existing 1848 model Dragoon and weighed just a few ounces more than the Navy model (upon which it was based). At the same time, Colt introduced their New Model Navy, which resembled the Army model in that it had a round barrel and instead of the old hinged lever ramrod of the original Navy pistol, it was now operated by a ratching system, and in appearance was more streamlined than its predecessors. But any Colt revolver was at a premium in the South, as indeed were other northern-made arms, particularly the Remington.

Eliphalet Remington, Jr, produced his first gun at Ilion Forge, New York, in 1816, and by the late 1850s the family firm had grown enormously. They entered the revolver market in 1858 with a pistol based upon a design by Fordyce Beals who assisted with other models. Then in 1863 the company produced the famous New Model Army pistol, a solid-frame .44 caliber percussion revolver that remained in production until 1875. Despite the lapse during the latter part of the war when a number of the pistols blew up, the majority of them were welcomed and much appreciated by soldiers and civilians alike.

The total disregard for human life displayed by the guerrillas during the war culminated in a period of retribution once hostilities ended, and a man was liable to keep quiet about his war activities. Only in later years, when nostalgia figured in most reminiscences, did the old-timers admit to their past, by which time reunions of surviving ex-guerrillas had become an annual event, some such gatherings occurring until the 1920s. And among those survivors were some of the men who continued their association with the gun by becoming outlaws.

Above: *Col. Charles R. Jennison, leader of the 7th Kansas Cavalry – 'Jennison's Jayhawkers' – from a rare Civil War portrait. Many of the men who rode with him became members of the 'Red Legs'.*

Above: *Clark Hockensmith, who tried to save Quantrill when they were attacked by Union cavalry on 10 May 1865. Both men were shot when trying to escape on the same mount. Quantrill died on 6 June.*

Above: *John Nichols, seen in jail just before he was hanged as a 'bushwacker' in September 1863. He and his gang were greatly feared. Note the ball and chain and the guard's Navy pistol barrel!*

COLT'S CARTRIDGE COMPETITORS

Among the numerous cartridge revolvers that appeared in the 1870s, when the Rollin White patent for bored-through cylinders expired, were a number that proved to be serious rivals to Colt's New Model Army Revolver, 'The Peacemaker'. During ordnance tests, however, what the Colt lacked in manufacturing precision it more than made up for in reliability in rough handling, which made it an ideal weapon for military and frontier use.

1. Prescott single-action six-shot Navy revolver in .38 caliber rimfire.
2. Pond pocket or belt pistol.
3. Merwin & Bray pocket pistol.
4. Uhlinger pocket revolver (sometimes credited to W.L. Grant) in .32 rimfire.
5. Bacon's Navy revolver, six-shot .38 rimfire.
6. Brooklyn Firearms Co.'s 'Slocum' pocket pistol in .32 rimfire.
7. Eagle Arms Company cup primed pocket revolver.
8. Two .22 caliber cartridges.
9. Bacon's .32 caliber rimfire pocket pistol. Short-lived because of infringement of Smith & Wesson's rights to bored-through cylinders.
10. Moore's 'Seven-Shooter' .32 caliber rimfire pocket revolver.
11. Remington New Model Army 1863 converted from percussion to cartridge.
12. Box of .45 caliber ammunition from Colt's Army revolver.
13. Remington double-action New Model belt pistol.
14. Remington New Model Army pistol converted to metallic cartridge.
15. Three .44 Remington cartridges.
16. A factory conversion of the 1863 Army revolver, engraved and fitted with ivory stocks.
17. Further Remington rounds.
18. Remington's No. 2 pocket revolver.
19. Allen & Wheelock's center hammer lipfire revolver. Notches were cut into the rear of the chambers to allow the hammer face to strike the cartridge 'lips'.
20. Belts complete with cartridge loops became common by the late 1870s. This ornate version is quite late.
21. The holster may not be contemporary to the belt, but it is of the type in common usage then.

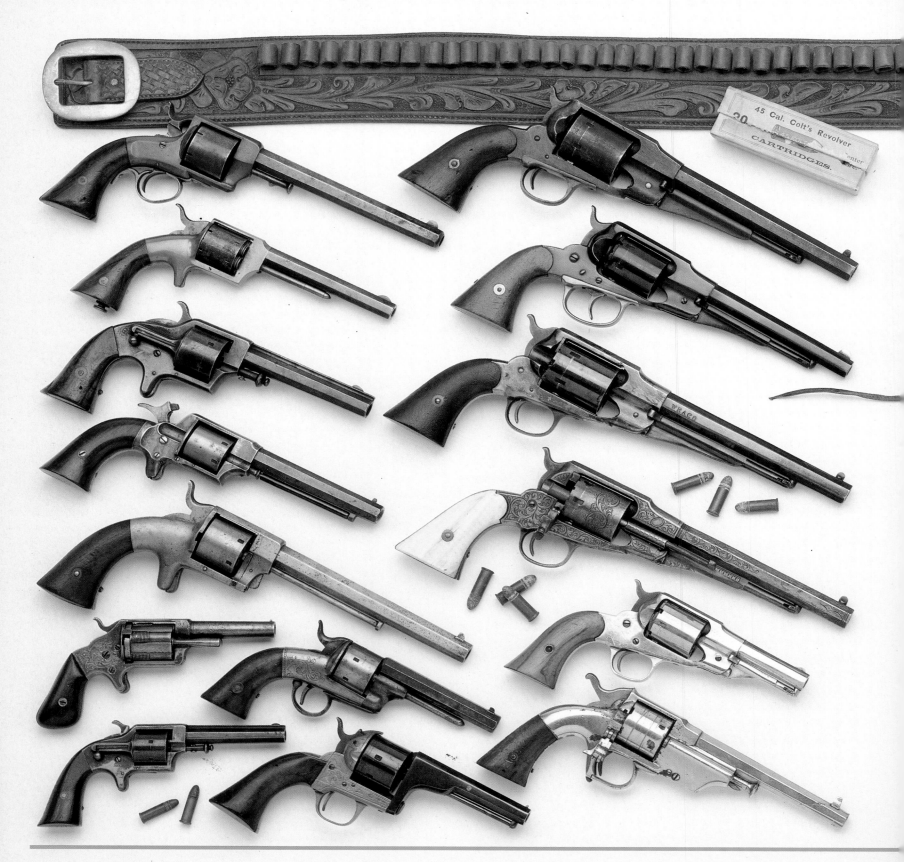

22. Merwin & Hulbert's open top Army revolver. This well-made pistol, beaten by the Colt Peacemaker in trials, was popular out West.
23. Box of reloadable cartridges made at the government's Frankford Arsenal.
24. Merwin & Hulbert's Army pistol nickel-plated.
25. Government-made cartridges.
26. Merwin & Hulbert's Army pistol with top strap.
27. Remington Model 1890 single-action Army revolver. About 2,000 of these were made.
28. Box of Winchester-made cartridges for Colt's .45 double- and single-action Army revolvers.
29. Smith & Wesson's No. 3 Model Army pistol in .44 caliber 'Russian'. So called because of special ammunition ordered by the Russians.
30. Smith & Wesson No. 3 'American' Model.
31. Schofield version of the Model No. 3 with improved barrel latch.
32. Smith & Wesson New Model No. 3 revolver in .44 Russian caliber.
33. .44 Russian cartridge.
34. Smith & Wesson's .44 double-action 1881 'Frontier' revolver.

(Artifacts courtesy of Buffalo Bill Historical Center, Cody, Wyoming.)

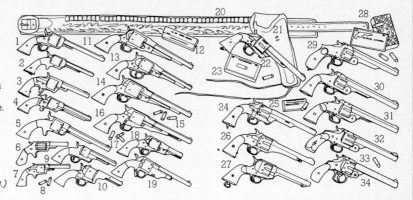

THE OWLHOOT TRAIL

The legend of the outlaw or social misfit has long had mass appeal, especially if it can be claimed that the individual was wronged and only turned to outlawry in order to fight injustice by righting the wrongs of others. This theme has permeated folklore for centuries, and is a familiar part of the Robin Hood myth. Similarly Jesse James, 'America's Robin Hood', would seem to be a natural successor. There the similarity ends, for the real Jesse James bore little resemblance to his legend. He was a product of an era that spawned many like him: survivors of the Civil War who had experienced the power of the pistol, when fighting on either side, men who found it difficult to adjust. In Jesse's case, it has been claimed by his descendants that because of his record he was refused a pardon. Instead, he was shot and wounded when he tried to surrender and this changed his whole life. His best biographer, William A. Settle, discovered that there is no record of Jesse ever attempting to surrender, and the story of his wound is not corroborated, although he does admit that Jesse may have been wounded about this time – perhaps from a late war engagement. Whatever the truth, the James brothers were rootless, moving from place to place. Jesse and Frank kept low for some time, but on 13 February 1866, almost a year later, they robbed the Clay County Savings Bank and were wanted men.

Jesse Woodson James was born on 5 September 1847, in Clay County, Missouri, the youngest son of Robert James, a Baptist minister, and Zerelda, a strong-willed lady who in later years proved to be a formidable opponent of those whom she thought had persecuted her sons. Frank James, Jesse's elder brother, was born on 10 January 1843, and although four years older than his brother in later life was dominated by him.

Robert James succumbed to gold fever in 1850 and left for California, where he contracted a proper fever and died. The widow James then remarried, but this was not a success and at her third attempt she married a quiet but prosperous man named Reuben Samuel. By the time the Civil War broke out in 1861, the family boasted several Negro slaves and were ardent in their support for the Confederacy. Frank is reported to have joined Quantrill, and later claimed to have been on the Lawrence raid. Most historians state that the James or Samuel family suffered at the hands of Union sympathizers, and on one occasion Reuben was dragged to a tree, a noose tied around his neck and he was 'lifted' off his feet in an effort to persuade him to impart information that he did not have. Sixteen-year-old Jesse witnessed this and swore revenge against the Yankees. Perhaps. But by 1864, he was reported to have joined Quantrill and for a time rode with 'Bloody Bill' Anderson. Some have

Above: *Jesse Woodson James from a tintype made in about 1864. He is sporting several of Colt's 1860 Army revolvers, worn in typical guerrilla fashion. Most of these pistols were captured during combat.*

Right: *N.C. Wyeth's classic painting of the James gang in hiding conveys a sense of the state of 'high anxiety' in which they lived. Jesse himself looks poised for action, as he stares into the Missouri landscape.*

suggested that it was his relationship with Anderson that eventually prevented his pardon. Be that as it may, a taste of killing and robbing had its effect, and the robbing of the Clay County bank was only the start of a career of robbery and murder that was to last almost fifteen years, by which time his reputation as a latter-day Robin Hood was assured.

Jesse James himself was an enigma. He married, had a family yet continued his career of outlawry. Claims that his latter exploits were directed at the 'robber barons' who ran the railroads and cheated people out of their property by claiming that they had 'right of way' to build tracks across their land were widely believed by those who were anxious to discredit the corporations behind the railroads. Similarly, 'crooked' banking houses were also targeted. It was claimed by some that it was the railroad and banking concerns who hired the Pinkerton Detective Agency to hunt down the James gang. In this latter respect, the activities of the Pinkertons do not inspire confidence. William Pinkerton's Civil War exploits have come in for some criticism, but it was the attack on Jesse's mother's home on 26 January 1875 that calls their role into question.

According to most sources, the Pinkertons set fire to the family home in an effort to drive them out. A fireball of burning cotton was discovered in the kitchen and when it was pushed into the fireplace it exploded, killing Jesse and Frank's nine-year-old half-brother and so seriously mangling his mother's hand that she had to have it amputated. The local press were incensed and the Pinkertons were widely condemned for the attack, and were described as 'fiendish'. Claims that the device was only a 'smoke bomb' were dismissed with contempt. Only very recently has it been discovered, following some research at the National Archives in Washington, that the Ordnance Department authorized the issue of a bomb containing what has been described as 'Greek fire' to the Agency, thereby confirming that there was an attempt to destroy the whole family.

Sympathy for Jesse, however, would be misplaced, for he cared little for those who might get in his way. He never trusted anybody, was ever watchful and suspicious of strangers. Some recalled that his eyes were constantly on the move and he blinked all the time. Others credited this to a complaint known as 'granulated eyelids', but it was far more likely that he suffered from trachoma, which was common at the time, that could cause pain and discomfort yet it did not necessarily endanger the sight, but did require treatment.

By the early 1870s, the James brothers and the Youngers (James, John, Robert and Coleman) had teamed up, and were including train robbery in their itineraries. No one knew for sure where they would strike next. In September 1872, Frank and Jesse were reported to

SINGLE- & DOUBLE-ACTION REVOLVERS

During Sam Colt's lifetime, all his pistols were single-actions. He experimented with self-cocking (by pulling the trigger and cocking and firing the hammer in one motion) but decided it was unreliable. Between 1850 and 1870 others followed his example and the accompanying group of arms indicates how closely they followed Colt. A number of makers used top straps instead of the open frame, but in other respects copied Colt's basic design.

1. Belts varied in width; some were plain, but by the mid-1870s cartridge loops were common. Before then most people carried saddle bags or ammunition pouches.
2. .36 caliber Whitney Navy pistol (s.n. 14457) that rivaled both Colt and Remington; well made and popular.
3. The pistol's original holster.
4. Whitney five-shot .31 caliber pocket model. On both the Navy and

Pocket pistols, the cylinder pin was attached to the rammer and held in place by a pin through the frame.
5. The Walch ten-shot .31 pocket pistol.
6. Massachusetts Arms Co.'s licensed copy of the British Beaumont-Adams .31 pocket pistol.
7. The MAC's version of the Beaumont-Adams Army Model in .44 caliber. A number of these were purchased by the Confederacy.

8. Remington-Beals Army pocket revolver.
9. Box of .31 caliber combustible cartridges.
10. Allen & Wheelock's center hammer Army revolver in .44 caliber.
11. Allen & Wheelock's center hammer pocket revolver in .28 caliber.
12. Six .44 caliber combustible cartridges for the Colt 1860 Army revolver.
13. MAC's Maynard primed belt revolver,

.31 caliber.
14. Maynard's cap primers.
15. Springfield Arms Co. pocket revolver in .28 caliber.
16. Remington-Rider double-action New Model belt revolver (1863) in .36 caliber.
17. Remington New Model pocket revolver (1863) in .31 caliber.
18. IXL revolver believed made before 1857, based upon the British

Adams.

19. Box of British-made Joyce percussion caps.
20. Another version of the IXL revolver. B.J. Hart of New York is often credited with their manufacture.
21. Another version of the IXL.
22. James Warner revolver.
23. Cooper double-action Navy revolver with a rebated cylinder; .36 caliber, five-shot.
24. Cooper five-shot .31 double-action pocket pistol.
25. Cooper pocket model; note close resemblance to Colt's pistols.
26. Package of combustible pistol cartridges. Sold in packs of six but larger quantities were available. Most civilians also had reserves of loose powder, ball and caps.
27. Pettengill's double-action hammerless Army pistol; six-shot, .44 caliber.
28. Manhattan's five-shot .36 caliber 'Navy' pistol that some confused with Colt's pistols.
29. Metropolitan Arms Co.'s copy of Colt's 1861 Navy.
30. Manhattan 6-inch barreled Navy pistol.
31. Manhattan .31 caliber five-shot pocket pistol.
32. Union Arms Company pocket pistol with fluted cylinder.
33. Hopkins & Allen pocket pistol.

(Artifacts courtesy of Buffalo Bill Historical Center, Cody, Wyoming.)

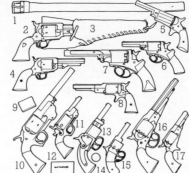

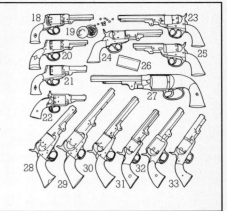

Above: *Thomas Coleman ('Cole') Younger, one of the gang's deadliest members. He rode with Quantrill and was present at the Lawrence, Kansas, massacre. He, too, rode with the James gang.*

Above: *Robert ('Bob') Younger was the 'baby' in the family, and followed his brothers when they joined Jesse James. Captured at Northfield after the abortive raid, he died in prison in 1889.*

Above: *James Younger, the least experienced of the gang; following his imprisonment after the Northfield raid, he was later parolled but committed suicide in St Paul, Minnesota, 1902.*

have held up the cashier's office at the State Fair and escaped with the takings. Later, when a young reporter gave them a glowing write-up in a Kansas City paper, describing them as 'heroes', he received a 'visit' and a present of a gold watch. He refused this, thinking it was stolen. 'Perhaps you can name some man around here you want killed?' He politely declined!

On 7 September 1876 came the final show-down. Eight members of the James–Younger gang tried to rob the Northfield, Minnesota, First National Bank. The staff resisted and, during a bloody battle in which local people joined in, several of the gang and some citizens were killed. Missourians might feel supportive when the James gang robbed banks or hit at the railroads, but in Minnesota there was no such support, and the killing of innocent people only strengthened their resistance. Jesse and Frank escaped, but a seriously wounded Bob Younger was captured. Cole and Jim, who were both wounded, refused to leave their brother and they too were captured. Bob died later in prison but Cole and Jim were paroled in 1901. Cole later teamed up with Frank James in an unsuccessful 'Wild West' show.

Jesse James was murdered by one of his own gang, Robert Ford, on 3 April 1882, at St

Right: *The infamous Richard ('Dick') Liddell, who was involved in the plot to kill Jesse James. As a result, he earned the undying hatred of Jesse's family. He is armed with a Whitney Navy pistol.*

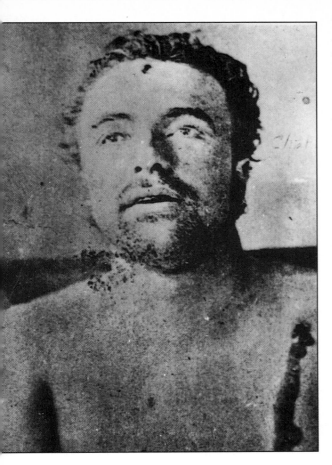

Above: *Clelland ('Clell') Miller, a member of the James gang and said to have worshipped both Jesse and Frank. Miller was shot dead in the street during the Northfield Bank raid in September 1876.*

Joseph, Missouri, where he was living under the alias of 'Howard'. Ford shot him in the back as he stood on a chair to adjust a picture. Ford, it was believed, had connived with the state governor, Thomas T. Crittendon, to murder Jesse and had been promised the $10,000 reward. Crittendon was later to deny any knowledge of such a plot but admitted that he was aware that Bob Ford was with Jesse when he was killed. The governor later became closely associated with the James family. As for the reward, it was divided up among several 'deserving parties'. The governor received one quarter of it – he had been instrumental in raising the money from the railroad companies – and one eighth went to Richard ('Dick') Liddell, a notorious member of Jesse's gang who sought to redeem himself at their expense and who suffered public humiliation when Mrs Samuel called him a 'traitor'. Other officials received their cut of the reward, which left one eighth for Bob and Charlie Ford. So the man who killed Jesse James received only a little more than $600, and with it a reputation as a back-shooting coward. Ford in turn was shot dead in 1892 by Ed Kelly.

Frank James, following several court appearances and aborted trials, escaped jail and survived until 1915, dying in bed at the old James farm.

Right: *James Copeland, whose exploits are said to have 'terrorized the entire southern states' during the 1840s and the early 1850s, was considered a very dangerous man. His hanging was well attended.*

MISSISSIPPI MISFITS

Apart from a cursory glance at the outlaws of California or the roughs and toughs who proliferated along the banks of the Mississippi and Missouri rivers, not much attention has been paid to southern outlaws. One of the most notorious of these was James Copeland, who terrorized parts of Southern Mississippi during the 1830s and the 1840s. So infamous was Copeland that he became a household name from Mobile Bay to Lake Pontchatarain as a man of violence, a robber and a killer who created trouble wherever he went.

Like many of his kind, Copeland was born to respectable folk, his father a veteran of the War of 1812. He was born in the Pascagoula River Valley near the Mississippi Gulf Coast, about ten miles from the Alabama border. John Guice, who rediscovered the *Life and Confession of the Noted Outlaw James Copeland* by Dr J. R. S. Pitts, published originally in 1858, in his introduction to the 1980 facsimile edition wrote that Copeland began his life of crime at the tender age of twelve. Copeland claimed that his mother upheld his 'rascality' when he was accused of stealing pigs from a neighbor. She and a man named Gale H. Wages, a notorious character from Mobile, convinced the boy that if the local courthouse were burned down, evidence against him would no longer exist!

From then on, Copeland, aided by Wages, turned to crime. Arson continued to be a favored means of acquiring wealth, together with grand larceny. So began a career that took Copeland from the ranks of a petty criminal to serious crime. These were the days before Colt's revolvers were readily available, and great reliance was placed upon single-shot pistols, shotguns and knives. But lack of firepower did not impair Copeland's rise to infamy. In 1841, accompanied by Wages and some other companions, he took a trip to Texas. From there the gang moved to Ohio, Louisiana and back to Mississippi, following a lucrative tour. During his nefarious career, Copeland attempted just about every crime in the book, including counterfeiting, rustling and the illegal sale of Negro slaves. But the net was closing. In the winter and spring of 1848, Wages and another gang member were shot by a man named James A. Harvey, who was himself murdered by Copeland. In 1849 Copeland was arrested and charged with larceny and sentenced to four years in the Alabama penitentiary. On his release in 1853, he was promptly re-arrested by the Mississippi authorities and charged with grand larceny. Following two years in the state pen, he was then handed over to the sheriff of Perry County, who placed him in jail to await trial for the Harvey murder. Two years later, in 1857, he was put on trial, found guilty and sentenced to hang. On 30 October, the morning of his execution, a large crowd gathered, some out of morbid curiosity, and others concerned at the news that he had dictated his memoirs to Pitts and that he had threatened to name accomplices. The effect was such, noted Dr Guice, that for 'Mississippians who trace their roots to the former haunts of the Copeland clan, the mention of the *Confession* draws an emotional response to this day'.

THE DALTONS

Copeland was typical of the breed that harbored criminal instincts from childhood and his like could be met almost anywhere. The James brothers on the other hand came from a stable background, but blamed the Civil War for their eventual outlawry. Another famous outlaw family, however, had no such excuse, for they started out law-abiding and some of them actually served the law. Then, for various reasons, things went wrong and they, too, rode the owlhoot trail. These were the Dalton brothers, whose exploits have long intrigued historians, novelists and filmmakers alike.

The Daltons were a very large family: fifteen children (ten boys and five girls) born to Lewis and Adeline Dalton. Most of the children were born when the family lived in Cass County, Missouri, where Lewis was a saloon owner. In 1882 they moved to the edge of Indian Territory and settled on a farm close to Coffeyville, Kansas. The eldest son, Frank, served as a deputy U.S. marshal attached to the formidable Judge Isaac Parker's court at Fort Smith, Arkansas, which for judicial purposes included Indian Territory as a part of its district.

Indian Territory at that time was considered one of the most dangerous places within the United States. More law officers were killed there than anywhere else, yet despite the hazards there was no shortage of would-be deputy marshals. Frank Dalton, eldest of the Dalton boys, was highly regarded as a deputy U.S. marshal, and revered by his younger brothers. Then came tragedy. On 27 November 1887 while attempting to serve a warrant on one Dave Smith for horse-stealing and the illegal sale of whiskey in Indian Territory, he was killed in the ensuing gun battle. Deputy U.S. marshal James R. Cole, who accompanied Frank, was wounded six times but not seriously. Frank, however, who had been shot in the chest by Smith (who had immediately been shot and killed by Cole), was then approached by William Towerly. Looking up at him, and the Winchester pointing at him, Frank begged him not to shoot again: 'Please don't fire; I'm preparing to die.' Towerly ignored him and placing the muzzle of his rifle into Frank's mouth he fired. A second round in his head finally killed him. A $1,000 reward was issued for Towerly for Frank's murder. Towerly's freedom was short-lived. With every available deputy on his trail, he was a marked man. Deputy marshals Moody and Stokley finally caught up with him at Atoka. Towerly killed Stokley, but Moody in turn killed him. Just before he died he admitted shooting Frank as he lay wounded. Moody, however, did not live to enjoy the reward; he was killed soon afterwards by Billy Bruner, an Indian.

Writing in 1918, Emmett Dalton recalled that Frank's death appalled his family and when an invitation came from the U.S. marshal for Indian Territory for Grat to become a deputy, he leapt at the chance. Soon Bob joined him. The Dalton brothers were at first very successful and respected in their roles as deputy marshals, but, according to Emmett, when the brothers discovered that they were being short-changed by the administration (alleging

that fees owed were not paid or were deferred through lack of funds), the brothers decided that they had had enough. 'Grafting as we of to-day know the term was a mild, soothing description of what occurred,' wrote Emmett. 'The government was fleeced by the men in authority, and the men in the ranks were fleeced as well.' So the brothers quit. Others, however, claimed that Bob had been taking bribes and he was fired. Later, rumors that Emmett and Grat had been mixed up in cattle-rustling on the side reached the ears of the court and they, too, were fired. Whatever the cause, the Daltons were beyond the law and so began a brief but hectic career of outlawry.

Emmett claims that all manner of crimes were laid at the door of the Dalton brothers, some committed hundreds of miles away, so none of them expected justice should they be caught. Plans for emigrating to South America

were shelved when Grat was jailed. But he escaped. While he was in California with brothers Bill and Littleton, Emmett and Bob tried their luck in New Mexico. Soon stories filtered back that the pair had robbed a faro game claiming that it had been fixed by a crooked bunch of house gamblers. The pair fled with wanted notices out after them. Bob went to California while Emmett drifted back to Oklahoma. In California Grat teamed up with a gang who tried to rob a train but were beaten off. Bob then moved to Kansas, where he soon became the leader of a gang that included his brothers Emmett, Grat and some equally tough characters, among them Dick Broadwell, Bill Doolin, Bill Power and others of like ilk.

Train hold-ups and other crimes kept them pretty busy until they planned what was to be their final hoist – two banks at Coffeyville, Kansas, to be robbed at the same time. On the

morning of 5 October 1892, Bob, Grat and Emmett, accompanied by Dick Broadwell and Bill Power set out for Coffeyville. David Stewart Elliott, editor of the Coffeyville *Journal*, who later published an account of the battle wrote that as the five horsemen reached the edge of town, all of them disguised with beards or moustaches a local farmer 'took them for a Deputy United States Marshal and posse, who frequently came up from the Indian country in such numbers, similarly equipped. No arms were visible on any of them. Their coats were closely buttoned and their broad-brimmed black slouch hats set forward on their foreheads.'

The plan was for Bob and Emmett to rob the First National Bank, while at the Condon Bank, Grat and Broadwell would make a similar large withdrawal from that one. Unfortunately for the gang, a passerby, a little more curious than most, recognized Bob and Emmett and

Left: *Emmett Dalton photographed prior to the Coffeyville raid. The lady is believed to be Eugenia Moore, his brother Bob's sweetheart. Some claim that Eugenia rode with the gang to Coffeyville.*

Below: *William M. ('Bill') Doolin lies dead on a mortuary slab riddled with bullets. He was the leader of a gang of outlaws known as the 'Oklahombres'. He was killed by a posse in Lawson, Oklahoma, in 1896.*

Below: *George ('Bitter Creek') Newcomb, ex-cowboy turned rustler and outlaw. His infatuation with Rosa Dunn (Rose of the Cimarron) led to his death at the hands of her brothers in 1895.*

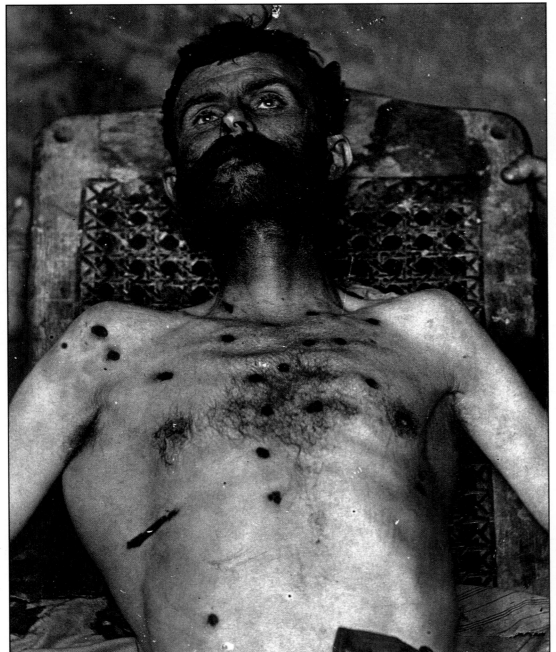

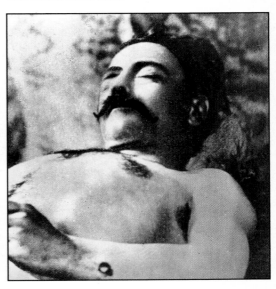

Below: *Roy ('Arkansas Tom') Daugherty, a well-known gunfighter from Missouri who teamed up at one time with the Doolin gang. His attire makes him look more like a successful banker than an outlaw!*

OUTLAW AND LAWMAN

The names of Doolin and Dalton, as we have noted, were notorious throughout Kansas and Oklahoma during the 1890s. The Daltons, originally on the side of the law (Frank, had been killed in the line of duty in 1887 and Grat, Bob and Emmett all wore badges briefly), became outlaws and were wanted men. Federal and state officers such as Ed Nix, Chris Madsen, Bill Tilghman and Louis Eichoff were soon on their trail.

Emmett Dalton was the one brother to survive the deadly attempt to hold up two banks at the same time in Coffeyville, Kansas, in 1892. Badly injured, he spent some years in prison before being pardoned. He later moved to Hollywood and became a technical adviser for 'Westerns', a short-lived movie hero and a real estate agent, as well as author of several books.

The lure of motion pictures that so attracted the likes of Buffalo Bill also interested men like Bill Tilghman who actually took part in the film depicting the capture of the Bill Doolin gang.

Louis Eichoff helped bring law and order to Oklahoma Territory. He is almost forgotten today, but Chris Madsen's solid gold presentation badge gives us some indication of the respect he earned among his peers. When Bill Doolin had the good sense to avoid involvement in the Dalton raid on Coffeyville, he continued to plague Oklahoma. Eichoff was one of the deputies ordered to bring him and his gang in.

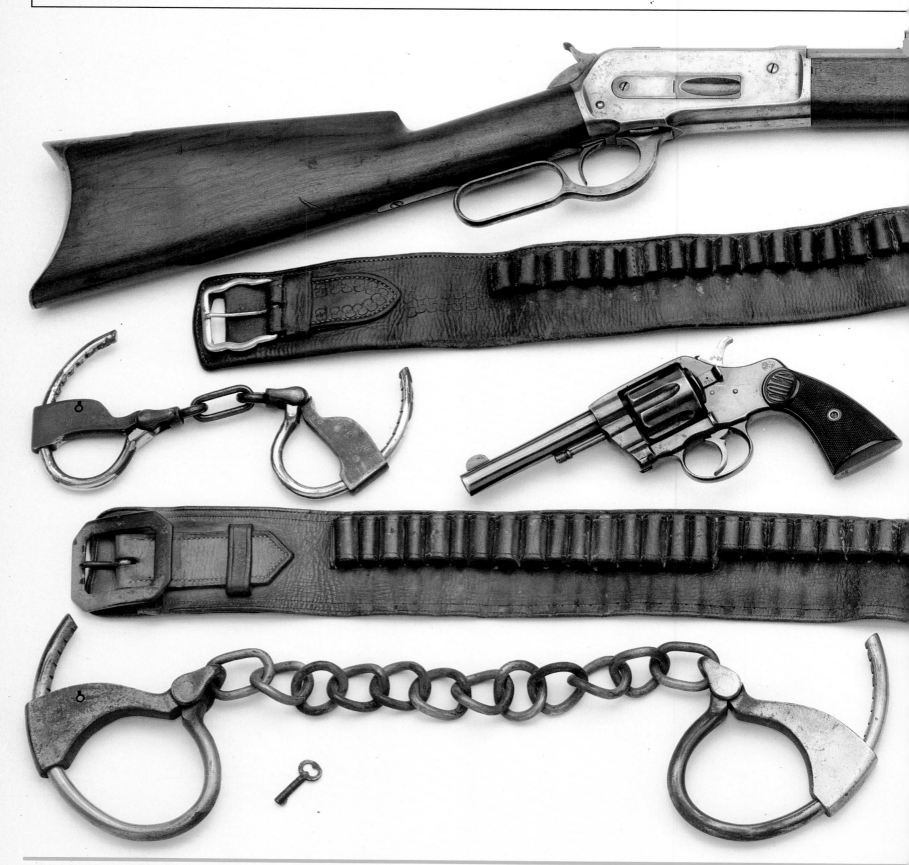

1. Winchester model 1886, caliber .40-82, carried in pursuit of Bill Doolin's gang by Louis Eichoff.
2. Handcuffs of the 1890s.
3. Colt Model 1889 double-action .41 caliber revolver, which belonged to Eichoff.
4. Revolver holster and cartridge belt used to carry Eichoff's Colt .41.
5. Solid gold badge inscribed 'To Louis Eichoff U.S. Deputy Marshal from C.M. [Chris Madsen]'. (Madsen was a former soldier who resigned from the service in 1891 to take up a post of deputy U.S. marshal in Oklahoma.)
6. Leg irons and key used in pursuit of the Doolin gang by Louis Eichoff.
7. Shackles and key used by Eichoff.
8. Revolver holster and belt which belonged to Emmett Dalton.
9. One of ten factory engraved Colt .45s shipped to St Louis from the factory with pearl grips. Emmett Dalton claimed that he and other members of the Dalton gang armed themselves with these guns when they tried to raid Coffeyville.

(Artifacts courtesy of Gene Autry Western Heritage Museum; Los Angeles, California.)

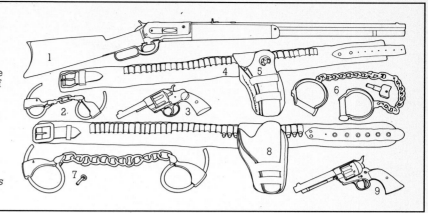

Above: *The end of the Dalton gang. Three of the brothers and Dick Broadwell lie dead and handcuffed outside the Coffeyville jail on 5 October 1892. Their attempt to rob two banks at once failed.*

Below: *The Condon Bank at Coffeyville, photographed at the time of the raid. It has changed little in one hundred years, and neither have other landmarks made famous by the Daltons.*

soon the cry 'The Daltons! The Daltons!' echoed up and down the street. Armed citizens led by city marshal Charles T. Connelly, were soon on hand, hiding themselves and laying in wait for the gang. Bob and Emmett successfully robbed the First National Bank, but when they rode to join their companions as they, too, emerged from the Condon Bank, they were met by a hail of bullets. In the ensuing fight four citizens were killed, among them Marshal Connelly. Hopelessly outnumbered, the gang fled into what is now known as Death Alley where they were hounded by the furious citizenry as they tried to reach their horses. When they first arrived in town they found that street works had made it necessary to place their horses at the farther end of the alley, where they hitched them to an iron pipe. Leading the attack was John J. Kloeher, a liveryman, and considered by many to be the hero of the aborted raid. Broadwell managed to get a mile from town, but fell from his horse dead. Bob, Grat and Power were also down in the alley, but seeing that Bob still moved, Emmett galloped to him and reached down to try and get him into the saddle. 'There was a convulsive shiver as he opened his eyes and muttered, "Good-bye, Emmett. Don't surrender: die game." ' At that moment, Emmett, already wounded, was hit again by a load of buckshot and passed out.

John Joseph Kloeher refused to accept that his behavior had been in any way heroic and always played down his part in the affair. In 1900 he was elected chief of police. When the Winchester company said that they wished to present him with an inscribed weapon, to avoid any mention of his own name he told them his real name was 'Jim Spears' which appears on the weapon that now holds pride of place in the local museum, just below Kloeher's photograph made when he was chief of police. As for the victims and the villains, during a visit to Coffeyville to celebrate the 100th anniversary of the raid, we found on display in the museum the local undertaker's burial book. I noticed that he had sent the bill for the outlaws' funerals to the mayor for payment. Their mass grave was unmarked for many years except for a piece of the iron pipe to which they hitched their horses (it is still there). Many years later Emmett personally paid for a stone to mark the spot.

Emmett's survival was miraculous. He later stood trial and following conviction was sentenced to life imprisonment at the Kansas State Penitentiary. Fourteen years later he was pardoned and thereafter led a blameless life. The Western writer and former cowboy, Earle R. Forrest, who knew Emmett very well, told this writer that he once invited him to dinner, which terrified his wife, but she found him to be a charming and a very erudite man. Emmett became involved with motion pictures, and in 1909 returned to Coffeyville to act as adviser when a film of the raid was made on the original location. Now available on video, it is an uncanny glimpse into the past. His own 'star' quality was recognized by an appearance in several early one-reel 'Westerns' playing an heroic role. Later, however, he became an adviser for the movies, and wrote several books and articles denouncing crime and criminals. He died in 1937.

THE GOOD BAD MAN

The theme of many a Hollywood Western is the 'good bad man', who either goes from bad to good in a scene of heart-warming reformation, or, rarely, goes from good to bad and ends up dead. William S. Hart, a Shakespearean actor turned Western star, specialized in such roles in the early days of films, but even he might have blanched at some of the characters who crossed or recrossed the thin line between good and bad. One of the most notorious of these was Henry Newton Brown, marshal of Caldwell, and former sidekick of Billy the Kid, who is remembered not for his association but for an attempt at bank robbery while a sworn police officer.

Henry Brown was born at Cold Spring Township, Missouri, in 1857, and had one sister. They were orphaned when quite young and reared by an uncle on his farm near Rolla, Missouri. The boy grew up full of tales about the pre-Civil War skirmishes between the Jayhawkers and the Missouri Border Ruffians, and the even more lurid escapades of the Civil War guerrilla bands that infested the state. Yearning for adventure, he left home aged about seventeen and worked as a cowboy, buffalo hunter, and later became involved in the Lincoln County cattle war, at first on the side of Murphy and later with Chisum, joining Billy the Kid in some of the more bizzare incidents. Following a brief career in law enforcement, during which time he earned a reputation as a man always looking for a fight, he ended up at Caldwell, Kansas, where he was appointed a deputy city marshal. This was in 1882, two years after Caldwell got into the cattle trade with the arrival of the Cowley,

Above: *Henry Newton Brown, flanked by William Smith and John Wesley (the tall form of Ben Wheeler is to their left), is captured on film hours before he and his gang were done to death by furious townsfolk.*

Below: *Members of the Medicine Lodge citizens' posse that pursued and captured Brown and his companions. Note that many of them carry Winchester rifles.*

Sumner & Fort Smith Railroad. Brown was soon promoted to marshal and he in turn appointed as his deputy Ben Robertson, a Texas hard case who went under the name of Ben Wheeler. The pair did such a good job that in 1883 Brown was presented with a brand new Winchester rifle. And the appearance in Liverpool, England, during the 1950s of a Colt .45 Peacemaker with Wheeler's name and Caldwell inscribed on the backstrap suggests that he, too, was rewarded with or perhaps purchased the pistol himself and had it inscribed.

Brown married in 1884 and most people regarded him as a solid officer and citizen. But he and Wheeler, together with two cronies from Oklahoma Territory had other ideas. On 30 April 1884, the four attempted to rob the bank at Medicine Lodge, Kansas, having convinced the mayor of Caldwell that they needed some days off to pursue a murderer headed for Indian Territory. The robbery was a failure. The gang killed several citizens before being pursued and captured by the infuriated townsfolk. Brought back to town they were photographed before being lodged in jail where Brown wrote to his wife telling her that it was 'all for you', but 'I did not think this would happen'. The four men were then remanded to await trial. Later that same evening, a number of men appeared at the jail where, despite some resistance, the four men were dragged outside. Brown tried to escape and was blasted to death with a shotgun. Wheeler was also wounded, but his pleas were ignored: the mob dragged him, William Smith and John Wesley to a tree and hanged them all. Greed and the criminal instinct, with its short-sighted view of life and emphasis upon now rather than the future, only led to misery. People power had again taken a hand: there was just so much that they would accept without taking drastic action. Brown and Wheeler should have known better. Instead, they risked all for nothing.

THE MISFITS

Social misfits, habitual criminals and so-called rebels or anarchistic individuals thrived in the Old West. John Wesley Hardin, whose parents had named him after the father of Methodism, could not possibly have imagined that he would grow up to be one of the most feared gunmen in Texas. Whether Hardin was the homicidal maniac some claim or a psychotic killer is a matter for debate; but his homicidal tendencies are reflected in his numerous encounters, most of which were the result of alleged insults directed at him or blood debts to cousins or close kin. As a result, he built up a reputation as a notorious killer.

Hardin's first known killing was that of a former slave named Mage, during a visit to his uncle's plantation at Moscow, Texas, in November 1868. He and the former slave fell out during a wrestling match and Mage is reported to have threatened Hardin. Soon afterwards, as Wes was preparing to return home, Mage appeared carrying a large stick. Without hesitation, Hardin pulled a pistol and shot the Negro three times. He died several days later. The murder was reported to the Union Army and three soldiers were ordered to bring Wes Hardin in. He ambushed and killed all three, the dead bodies were hidden by former Confederate sympathizers and Hardin escaped. In examining the killings credited to John Wesley Hardin, it is apparent that he devised devious schemes to get the drop on any opponent, rarely facing down a man in the traditional manner. For someone reputed to be a wizard with a six-shooter, and who could have earned a living in a circus as a trick shot, he seems to have been surprisingly reluctant to

Right: *John Wesley Hardin from a tintype believed made at Abilene in 1871. Wes is 'all dressed up' for the occasion; but his bemused expression does not suggest that he was too happy about the experience.*

Below: *Texas Ranger John Armstrong who pursued Wes Hardin to Florida following a tip-off. He owed his survival to the fact that when Wes went for his gun it was caught in his suspenders!*

Above: *El Paso, Texas, in its early days. The wooden false-fronted buildings are typical of the period and some remained long after bricks and adobe dwellings became common. Note the canvas hoarding.*

Right: *John Selman, whose main claim to fame is that he killed John Wesley Hardin in 1895. But his own exploits included periods on both sides of the law. He was killed by Scarborough in 1896.*

engage in face-to-face conflict. He was finally cornered on a train at Pensacola, Florida, on 23 August 1877, by the Texas Rangers who had received a tip off that he was posing as 'J. H. Swain, Jr', and that he would be on the train. Hardin went for his pistol but it jammed in his suspenders. James Mann, a nineteen-year-old companion who sat next to Hardin, managed to pull his pistol and put a bullet through Ranger John Armstrong's hat. Armstrong promptly shot him in the chest. The boy jumped from the train, staggered and died on the platform. Hardin was disarmed after a short struggle, during which he was hit over the head with a six-shooter. Back in Texas he was put on trial and sentenced to the state penitentiary at Huntsville.

Unlike many who were similarly sentenced, Hardin studied law and eventually passed his bar exams. Shortly before he was due for release in 1894, his wife died. This had a devastating effect on him. Hardin opened a law practise at Gonzales, Texas, where he spent some time with his children. Later, he moved to Junction where on 8 January 1895 he married a young girl named Callie Lewis, said by some to have only been fourteen at the time. She was captivated more by his reputation than the man and within hours of the marriage she had fled.

Hardin next showed up at El Paso where he again hung up his shingle but with little success. Too many people recalled his erstwhile reputation, and he gradually drifted into a life of dissipation. A fracas in a saloon over a game of cards in which he was accused of robbing the pot at gun point did not endear him to the hardcore faction, and they shed no tears when, on the night of 19 August 1895, as he stood at the bar of the Acme saloon, he was shot down from behind by John Selman, a gunman and part-time policeman from El Paso. Selman apparently wanted to boost his own reputation. The previous year he had killed Bass Outlaw, another hard-drinking, hot-tempered individual with a reputation and a past. Selman, however, himself became another notch on the pistol of George Scarborough who killed him during an argument in 1896.

Hardin's present reputation is not good; many believe that had he been born in a more peaceful era, and his aggressive instincts been channeled toward the law at an earlier age, he might have ended up a much respected advocate. Instead he is remembered as a killer who boasted of 'forty notches'.

Possibly one of the most intriguing characters who went from bad to worse was William ('Billy') Brooks, who achieved considerable fame as a gunfighter, peace officer, stagecoach driver, and finally as a horse thief. According to an 1870 Census he was born about 1849, somewhere in Ohio. Whether he

Above: *Bass Outlaw, who hailed from Georgia, and was well educated. He served as a Texas Ranger and won rapid promotion. Found drunk on duty he was forced to resign. He was killed by Selman in 1894.*

Below: *A photograph said to depict George Scarborough and Jeff Milton (right). Jeff Milton was said to be 'a good man with a gun' and was considered one of the Old West's truly great lawmen.*

A CIRCLE OF VIOLENCE

The fact is that John Wesley Hardin was a hardened criminal who killed and served time for doing so. It is equally certain that lawman John Selman walked up to Hardin in an El Paso establishment – the Acme saloon – in August 1895 and shot him dead. There is also no doubt that Selman's sometime deputy and associate in petty crimes, George Scarborough, killed Selman in a darkened alley. On 6 April 1900, four years to the day that Selman was killed, George Scarborough himself died after being shot in the leg (it required amputation) during the pursuit of outlaws in Arizona. These three examples of violent people living in violent times help to contradict all too popular notions that the life of the lawman was a romantic part of the history of the West. Their guns prove testimony to the toughness of the times.

Despite all the violence in his life, John Wesley Hardin, one of the most notorious gunfighters in the Old West, still managed to have a family. The death of his wife Jane just a year before his own demise devastated him. Toward the end of his life, he wrote an autobiography, published posthumously by his children. These same children grew to be good citizens and there are many relations of John Wesley Hardin living in Texas today who are proud of their gunfighting ancestor. Records show that Hardin was active in many parts of Texas during his heyday in the 1870s, in places such as Smiley, Cuero and Trinity City.

THE STATE OF TEXAS

To the Sheriff or any Constable of El Paso County or to the Chief of Police or any Policeman of the City of El Paso—GREETING:

WHEREAS _George Scarborough_ stands accused in the _before me_ Recorder's Court of the City of El Paso with the offense of _assault with intent to murder_

This, then, is to command you that you arrest and take into your custody the body of the said _Geo Scarborough_

and that you forthwith bring the body of said _Geo Scarborough_ before me at my office in the city of El Paso, El Paso county, Texas, to be dealt with according to law.

Given under my hand this _5_ day of _April_ ,1896

JOHN W. HARDIN Esq.
ATTORNEY AT LAW

OFFICE:
200½ El Paso
Wells Fargo Bldg.

PRACTICE IN
ALL COURTS

1. Winchester model 1887 shotgun belonging to George Scarborough. GS stamped on the right side.
2. Colt with pearl grips carried by George Scarborough.
3. .41 caliber Colt Lightning which belonged to notorious Texas gunman John Wesley Hardin.
4. Hardin's single-action Army Colt has had the ejector rod removed. The grips are ivory.
5. Lawman John Selman cut the barrel of his Colt .45 to 5 in., making it easier to draw, hide, and carry.
6. Hardin demonstrated his shooting skills and gave away signed and perforated playing cards.
7. Teaching himself the law while in prison, Hardin could then hand out a different type of business card.
8. Warrant for the arrest of George Scarborough,
dated 5 April 1896.
9. Warrant for the arrest of a witness to testify on behalf of the defense of Scarborough, 3 June 1896.
10. Statement dated 5 April 1896 charging that George Scarborough did 'with malice a-fore-thought kill one John Selman with a pistol'.

(Artifacts courtesy of Gene Autry Western Heritage Museum, Los Angeles, California.)

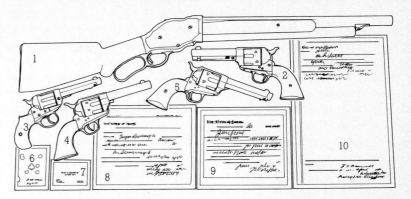

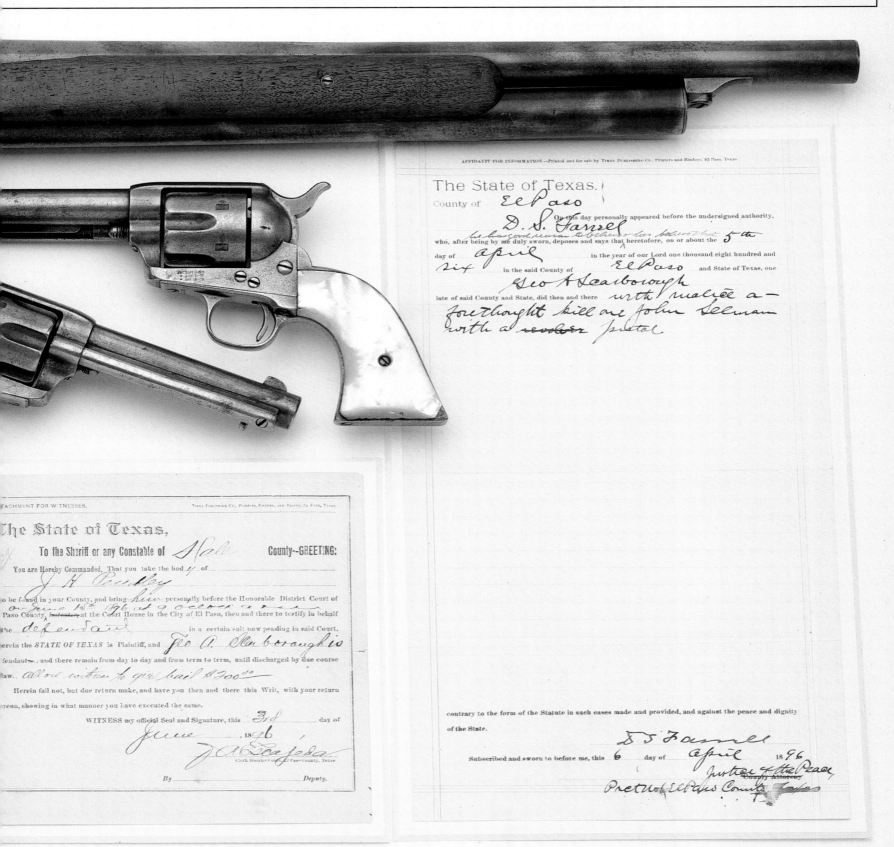

grew to adulthood there or migrated with his parents to Kansas soon after his birth is not known, but by 1870 he was already possessed of a reputation as a tough character. He is also reported to have been a noted buffalo hunter and to have been dubbed 'Buffalo Bill' (which confused him with William F. Cody, the best known, or William Mathewson, the original Kansas 'Buffalo Bill' who was known as 'Buffalo Bill' as early as 1860). Whatever the truth, by 1870 Brooks had a growing reputation as a gunfighter. In appearance he was about five feet eight inches tall, and was reported to wear his hair shoulder length in the manner of Wild Bill. Indeed, his custom of carrying a pair of Colt's Navy pistols was reminiscent of Hickok. But the only alleged photograph of Brooks depicts him with short hair and sporting a narrow-brimmed high-crowned hat. Around his waist is a cartridge belt and one single ivory-stocked Colt revolver that must have been a conversion from percussion to rim-or center-fire.

Brooks appeared at Wichita in 1870, two years before the railroad arrived and with it the cattle trade. Nevertheless, Wichita already had an unenviable reputation as a tough town. Employed as a driver by the Southwestern Stage Company, Brooks drove a six-mule team with great skill. For a while he settled at El Dorado, and when the railroad reached Newton, the stage company switched routes. Brooks then drove his stagecoaches between Wichita and Newton.

Here Brooks found that the cattle trade was in full swing. It would be short-lived, however, for soon Wichita would take over. In the mean-time, it was badly in need of law enforcement. Early in 1870 the place was incorporated as a third-class city, and the city council wasted no time in appointing a police force. Brooks' reputation as a tough character led to his appointment as town marshal on 1 April, and as his assistant he had Charles Baumann, of Germanic origin and a quiet but determined individual. His term in office was short: a fight with the notorious half-blood Indian Dan ('Cherokee Dan') Hicks, who had got himself drunk and shot up a saloon, left him with a severe leg wound, and he was dismissed. Hicks was killed later in a fight with saloon owner Harry Lovett. Brooks was now on his own.

On 9 June a bunch of cowboys raised a ruckus in Edward T. ('Red') Beard's saloon, and Brooks was sent for. He persuaded them to leave the place and escorted them to the edge of town. Suddenly, one of them pulled his pistol and shot Brooks in the right shoulder. They then fled toward the stockyards. Brooks gave chase and in a running gunfight that lasted for ten miles he was shot twice more. The Texans escaped and Brooks returned to have his wounds seen to. On 14 June, the *Eagle* declared that 'Bill has sand enough to beat the hourglass that tries to run him out'. Brooks, however, had had enough. For the $75 per month they paid him he did not think it worth laying his life on the line. He next appeared at Ellsworth where he was employed as a policeman. He soon moved on to a place that would one day become world famous – Dodge City.

The place was situated on the tracks of the Atchison, Topeka and Santa Fe Railroad, and

Below: *Wichita, Kansas, in 1871. Main Street is still a collection of false-fronted wooden shacks with the occasional two-story structure. Note the dusty street and hitching racks for horses.*

Above: *The embryonic Dodge City in about 1872, looking west. Built close to the Santa Fe Trail and Fort Dodge, it attracted much attention in the press. Today it is remembered as the 'Cowboy Capital'.*

Right: *This photograph is reported to be of William L. ('Billy') Brooks, one of the West's most famous 'good-bad men'. No valid proof has been found, however, to verify the claim that it actually is Brooks.*

close to Fort Dodge on the Santa Fe Trail. At first the haunt of buffalo hunters, it gradually attracted people and merchants who dabbled in the hide business – some two hundred thousand are reported to have been shipped east in the winter of 1872–3. When Brooks arrived, the town was thriving. It was also a very violent place. J. B. Edwards, of Abilene, who spent some time at Dodge in its early years, recalled that there was no organized law at the time. It was also a time when the local Boot Hill became very populated. 'I helped bury a few of the first ones killed there on Boot Hill.'

Confusion rages over who was the first so-called marshal of Dodge. Jack Bridges, himself a noted character and police officer, is thought by some to have been the first marshal. They point out that he was already a serving deputy U.S. marshal. This would have had no effect on any civil appointments, but it would count when the city fathers considered candidates. We know that he and his wife Ella and his daughter were living in Dodge at the time, where he was engaged in a federal offensive against horse thieves. In any event, it was some time before Brooks' status as an 'assistant marshal' was mentioned. But by that time, his reputation was against him. Henry H. Raymond, then a young buffalo hunter, recalled many years later that one of the first sights that greeted him when he first arrived at the place was a crowd around a table playing cards in a saloon. 'The man sitting with his back to the door as I entered wore two big revolvers, whose ends showed beside the stool on which he was sitting. I learned afterwards that he was Bill Brooks, a gambler and all round crook.'

Brooks (some called him 'Bully Brooks' but not to his face) became a notorious character in Dodge, and his name was linked, but only in hearsay, with several unexplained killings. Brooks was reported to be involved in a possible saloon-owning partnership with a man named Sullivan who was himself involved in allegations of cheating, and in November 1872 it was reported in the Newton *Kansan* on the 21st that some Texans had tried to walk off with the ante in protest. Sullivan pulled a pistol and struck one of them over the head with it, the hammer spur piercing his left temple and into his brain, from which wound he died. His friends rushed to his aid, but Brooks opened fire killing one of them. Sullivan then joined in, seriously wounding another. Later a Matthew Sullivan (who may or may not have been the same man), described as a saloon keeper, was killed when someone shoved a pistol through a window and shot him dead. For some reason Brooks was believed responsible. The Topeka *Daily Commonwealth* of 31 December even stated that 'It is supposed that the unknown assassin was a character in those parts called Bully Brooks, but nothing definite is known concerning the affair, or what led to it.' Brooks was later involved in a shootout with a Mr Brown, former yardmaster at Newton. According to the Wichita *Eagle* of 2 January 1873, '"Bully" Brooks, ex-marshal of Newton, and Mr Brown . . . fired three shots each, Brown's first shot wounded Brooks, whose third shot killed Brown and wounded one of his assistants. Brooks is a desperate character, and has before, in desperate encounters, killed his man.' Later, it was reported that

HANDGUNS AND HOLSTERS

Not everyone in the West carried a gun. Those who did needed some kind of container or holster to make carrying the gun comfortable and to ensure that the firearm would be protected and easy to draw when needed. Single-shot percussion or flintlock pistols prior to the 1830s could be carried in a belt sash or might have a metal clip on the side to hook the gun onto the belt. In the 1830s it was common for both military and civilian personnel to drape a pair of pommel holsters over the front of the saddle to carry pistols and holsters on horseback. Civilian use of pommel or saddle bags which had built-in holsters continued until well after the turn of the century.

As the number of handguns proliferated, holster styles rapidly developed and changed. Earlier civilian styles reflected military influences in the use of flap covers. Saddle makers manufactured holster styles which in the 1860s/70s were form fitting and held the revolver snuggly in place.

1. U.S. military issue pommel holsters for 1855 pistol carbine on one side and Colt Walker on the other, about 1855.
2. The Colt Walker's massive weight made it impractical to carry on the person. Pommel holsters were desirable for such revolvers.
3. Standard military issue flap holster used with Colt dragoon and army revolvers, 1850s–60s.
4. Civilian half-flap holster with an 1851 Colt Navy revolver, complete with belt and attached steel for starting fires.
5. Civilian half-flap holster for an 1861 Colt Army.
6. Form-fitting civilian holster, open top for 1860 Army.
7. Inexpensive civilian holster of the 1860s.
8. Mail-order Montgomery Ward holster for Colt single-action Army revolver.

9. Typical Colt .45, also available by mail from Montgomery Ward.
10. Left-handed holster, about 1880, made in Dodge City, Kansas, by S.C. Gallup.
11. Colt .44-40 frontier revolver.
12. Colt .45 single-action, 1880s.
13. Experimental Bridgeport devise, tested by the army. An enlarged hammer screw on the revolver slid into the metal plate, holding the gun so that it could be pivoted and fired.
14. Typical civilian tooled holster for the Colt single-action.
15. Belt holster for the Colt Lightning double-action revolver.
16. Patented pocket holster for concealing double-action revolver.
17. This 1860 .44 caliber Colt Army revolver and its matching holster have been cut down to create a powerful but concealable belt gun.
18. Colt single-action Army .45 of the 1890s.
19. Shoulder holster for the Colt single-action Army, 1890s.
20. Smith & Wesson hammerless double-action revolver.
21. Shoulder holster.

(Artifacts courtesy of Gene Autry Western Heritage Museum, Los Angeles, California.)

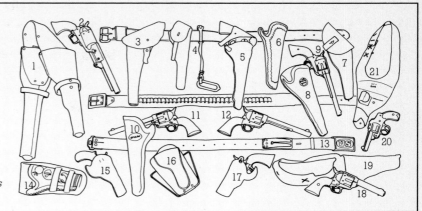

Brown was not killed and that the reason for their fight – a nineteen-year-old prostitute named Jessie or 'Captain Drew' had deserted Brooks for Brown and had also nursed him back to health.

Much of Brooks' subsequent career is a mixture of hearsay, alleged gunfights and tall tales. But on one occasion, when he ran foul of the buffalo hunter Kirk Jordan, it could have been his last. On 4 March 1873, Jordan rode into Dodge looking for Brooks, a long-barreled buffalo rifle in the crook of his arm. He lay in wait for Billy and when he stepped from a saloon, up went the barrel. But Brooks saw the glint as the sun flashed along it, and threw himself behind a water butt as the huge ball thudded into it. His only 'injury' was a dousing from the water that splashed down his neck. Various stories claim that the pair were persuaded to shake hands, or that Jordan skipped town. But Billy's reputation suffered from the implied criticism of his action in hiding rather than defending himself against Jordan.

By 1874, Brooks had turned to outlawry and horse thievery full time and it came as no surprise to learn that he and several cronies had been arrested by Sheriff John G. Davis and posse following a siege near Caldwell. Taken to Wellington, Brooks was placed in jail. But late on the night of 30 July, he, Charlie Smith and L. B. Hasbrouck, by profession a lawyer who had somehow gotten himself embroiled with the outlaws, were removed from the jail by a large gang of silent men who took them to a tree on the main road between Caldwell and Wellington. Despite pleas for mercy and a fair trial, the three men were hanged. Brooks is reported to have begged for mercy. The *Sumner County Press* report, published within hours of the hanging, remarked: 'The distorted features of Brooks gave evidence of a horrible struggle with death. The other men looked naturally, and evidently died easily.'

For the many who gawped at the bodies as they were laid out in a store room prior to being wrapped in blankets and hastily buried in unmarked graves, it was both a warning and a revelation. Brooks inspired little comment in the press. Only long after his death would he be remembered for what he had done in the early days before civilization overtook and engulfed the short-lived wilderness that had spawned him.

Lawmen who turned bad were by no means in the minority, and Henry Brown and Ben Wheeler were not typical. Neither for that matter was James Timothy Isaiah Courtright, better known to his cronies and to history as 'Long-haired Jim'. Born in Iowa in 1848, he came to prominence in the years following the Civil War in which he served briefly toward its end. Hearsay records that he led a checkered career as a military scout, mine guard, ranch foreman and later as a lawman. Others contend that during this period and later he was also a racketeer, having his hand in several ventures that bordered upon or were outright crooked. But it was as marshal of Fort Worth from 1876 until 1879 that he is best remembered. In *Fort Worth: Outpost on the Trinity*, Oliver Knight recorded that Courtright was known as a man of ice-nerves and with a 'capacity for inspiring loyalty'. He was the first city marshal to serve more than one term. In appearance he was quite tall and, in common with some other gunfighters and Indian scouts, sometimes wore his hair shoulder length. His right hand was 'slightly crippled' which may account for him carrying two six-shooters, butts forward in the approved plains manner. Dr Will Woody, who had been a small boy when Courtright ruled the roost at Fort Worth, told Dr Knight in 1949 that Courtright did not use a cross draw, but 'drew from the right hip with the right hand, claiming it was faster that way. When indoors, he carried his pistols in a sash.' Courtright was obviously well versed in the use of the plains or reverse draw that not only proved to be quick but was perhaps the safest means of drawing and firing a pistol.

Jim Courtright proved to be a good officer, but he was not as rigid in his attitudes to his deputies, turning a blind eye when they occasionally drifted into variety houses or brothels when they should have been patrolling the streets. Here he epitomizes the conflict between duty and devotion that so beset the old-time peace officers. Sworn to do their duty according to city and state statutes or ordi-

Below: *Henry Brown (left) with Fred Waite, before Brown became a cowtown lawman. Both men were involved with Billy the Kid in the killing of Sheriff Brady in Lincoln, New Mexico, in 1878.*

nances, they sometimes had problems when it came to enforcing gambling and prostitution laws, especially if it meant offending someone who might prove helpful in a crisis. He himself was a gambler and Knight reports that he was once hauled into court for playing pool.

Courtright went to Silver City, New Mexico, when his term as marshal of Fort Worth ended. Here he did his stint as a guard at the American Mining Company. He and fellow guard Jim McIntire of Wichita Falls were implicated in the deaths of several Mexicans who were alleged to have attempted to rob a train carrying silver. Later, when two ranchmen were murdered, and questions were asked, the pair fled to Texas.

Back at Forth Worth, Courtright opened his T.I.C. (for his initials) Detective Agency. Somewhere along the line 'Tim' had been corrupted into 'Jim.' For some weeks things remained quiet, but Courtright was aware that he might well have problems following his New Mexico exploits. This came about on 17 October 1884, when two Texas Rangers and the Chief of Police of Albuquerque called upon him. To allay his suspicions, they invited him to their hotel to examine photographs of wanted criminals. Courtright, not entirely duped, asked a friend, deputy sheriff James

Above: *James Courtright, known as 'Long-haired Jim', served as Fort Worth's marshal and later opened his own detective agency. His death in a gunfight with Luke Short was a sad end for one who deserved better.*

Maddox to accompany him, but on a pretext he was kept in the hall while Jim entered the room. He was then arrested and they decided to keep him hidden until the 9 p.m. train arrived when they would smuggle him on board.

Unfortunately for the lawmen, when the train arrived a passenger reported that the Rangers had arrested McIntire in Wichita Falls and were after Courtright. The news flashed around town. Maddox then remembered the hotel visit. When Courtright failed to return he had gone home. Once it was learned that Jim was indeed confined in a room on the second floor of the Ginnochio Hotel, a mob besieged the place. There were many who sympathized with him, influenced by his previous good name and reputation. The officers slipped through the crowd at the rear of the hotel and shoved him into a waiting carriage and sped to the jail, where he sat in the sheriff's office awaiting events.

The Fort Worth *Gazette* of 20 October 1884 reported that Courtright expressed the opinion that because of the 'bitter feeling between Americans and Mexicans, I am convinced that I could not have a fair trial. The assertion that I am wanted as a witness is only made to allay the public feeling in this city.' This was later confirmed. On the evening of the 19th, prior to the publication of the above statement, Jim had been having a meal in the Merchants Restaurant, escorted there under guard. When he dropped his napkin and asked the guard if he would like to pick it up,

Below: *This view of main street Silver City, New Mexico, dates from the early 1870s. Ox trains were a common sight. Many Texas longhorns ended up teamed with oxen, and proved very durable.*

CARRYING LONGARMS

Any hunter, lawman, cowboy, or gunfighter carrying a rifle or shotgun would want his weapon to be protected from the elements, and also to be easily to hand. At the same time, such weapons were heavy and bulky. A quality scabbard helped to protect the weapon and made it easier to carry.

Buckskin scabbards, often embellished with fringe or beading, could be easily made or purchased from Indians or traders. Sheathed in such covers, rifles could be carried across the pommel of the saddle, in hand and ready for use. By the 1870s leather scabbards, both plain and fancy, could be purchased from saddle and harness makers with buckles and straps to attach them to the saddle. Personal taste dictated which side of the horse the scabbard was attached to and the different opinions held whether the butt of the gun should face to the front or the back. Long-range rifles and sporting shotguns could be fitted to more rigid cases and boxes which could be stored or carried in wagons or other conveyances. Most gunfighters, however, were more concerned with pistols than longarms, although many of them owned such weapons, and on occasion owed their lives to them. For out on the plains there lurked many dangers. A pistol was fine for close-range shooting but of little use when confronted by hostile Indians whose ambition was to get up close. A rifle made sure they kept their distance.

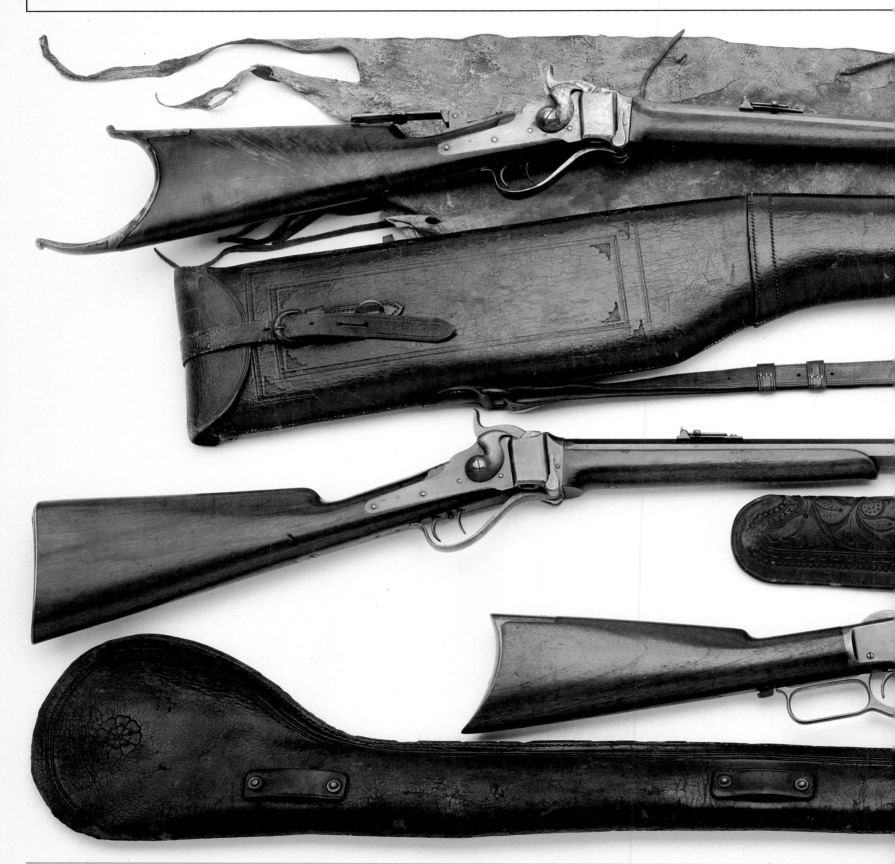

1. Indian tanned antelope skin scabbard of about 1875, which was used by 'Antelope' Ernst Bauman.
2. Sharps rifle used for market hunting by 'Antelope' Ernst Bauman on the eastern plains of Colorado in the late 1870s.
3. Rare factory supplied leather case for the heavy 1874 Sharps buffalo rifle, made in 1877.
4. Typical 1874 Sharps hunting rifle, caliber .45, 2⅞ in., made on special order from E.Z.C. Judson, better known as Ned Buntline, author of dime novels and promoter of the West.
5. Scabbard for a lever-action rifle of the 1880s or 1890s, made by F.A. Meanea, Cheyenne, Wyoming; there would have been an extra charge for the fine leather tooling.
6. Winchester model 1873 rifle in .44-40 caliber, bought in Texas and probably used for hunting by a railroad locating engineer.
7. Standard rifle scabbard of about 1880 purchased for use with the above Winchester 73; a plain but serviceable weapon.

(Artifacts courtesy of Gene Autry Western Heritage Museum, Los Angeles, California.)

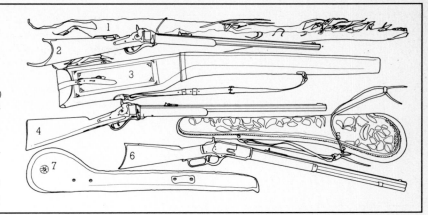

he snapped: 'Pick it up yourself!' Jim stooped to
retrieve it and came up instead with a brace of
pistols. As he shoved back his chair he lined
them up on the guards. 'It's my turn now,' he
said quietly. Minutes later, and mounted on a
swift horse, he was away, accompanied by the
shouts and cheers of his supporters. The
County Attorney, W. S. Pendleton, infuriated
by the escape and the apparent reluctance of
the guards to lock him in a cell and feed him,
was reported by the *Gazette* on the 20th to
have bemoaned the fact that his friends had
served him 'boiled fish, quail on toast, and
pistols under the table for dessert'.

Courtright succeeded in escaping by rail
and ship to New York from where he kept in
touch with friends at Fort Worth. He returned
later to New Mexico where he was cleared of
all charges. Oliver Knight reports that when he
did return to his wife and family at Fort Worth,
he was met by a large crowd that gave him a
rousing welcome. He then reopened his
detective agency.

Luke Short, fresh from his dispute with
Dodge City (described elsewhere) had set up
in business in Fort Worth, and his presence
irritated Courtright, or at least that is the impression one gets from some sources. Others,
however, point out that Jim's activities as a
racketeer were hidden behind his detective
agency and he acted as a front man for others.
On the evening of 8 February 1887, Courtright
appeared at the White Elephant saloon run by
Short and Jake Johnson. Courtright spoke for
some minutes to Johnson who then called Luke
out, and the trio walked down the street and
stopped outside the Ella Blackwell shooting
gallery. Later reports suggest that Courtright
wanted money that Luke was not prepared to
pay. The pair were standing about four feet
apart when, according to Johnson's statement
published in the *Gazette* on the 10th, the
trouble started. 'Luke had his thumbs in the
armholes of his vest,' Johnson said, 'then he
dropped them in front of him, when Courtright
said, "You needn't be getting out your gun."
Luke said, "I haven't got any gun here, Jim,"
and raised up his vest to show him. Courtright
then pulled his pistol. He drew it first, and then
Short drew his and commenced to fire.'

Courtright failed to pull the trigger. Luke
fired, and Jim fell. Luke then put another four
shots into him. It was later discovered that Jim's
cylinder was jammed. Short was given a preliminary hearing and released on a two thousand dollar bond but never faced trial. Courtright was given a fine funeral, for he still had
many friends in town. His wife and children
later moved to California. Just how crooked
Courtright really was or if in fact he was
maligned is a matter for speculation. But his
demise and reputation exemplify the manner
in which such men hovered on the edge of
social acceptance or stigma, often on the whim
of hearsay, prejudice or downright hypocrisy.

Another so-called badman whose exploits
have long interested the public was Tom Horn.
His involvement in the Graham–Tewskbury

Right: *Luke L. Short, noted gambler and
gunfighter, dressed like a New York dandy.
It was said of Luke Short that he was the
undertaker's friend, for he 'shot 'em where it
didn't show.'*

war and later the Johnson County war, together with a reputation as an army scout, gave him a status that kept him in the public eye. He was born on 21 November 1860, at Memphis, Missouri, and, like many others, drifted from job to job. He is reported to have worked on railroads, driven stagecoaches, been a teamster and generally worked his way across westwards before securing employment as an army scout in 1875. He became highly proficient and also learned to speak fluent Apache. This brought him to the attention of Albert Sieber, chief army scout at the San Carlos reservation, and Horn worked for him on and off until about 1886 when, according to Horn, he was responsible for arranging Geronimo's surrender to General Nelson A. Miles.

Horn was also an adept horseman, taking part in several early rodeos – winning the steer-roping contest at Phoenix in 1891. He is also reported to have gone to Cuba with the Rough Riders as a mule-pack-train operator during the Spanish–American War. But it was his Western exploits that brought him most attention. From 1890 until 1893, he worked for the Pinkerton Detective Agency, and then he hired himself out to the Swan Land and Cattle Company, where his reputation as a killer was founded. It was claimed that he ambushed would-be or alleged 'rustlers' using a high-powered rifle. It is also reported that his trade mark was a couple of rocks placed beneath his victim's head to guarantee his six hundred dollar fee.

How true many of these stories were has never been satisfactorily explained, but in his recent book *Tales Never Told Around the Camp Fire*, Mark Dugan introduces material that provides a more balanced view of Horn's activities. He certainly was a killer, yet he had his share of courage. His weakness, however, was his tongue, and when in his cups he said things that were boastful. When two local

Above: *Tom Horn photographed shortly before he was hanged for the murder of Willie Nickell. Convicted on circumstantial evidence and an alleged confession when drunk, many believe he was 'railroaded'.*

ranchers name Lewis and Powell were murdered, Tom Horn was blamed on hearsay evidence. William Lewis was generally disliked by his neighbors, who were convinced that he was rustling cattle. Arrested and indicted, he managed to evade trial on legal technicalities, and when he finally came to trial the jury acquitted him. Lewis promptly sued for costs. On 31 July 1895, as he was loading a skinned calf into a wagon, three .44 caliber slugs from a rifle slammed into him, and it was

three days before his partly decomposing body was found. Although a reward was offered for information on the killing, local press reports indicate that 'all the people within a radius of fifteen miles of Lewis' place say they are glad he is dead'. No one, it seems, had any sympathy for him.

Fred Powell, if anything, was worse than Lewis in his attitude to his neighbors and their possessions. Dugan cites a number of instances which illustrate how detested the man was, including this anonymous letter addressed to Powell and published, following his death, in the Cheyenne *Daily Leader-Sun* of 11 September 1895:

> Laramie, Wyo., September 2, 1895
> Mr Powell – This is your third and last warning. There are three things for you to do – quit killing other people's cattle or be killed yourself, or leave the country yourself at once.

Before Powell could make any decision, however, he too was the victim of an unknown rifleman at 7.30 on the morning of 10 September. His hired man stated that they were alone on the ranch when the shot was fired, hitting Powell in the chest. He gasped out 'Oh! My God!', clutched at his breast, then fell dead. Again, speculation was rife over who killed Powell. His wife Mary, herself a very tough lady, later claimed to have known who killed her husband, and she was adamant that it was not Tom Horn.

Horn's nemesis was an equally shady character named Joe LeFors, a lawman put on his trail late in 1901 following the killing of a fourteen-year-old boy named Willie Nickell on 18 July. Horn had been employed earlier in the year by John Coble, owner of a large ranch north of Laramie. He had reached that stage in his life when he looked to the future. He had also become friendly with a local school

Below: *An alleged photograph of 14-year-old Willie Nickell, the boy whose murder led to the arrest and execution of Tom Horn in November 1903. Horn denied murdering the boy, but to no avail.*

Below: *Joe Lefors, the shadowy lawman who tracked Tom Horn down to his Denver lair and got him drunk enough to 'confess' to the murder of Willie Nickell. Only Lefors knew the truth about the 'confession'.*

Below: *Sheriff Ed Smalley was involved in the capture and ultimate execution of Tom Horn in Cheyenne in November 1903. Before long, a name such as Horn's would seem an anachronism in the 20th century.*

OUTLAW GUNS

Accounts of Western outlaws often include descriptions of their equipment and tales of their skill with a gun.
As is the case with more law-abiding citizens, breakers of the law tended to favor the most reliable weapons they could get their hands on. Hence, Colt or Remington revolvers are common. Winchesters, the Sharps, and other shoulder arms served best for long distance work. Ultimately the sawed off shotgun was considered the most deadly of weapons – a tool to demand respect and compliance with such orders as 'put up your hands' or 'surrender your money'.

Some outlaw guns have survived because they were given as gifts or were captured. Frank James presented his revolver, belt, and holster to Dr A.H. Conkwright at Sedalia, Missouri, before surrendering to the authorities. Black Bart's shotgun was captured at the time he was tracked down, following the evidence of laundry marks present on garments left at the scene of the hold-up. (Black Bart made something of a habit out of holding up Wells Fargo stagecoaches but the company got even: they hunted him down and kept the gun as a souvenir.) The revolver which belonged to Belle Starr was given away by a granddaughter in the 1940s. Pancho Villa gave his Colt to a friend, while Harvey Logan of the Wild Bunch presented his revolver to a younger member of the gang who kept it until the 1970s.

1. Leather cartridge belt with .44-40 cartridges worn by Frank James. The matching holster held the outlaw's Remington revolver.
2. Remington model 1875 revolver, caliber .44-40, carried by Frank James.
3. Belle Starr's .45 caliber Colt single-action Army revolver, carried by her near the end of her career.
4. Invitation to a hanging.
5. Colt Bisley, .44-40, which belonged to Pancho Villa, and was carried by General Jose Ruiz.
6. William 'Bill Kick' Darley was a youngster when he joined the 'Wild Bunch'. Harvey Logan, better known as 'Kid Curry', gave him this Colt .45 with nickel finish. Abrasions on the barrel are from twisting barbed wire around it.
7. This Wells Fargo wanted poster for Black Bart included descriptions of the outlaw and his various hold-ups.
8. Loomis IXL no. 15 shotgun with a short barrel. Charles Boles, alias 'Black Bart', carried it during numerous hold-ups of stages in California.

(Artifacts courtesy of Gene Autry Western Heritage Museum, Los Angeles, California.)

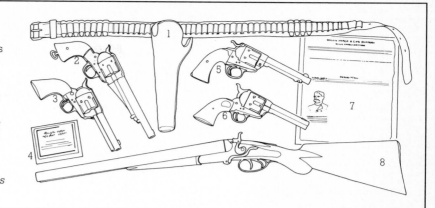

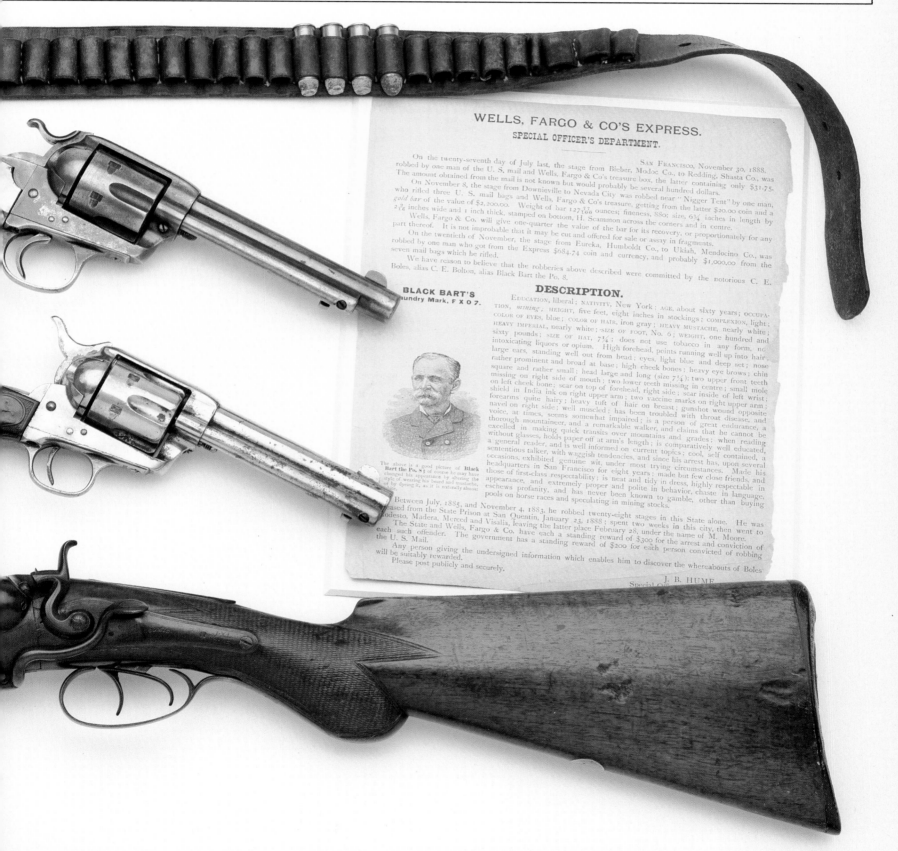

WELLS, FARGO & CO'S EXPRESS.
SPECIAL OFFICER'S DEPARTMENT.

SAN FRANCISCO, November 30, 1888.

On the twenty-seventh day of July last, the stage from Bieber, Modoc Co., to Redding, Shasta Co., was robbed by one man of the U. S. mail and Wells, Fargo & Co's treasure box, the latter containing only $31.75.

The amount obtained from the mail is not known but would probably be several hundred dollars.

On November 8, the stage from Downieville to Nevada City was robbed near "Nigger Tent" by one man, who rifled three U. S. mail bags and Wells, Fargo & Co's treasure, getting from the latter $20.00 coin and a gold bar of the value of $2,200.00. Weight of bar 127 10/16 ounces; fineness, 880; size, 6¾ inches in length by 2⅞ inches wide and 1 inch thick, stamped on bottom, H. Scammon across the corners and in centre. Wells, Fargo & Co. will give one-quarter the value of the bar for its recovery, or proportionately for any part thereof. It is not improbable that it may be cut and offered for sale or assay in fragments.

On the twentieth of November, the stage from Eureka, Humboldt Co., to Ukiah, Mendocino Co., was robbed by one man who got from the Express $684.74 coin and currency, and probably $1,000.00 from the seven mail bags which he rifled.

We have reason to believe that the robberies above described were committed by the notorious C. E. Boles, alias C. E. Bolton, alias Black Bart the Po. 8.

BLACK BART'S Laundry Mark, F X O 7.

DESCRIPTION.

EDUCATION, liberal; NATIVITY, New York; AGE, about sixty years; OCCUPATION, *mining*; HEIGHT, five feet, eight inches in stockings; COMPLEXION, light; COLOR OF EYES, blue; COLOR OF HAIR, iron gray; HEAVY MUSTACHE, nearly white; HEAVY IMPERIAL, nearly white; SIZE OF FOOT, No. 6; WEIGHT, one hundred and sixty pounds; SIZE OF HAT, 7¼; does not use tobacco in any form, no intoxicating liquors or opium. High forehead, points running well up into hair; large ears, standing well out from head; eyes, light blue and deep set; nose rather prominent and broad at base; high cheek bones; heavy eye brows; chin square and rather small; head large and long (size 7¼); two upper front teeth missing on right side of mouth; two lower teeth missing in centre; small mole on left cheek bone; scar on top of forehead, right side; scar inside of left wrist; shield in India ink on right upper arm; two vaccine marks on right upper arm; forearms quite hairy; heavy tuft of hair on breast; gunshot wound opposite navel on right side; well muscled; has been troubled with throat disease, and voice, at times, seems somewhat impaired; is a person of great endurance, a thorough mountaineer, and a remarkable walker, and claims that he cannot be excelled in making quick transits over mountains and grades; when reading without glasses, holds paper off at arm's length; is comparatively well educated, a general reader, and is well informed on current topics; cool, self contained, a sententious talker, with waggish tendencies, and since his arrest has, upon several occasions, exhibited genuine wit, under most trying circumstances. Made his headquarters in San Francisco for eight years; made but few close friends, and those of first-class respectability; is neat and tidy in dress, highly respectable in appearance, and extremely proper and polite in behavior, chaste in language, eschews profanity, and has never been known to gamble, other than buying pools on horse races and speculating in mining stocks.

Between July, 1885, and November 4, 1883, he robbed twenty-eight stages in this State alone. He was released from the State Prison at San Quentin, January 23, 1888; spent two weeks in this city, then went to Modesto, Madera, Merced and Visalia, leaving the latter place February 28, under the name of M. Moore.

The State and Wells, Fargo & Co. have each a standing reward of $300 for the arrest and conviction of each such offender. The government has a standing reward of $200 for each person convicted of robbing the U. S. Mail.

Any person giving the undersigned information which enables him to discover the whereabouts of Boles will be suitably rewarded.

Please post publicly and securely.

J. B. HUME,
Special O...

The above is a good picture of **Black Bart the Po. N 1** of course he may have changed his appearance by altering the style of wearing his beard and mustache, or by dyeing it, as it is naturally abundant.

teacher named Glendolene Kimmel. Her family were involved in a feud with Kels P. Nickell, and since Coble also had a dispute with him it seems Tom got involved. When news of the boy's killing was made known, rumors spread that it was identical to the Powell and Lewis killings. Once again Horn came under suspicion. However, he was in Denver by this time, where he used to go just to let off steam. Unfortunately, when he got drunk he said many things that were just bravado. LeFors tracked him there, became friendly and got him drunk. On the basis of that 'confession' Horn was arrested and put on trial. He denied killing the boy and the others, but despite pleas on his behalf by Miss Kimmel and some of the cattlemen (who paid for his defense), he was sentenced to hang. An attempted break out from jail was foiled, and he then spent the remainder of his time in writing a one-sided account of his adventures. On 20 November 1903 (the eve of his 43rd birthday) Tom Horn was hanged. Many years later, when Dean F. Krakel came to write his book *The Saga of Tom Horn*, the first edition had to be withdrawn and some names omitted. Even after fifty years there were those who still did not wish Tom Horn's alleged involvement in the Nickell murder to be discussed. Horn, however, continues to intrigue those who seek to understand the 'good-bad' characters that populated the Old West.

John Wesley Hardin's rise to fame amid claims that he had been forced into killing and outlawry by circumstances, can be matched

Above: *The original of this photograph depicts Tom Horn, full length, standing in the door of his cell. He busied himself making lariats – some even claimed that he spliced his own 'necktie'!*

Below: *Tom Horn's brief escape from jail was quite an event. Here he is being returned accompanied by an excited crowd. The bicycles serve only to show that not only times but transport was also changing.*

by another Texan of similar ilk. Indeed, many thought him Hardin's equal. But unlike Hardin, he did not live long enough to prove it. This was William Preston Longley, who was born on 16 October 1851 (two years before Hardin). Bill Longley also used the 'Reconstruction' of Texas as his excuse for violence. However, his apparent ease when it came to squeezing the trigger suggests that there were other factors involved. Born on Mill Creek in Austin County, he grew to manhood with a local reputation as a tough character. Before he reached the age of twenty he is reputed to have shot several men. Working as a cowboy, horse-breaker and with some farming experience, he spent most of his formative years at Evergreen, Texas, where the family had moved when he was two years of age. His first killing is alleged to be that of a Negro soldier (again the similarity with Hardin). Soon he was wanted for other crimes. He left home, and eventually joined up with the infamous Cullen Baker's gang. Baker's death on 6 January 1869, in Arkansas at the hands of a posse, forced Longley to change his base and he returned to Texas and to Evergreen. Before long, he resumed his murderous career and was eventually captured in Louisiana and returned to Texas. Put on trial at Giddings he was sentenced to hang. He complained to the governor of the state that his alleged 'crimes – if such they were' compared with those of John Wesley Hardin, yet Hardin was only given a sentence in the penitentiary, whereas he, Longley, was to hang. What justice was that?

On 11 October 1878, Bill Longley was hanged at Giddings, just five days short of his twenty-seventh birthday. Many legends have grown up around the event. Some claim that when he was hanged, his legs touched the ground. He was not immediately hauled up again as reported, but cut loose and smuggled away. And so the stories go on. Some recent writers have dubbed him 'Wild Bill' a name, his family have assured this writer, that was never used in his own lifetime.

Individuals who went bad were common but when a number of them joined forces, then heaven help those who encountered or opposed them. The notorious 'Wild Bunch' led by Robert Leroy Parker, alias 'Butch Cassidy' was a fine example. Parker, their leader, was born near Circleville, Utah, in 1866, to devout Mormons. The young man, however, who was raised on a ranch, was more concerned with material rather than spiritual pursuits, and he became infatuated with a cowboy turned rustler named Mike Cassidy who persuaded him to leave home. It was not long before Robert turned rustler himself, adopting his mentor's name as his own alias. This led to a career of rustling, bank robbery and other crimes. Unlike others of his ilk, Butch was never known to kill anyone. Captured in Wyoming in 1894, he was sentenced to the state penitentiary. In 1896, however, on the alleged promise that he would 'never worry Wyoming again', he was paroled. Many believe this story to be hearsay, but it is true that Butch was never again in trouble in Wyoming.

Above: *William P. Longley following his capture. Original prints of this photograph have not been found; the only known copy is this badly retouched version. Longley stares hard at the lens.*

Below: *The Wild Bunch dressed to kill – note the assortment of single- and double-breasted waistcoats or 'vests'. Robert Leroy ('Butch Cassidy') Parker is the smiling figure to the right. 'Sundance' is on the left.*

CABIN FROM 'HOLE IN THE WALL'

The 'Hole in the Wall' country is a remote, vast and picturesque region located at the southeast corner of the Big Horn mountains in north central Wyoming. A few miles to the east, the great red wall parallels the mountains for about thirty miles. A section of the vertical wall runs for many miles and is impassable for man or horse, except for a steep V-shaped notch or pass, referred to as the 'Hole in the Wall'. Through this pass riders could come and go relatively unobserved.

Buffalo Creek valley lies between the mountains and the red wall and is wonderful country for livestock. By the late 1880s there were a number of small and large cattlemen living in and using the area. Because the region offered good places to hide cattle, it was also ideal for rustlers and outlaws.

There were basically three periods of outlaw use in the Hole in the Wall country, the first during the late 1870s when stagecoach bandits occupied it between raids on coaches carrying gold from the Black Hills mines to the railroad at Cheyenne. The second period was during the late 1880s when cattle rustling operations were growing, which led to the Johnson County war of 1892. The third period was from about 1895 to 1910, during the time that the 'Wild Bunch' or Butch Cassidy's 'Hole in the Wall gang' was in operation. Their main pursuits were horse stealing and bank and train robberies.

The cabin shown below and overleaf is called the Ghent cabin, after Alexander Ghent, a Hole in the Wall resident who rode with the Currys and other gang members. It was moved by the present owner of the Willow Creek ranch up Buffalo Creek to a spot nearer the original Hole in the Wall ranch buildings, which had been washed away by floods in the early part of the century. In the early 1970s, the cabin was acquired for Old Trail Town and in the spring of 1973 was reconstructed and restored there. The roof and floor boards had to be repaired and new windows were installed. The cabin and its simple contents evoke memories of a time now gone.

(Courtesy Bob Edgar, Old Trail Town, Cody.)

Brown's Hole, which bordered the states of Wyoming, Utah and Colorado, and the nearby 'Hole-in-the-Wall' region proved to be ideal for outlaw activities. Its remoteness deterred most pursuers. Here Butch met up with such diverse characters as George ('Flat Nose' or 'Big Nose') Curry; Harry ('The Sundance Kid') Longabaugh; Benjamin (the 'Tall Texan') Kilpatrick; Harry Tracy; Harvey ('Kid Curry') Logan and others who formed the infamous Wild Bunch. The gang's exploits received a great deal of nationwide publicity, attracted large rewards and the attention of the Pinkerton and other agencies. Modern technology, however, in the form of the telephone and telegraph systems, gradually eroded their escape routes and by 1901 the gang had split up. Cassidy and his closest friend 'Sundance' decided to quit the United States. Accompanied by Sundance's girl, Etta Place, they decided upon a sea voyage.

It is claimed that the trio went to England where one of them had relations living in Preston, Lancashire, before returning via New York to Latin America. For a time they lived in Brazil, close to the Chilean border, where they aroused no interest. Etta, unwell, returned to the United States in 1906, accompanied by Sundance, who returned on his own some time later. Etta then disappeared. In 1911, Butch and Sundance, following a series of bank robberies, were reported to have been killed by Bolivian soldiers during a gunfight in a remote village. Butch's sister, who died in recent years, claimed that he escaped the troops and returned home where he lived in obscurity. Another claim was that he changed his name to William K. Phillips and died in 1937 at Spokane, Washington. Longabaugh is also said to have returned, sought out Etta, married

Below: *Robert Leroy Parker, alias 'Butch Cassidy', at about the time he was in the Wyoming Penitentiary. Despite his tough reputation, there is no evidence that he ever killed anyone.*

Above: *Harvey Logan in a relaxed pose. Known at 'Kid Curry', he was considered to be one of the most dangerous members of the Wild Bunch. He met his end in 1904 following an abortive train robbery.*

Below: *Logan wrecked this train on 8 June 1904, but got away with little money. He and his companions were pursued and surrounded. Rather than be captured, Logan took his own life as the posse closed in.*

her, and lived under an assumed name until his death in 1957. He is reported to be buried at Casper, Wyoming. In 1992, however, human bones were removed from a grave in the village where the two 'American desperadoes' were killed and buried in 1911. These were despatched to the United States for forensic study. The evidence produced early in 1993, however, suggests that they are *not* the bones of Butch and Sundance.

The infatuation some people have with outlaws and outlawry has intrigued historians and sociologists for years. It is not enough to suggest that their lives were exciting. Rather, one must examine the implications of their acts. For even the most cursory study will reveal the fact that it was often rebellion against authority, organized existence and so-called 'normal' living that prompted some to kick over the traces. Others, however, would have gone

Below: *The Union Pacific organized a squad of hard cases to pursue the Wild Bunch. Here, looking relaxed but alert and armed with an assortment of weapons, they sit among saddles and equipment.*

bad no matter what the circumstances, for they were convinced that the world owed them something and its riches were theirs for the taking. Some matured, reformed and led respectable lives. Others, however, continued their nefarious existence and paid the price.

The likes of the James brothers, the Daltons and a host of other noted characters may have relished their reputations, but they well knew that they did not have the freedom of their more honest neighbors. Living in fear of betrayal from other gang members, recognition by someone who might have witnessed a crime or known them in former years, induced a state of tension that was hard to live with. Jesse James came to realize that his only hope of survival was to disappear, but he did not get the chance. Frank, however, was more fortunate. He managed to evade jail on legal technicalities and live a near normal life boosted by a reputation that kept him in the public eye for the remainder of his life. But he was by no means a happy man. The same could be said of many others who rode the owlhoot trail: the spoils might be good, but the prospect of a tight noose or a bullet made for a poor investment. Also, public reaction to outlawry was mixed. When the 'James boys' appeared to be getting back at the railroad barons, they were the darlings of the dispossessed and others who had lost their homes to the advancing iron rails. Government intervention and legal wrangling eventually controlled the speculators, and the growing need for law and order over six-shooter advocacy also turned public opinion against the lawless. It was then the turn of the dime novel, the movie and, much later, television to perpetuate the myth of the outlaw as a Robin Hood rather than a social misfit.

Below: *Reuben ('Rube') Houston Burrows. His early life was blameless; he married and had a family, and was involved with the masons. But he later met his end at the hands of a railroad detective in 1889.*

Below: *William Ellsworth Lay, alias 'Elzy' and 'William McGinnis', rustler, train and bank robber. This photograph was made when he was captured. Reformed he went straight and died in 1934.*

Below: *Thomas ('Black Jack') Ketchum. Following a career of outlawry with Lay and others, he was arrested and hanged for murder. The drop was too long, and his head was torn off, one of the West's worst hangings.*

FEUDS AND RANGE WARS

'The cattle–sheep dispute
triggered the Graham–Tewksbury
feud but prejudice and hatred
fanned the flames that kept it alive.
It was a hatred that passed from
generation to generation even
though the majority of the
combatants were long dead.'

Right: *A re-staged photograph of the
Dewey–Berry fight in Kansas in 1903.*

Below: *A nickel-plated .41 caliber Colt
Thunderer; 2½-inch barrel minus ejector.*

THE LUST FOR LAND

Greed, power and the lust for land: they were the ingredients that led men to fight each other in a bid for supremacy in the race for possessions in the West. Range wars and feuds took their toll, adding to the hazards of frontier life. Probably the most famous, or infamous, of these was the Lincoln County war of 1878–81. Its present-day fame is very much a part of the Billy the Kid myth, although the 'Kid' himself was only a minor character.

Some writers believe that the 'war' was really a conflict between individuals rather than a social or blood feud between divided factions. In fact, the actual war came at the end rather than the beginning of what had been an increasingly anarchical dispute for more than a decade. New Mexico at that time was a melting-pot for the races. Inhabited for centuries by the Pueblo Indians and various Navajo and Apache tribes, it had witnessed Francisco Vasquez de Coronado's march northwards in the 1540s, and in the years following had been 'invaded' many times by exploring parties from Spain and later by the French. Then, in 1848, following the Treaty of Guadalupe Hidalgo, which ceded California to the United States, New Mexico was included. It was not until 1850, however, that a formal territorial government was organized. The area was vast and led to disputes with Texas, a state of affairs which was only resolved when the Lone Star state accepted $10 million to surrender its claim. In 1853, a niggling dispute with Mexico over an international boundary was settled by the Gadsden Purchase. This particular treaty enabled the United States to push a railroad link to California via southern New Mexico. Finally, the territory of Arizona was formed from land ceded by New Mexico in 1863.

The country had long appealed to cattlemen, and one particular region of it attracted considerable attention – Lincoln County, a rather remote part with a reputation for

FEUDS AND RANGE WARS

The great cattle ranges of Texas, Montana and Wyoming were also the scenes of range wars and family feuds. Some feuds were short-lived, while others lasted for generations until in the end few of the participants were really sure what started it all. The 'blood feud' became almost a way of life to some people who felt obliged to carry on the fight no matter what. The likes of John Wesley Hardin, who joined in on the side of the Taylors in the Sutton–Taylor feud, claimed it was because they were 'kin'; but his love of violence may well have been the real reason.

The cattle empires, where cattle took precedence over people, accounted for a number of bloody conflicts. The land on which vast herds of cattle or sheep were run, was comparatively flat, well-grassed and watered. In short (for the time), it was as valuable as oil is to the present generation. Fortunes were made in the rearing of beef and mutton. The benefits were not confined to the United States. A number of English and Scottish companies invested in the cattle business, particularly in Wyoming. Like the Americans involved, they bitterly resented the intrusion of the 'nesters' or 'homesteaders' whom they regarded as interlopers or 'sod-bustin' rustlers'. The Johnson County cattle war was the result of such feeling. In Lincoln County, New Mexico, the 'intrusion' of the Englishman John Tunstall was not welcomed by some, but his death was another incident in a situation that had been building for some time. The later involvement of Billy the Kid in the Lincoln County war was minor at the time. In later years his part was glamorized in legend, an ingredient that aided the legend builders in their efforts to enhance his myth.

The Pleasant Valley war, with its racial as well as community conflict, provided a backdrop of violence and human misery that was to inspire a number of fictional imitators. In fact, the war was the ideal scenario for favorite themes, especially the eternal distrust between cattle and sheepmen.

FRANK WOLCOTT
(dates unknown)
Wyoming

FRANK CANTON
(Joseph Horner)
(1849–1927) Wyoming

REGULATORS
(1840s and 1870s Texas)
(1880s–90s New Mexico, Wyoming)

CATTLE KATE
(1862–88)
Wyoming

NATE CHAMPION
(1857–92)
Wyoming

JOHN TEWKESBURY
(18??–1887)
Arizona

THOMAS GRAHAM
(1864–92)
Arizona

COMMODORE PERRY OWENS
(1852–1918) Arizona

Buffalo

WYOMING

Casper •
North Platte R.

Laramie •

De

UTAH

NEVADA

Colorado R. **ARIZONA TERRITORY**

Holbrook •

Tonto Basin
Globe •
Gila R.

Tucson • Southern

violence and lawlessness. John Chisum, a typical cattleman of the time, had run cattle in the area since the early 1870s and had a reputation for pre-empting government lands and for getting what he wanted. This did not sit well with some, in particular Lawrence G. Murphy, a hard-nosed entrepreneur who saw a future not in cattle but merchandise and property.

Chisum believed that control lay in government beef contracts and provisions, which would include meat for Indian reservations and lucrative eastern and western markets. However, his plans were thwarted by the so-called 'Santa Fe Ring', a political group of prominent Republican businessmen based at Santa Fe. They supported Murphy and, with their help, he acquired many of the government contracts that Chisum had his eyes on. The Ring sought control of the economics as well as the politics of New Mexico. So determined were they that they even supported Democrats who shared their aims, which is how James J. Dolan and others came to join Murphy to virtually monopolise the economy of the territory. Their power did not stop there: control and influence extended even to the law enforcement, and lucrative positions were reserved for those who supported their views and ambitions.

John Chisum, whose baronial empire included vast herds of cattle, felt threatened, and he determined to sidestep the Murphy–Dolan faction and seek government contracts on his own. Meanwhile, a former Kansas lawyer named Alexander McSween had arrived and initially he joined the Murphy camp. Later, he changed his mind and in 1876 he joined forces with an Englishman, John Tunstall, and formed a rival merchandise outfit that not only rivalled the Murphy–Dolan partnership but aligned itself up with Chisum.

Murphy eventually sold out to his partners, Dolan and James H. Riley, who found themselves unable to compete with the Tunstall–

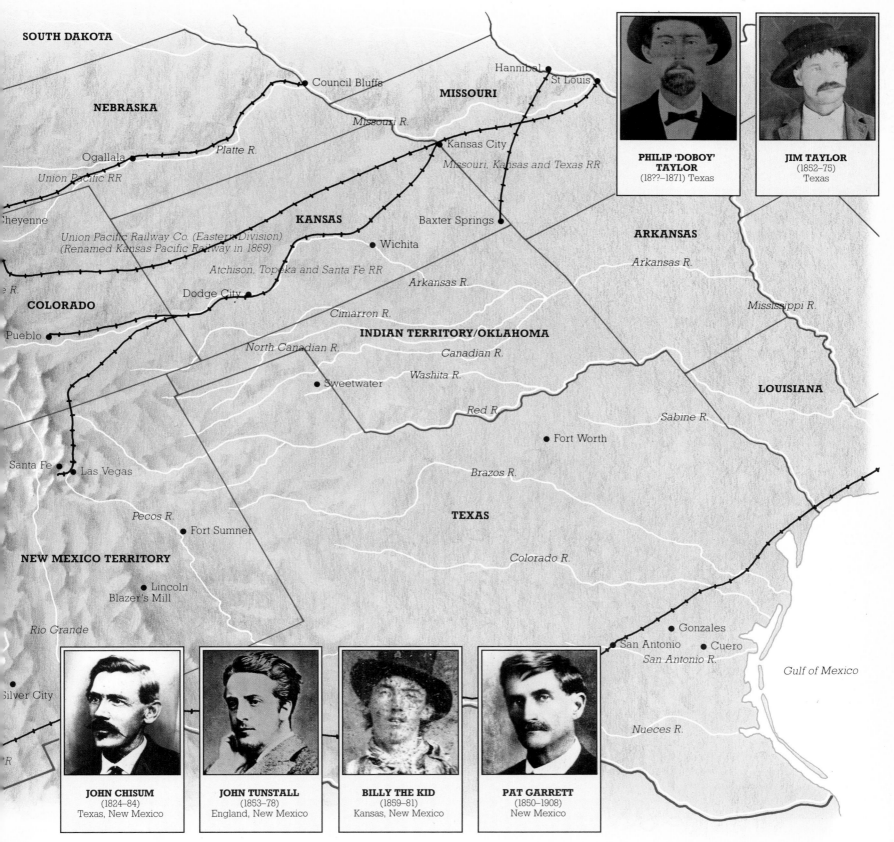

PHILIP 'DOBOY' TAYLOR
(18??–1871) Texas

JIM TAYLOR
(1852–75)
Texas

JOHN CHISUM
(1824–84)
Texas, New Mexico

JOHN TUNSTALL
(1853–78)
England, New Mexico

BILLY THE KID
(1859–81)
Kansas, New Mexico

PAT GARRETT
(1850–1908)
New Mexico

McSween business. The Ring then supported Dolan and Riley and began to bring political and economic pressure on Tunstall and McSween. This soon led to public utterances and local ranchers began taking sides.

Meanwhile, Chisum's pre-empting of public lands continued, which served to alienate many of the smaller ranchers, some of whom changed their allegiance to Dolan. It was no comfort to the Tunstall–McSween partnership to know that many of those who expressed allegiance to Dolan did so out of sufferance, for they were in his debt for patronage or simply because they owed him money. On the other hand, a lot of the Spanish-speaking home-steaders and small land owners rallied to Tunstall simply because he represented the opposition to the unpopular Dolan group.

Rumors began to spread that Dolan was dealing in stolen cattle. Proof was not forthcoming, because, so it was claimed, as soon as the cattle were rustled they were slaughtered or the brands were altered if they were moved on the hoof. Whether this was malicious gossip or part fact was not explained; but it was also believed that no action was taken simply because Dolan controlled the local law enforcement.

Historian Philip J. Rasch discovered an unpublished affidavit by one Andrew Boyle claiming that, when Tunstall hired Richard M. ('Dick') Brewer as his foreman, he sent him out to buy stock at below the going rate, making it clear that he was not too concerned about their

Above: *John Chisum, one of the Old West's legendary cattle barons, whose exploits have inspired novelists and Hollywood in their depiction of the sort of men who created and ruled vast cattle empires.*

origin just so long as they did not come from Chisum's herds. Such rumors abounded, and perhaps on the pretext of one of them the Dolan crowd served a notice of attachment on Tunstall's stock. Deputy sheriff Jacob B. Miller attempted to serve it, but excluded some horses.

On 18 February 1878, Tunstall set out to drive the horses to Lincoln. Accompanying him was Brewer, John Middleton, Robert Widenmann and a young man known variously as Henry McCarty, William H. Bonney or 'Kid Antrim,' but since immortalized as Billy the Kid. Two of the group, Widenmann and Brewer, rode ahead looking for wild turkeys. They happened to glance behind and in the distance they could see dust and riders. They shouted a warning and Billy and the others rode to them, taking cover behind some rocks, thinking that Tunstall was with them. Realizing their error, they turned and raced back. But they were too late. Jesse Evans, Tom Hill, Frank Baker and William Morton had caught up with Tunstall and started an argument. They pulled their pistols on him and opened fire, claiming later that he had 'resisted arrest'. By the time the Kid and his companions arrived, Tunstall lay dead and the killers were gone. Tunstall's murder sparked off the Lincoln County war.

Following the murder, Justice of the Peace John B. Wilson unwisely appointed Brewer a special constable with authority to arrest the murderers. Among the possemen was Billy the Kid. Rasch reports that on 6 March the posse

Below: *James J. Dolan and Lawrence G. Murphy photographed in a typical formal pose at Christmas 1871, at Fort Stanton. Both were ruthless and determined hard-headed business men.*

captured Morton and Baker and took them to Agua Negra where they were 'executed'. A man named McCloskey, a friend of Morton's, was also killed, presumably because he got in the way.

Billy the Kid's role in what followed was minor but made major by his reputation as a gunfighter and a man of violence. He was born on 17 September 1859 in New York City, and he was the son of Patrick Henry McCarty and Catherine Devine McCarty. (The date was established several years ago by historian Jack DeMattos.) His father is believed to have died in the early 1860s, leaving his mother with Henry, another son Joseph and a daughter Bridget (she has so far eluded researchers). Catherine moved west where for a while she lived in Wichita, Kansas, and later went to Silver City, New Mexico. Here she married William Antrim, an alias occasionally adopted by his notorious step-son. Following his mother's death in 1874, Henry McCarty went from scrape to scrape and eventually achieved a reputation as a man-killer, being credited in legend with twenty-one men – one for each year of his life. But the true tally was closer to six. He is reported to have killed personally some of the men who gunned down Tunstall, and his meteoric career as an outlaw-cum-gunfighter was finally stopped by Sheriff Pat Garrett at Fort Sumner during the night of 14–15 July 1881. Garrett was waiting in the dark as the Kid wandered into his host Pete Maxwell's bedroom and, seeing a shadow, called

Left: *Henry McCarty, alias Antrim, alias William H. Bonney – 'Billy the Kid'. He may look half-witted, but he was both a cunning and very dangerous man to cross. And one who killed in cold blood.*

Below: *The 'Maxwell House' where coffee and accommodation was one of Pete's specialties. It was here, during the night of 14–15 July 1881, that Pat Garrett sat in Pete's bedroom and shot the Kid.*

Above: *Left to right are Pat Garrett, John W. Poe and James Brent, all of whom were involved in the hunt for the Kid and his gang. Deputy sheriff Poe later wrote a book about The Death of Billy the Kid.*

PAT GARRETT AND BILLY THE KID

Few Western characters have attracted as much attention as Billy the Kid and Pat Garrett. They have been the subjects of books, dime novels, stage plays, and films. Sorting out the real individuals from the myths which have grown around them becomes increasingly difficult with the passage of time. Actual objects which belonged to either man are rare reminders of the drama, tensions, and violence which were played out in the course of their real lives.

It is agreed that Pat Garrett used a .45 caliber Colt single-action to kill the Kid. As a life-time lawman, however, Garrett owned a variety of guns – many of them presents from admirers. He ultimately was murdered, shot from behind with his own shotgun. Many of the mementoes of Garrett's career were kept for years by his son Jarvis.

Billy the Kid carried a variety of Winchester rifles and Colt revolvers during the course of his career. However, it is also claimed that in about 1880 he swapped his Peacemaker for a Colt .41 caliber double-action 'Thunderer'. The film actor William S. Hart once owned a Kid pistol, but it was manufactured in 1887 – six years after his death!

The Whitney-Kennedy lever-action carbine (4) is purported to have been presented by the Kid to deputy U.S. marshal Eugene Van Patten for treating him fairly when in his charge. Van Patten treasured the gift, recalling the part he played in the Kid's life.

1. Box embossed on the lid, Pat. F. Garrett, for Merwin and Hulbert revolver.
2. Merwin and Hulbert revolver, .38 caliber, ivory grips with the name Pat F. Garrett.
3. Silver cased pocket watch engraved, 'From Grateful Citizens, Lincoln County, September 1881 To Pat Garrett'.
4. Whitney-Kennedy lever-action .44-40 caliber carbine given by Billy the Kid to deputy U.S. marshal Eugene Van Patten.
5. Hopkins and Allen, .32 caliber revolver, inscribed, 'Patrick Floyd Garrett'.
6. Warrant issued to Pat Garrett to arrest Thomas Mooney 'for assault to kill', Lincoln, New Mexico, to appear 6 June 1881.
7. Letter from U.S. marshal to Robert Ollinger, conveying warrant to arrest William Bonney, 5 April 1880. The Kid later killed Ollinger with his own shotgun before escaping from jail.
8. Pat Garrett carried out this warrant on 22 March 1882, arresting one Daniel Dedrick and charging the court the sum of $16.12 for his expenses.

(Artifacts courtesy of Gene Autry Western Heritage Museum, Los Angeles, California.)

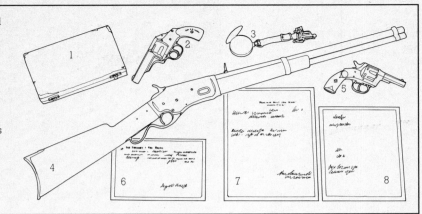

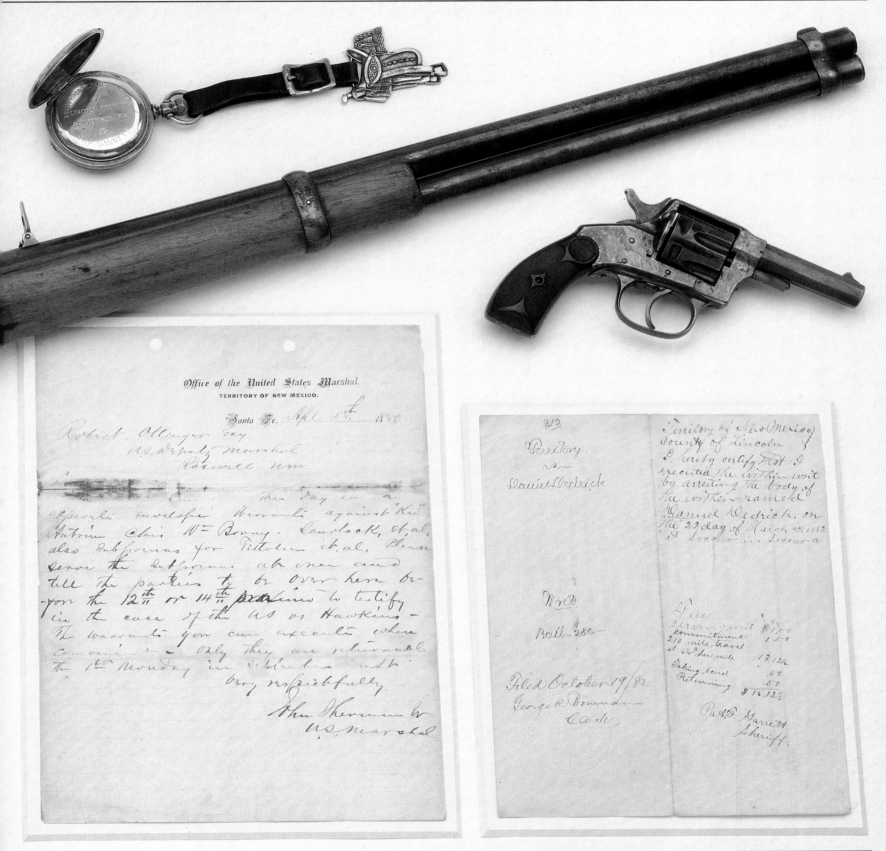

out '*Quien es?*' ('Who is it?'), to be answered by a shot from Garrett's pistol.

The McSween–Chisum association continued following Tunstall's murder, and it is reported that their supporters, sometimes called Regulators, or Modocs (or indeed the Mexican Party according to some contemporary accounts), at one point numbered about sixty-three men. Among those who were involved were said to be about thirty Mexicans. Billy the Kid accompanied McSween when he and about fifty men rode into Lincoln on 15 July 1878 and repossessed a store owned by him. Until the night of the 19th the group were under siege. The Dolan faction managed to hoodwink the commanding officer at Fort Stanton into believing that McSween's party were all outlaws and when troops arrived their commanding officer showed a marked partiality toward the Dolan faction. When the place was set on fire, the Kid and some of his companions escaped, but McSween was killed, shot down while unarmed and attempting to surrender.

During this conflict, the McSween faction had not been entirely blameless. On 4 April the Kid, Dick Brewer and about eleven others had ambushed and killed Andrew ('Buckshot Bill') Roberts, a member of the Matthews posse. But Roberts had proved hard to kill. In what was later remembered as the 'Gunfight at Blazer's Mill', he was fatally wounded by Charlie Bowdre, but managed to shoot off two of George Coe's fingers, blast John Middleton through the chest, and blow Brewer's brains out before succumbing to a hail of bullets. Roberts was attacked because it was alleged (but not proved) that he had been involved in Tunstall's murder.

Later, Sheriff William Brady (who also held a commission as a deputy U.S. marshal) was also implicated in the Tunstall killing, and as a known partisan of the Dolan's he was on the hit list of the Kid, who killed him from ambush. The killings and the publicity convinced territorial governor Samuel B. Axtell (a known sup-

Above: *Charlie Bowdrie and his wife Manuela Herrera, from a cartes-de-visite made by Furlong of Las Vegas, N.M., circa 1880. His garb depicts the fashion of the time: button-over shirt front, fancy necktie, and a 'waist armory' that includes a Colt Peacemaker in a handsome hand-tooled holster; double cartridge belts (for pistol and rifle ammunition) and a Winchester lever-action rifle. Charlie was another victim of Garrett's posse.*

Above: *The Murphy–Dolan store from a photograph believed made in 1884. The row of 'Lincoln County Officials' includes John W. Poe (extreme left) and center is Jim Brent who succeeded Poe as sheriff in 1886.*

Below: *Despite its damage this photograph, made circa 1879, is a good likeness of Robert ('Bob') Ollinger whose murder by the Kid in 1881 aroused much anger. Dwarfed by the tall lawman is James Dolan.*

Above: *Robert Beckwith, one of the Kid's followers, who was killed in the fight at McSween's store. When McSween refused to surrender, both he and Beckwith were cut down in the fusilade that followed.*

porter of the Ring) that he should not get involved, and he kept a very low profile. He was later replaced by General Lew Wallace, at that time engaged upon his life's work – the novel *Ben Hur*, the epic work which depicted conflict in the Roman Empire.

Although violence subsided following the McSween killing, Governor Wallace was anxious to rid the country of the outlaws. He called Pat Garrett, the newly elected sheriff of the county who had known the Kid for some time, and ordered him to find Billy, and is reported to have promised him an amnesty if he would surrender. But a series of events determined a different course. The Kid is thought to have fallen foul of Chisum, whom he alleged had failed to pay him for his support of Tunstall. Some have even suggested that Billy regarded the Englishman as a surrogate father, which might account for his revenge killings. However, to spite Chisum, Billy rustled his cattle. He was also involved in several shootouts which had origins going back prior to the war. When he was finally captured by Garrett in December 1880, any hope of amnesty was long gone. Tried and sentenced to death, Billy the Kid was due to hang on 13 May 1881. Aware of the feeling for and against him in the territory, his guards were extra vigilant. But someone hid a pistol in the jail's outhouse, and when Billy got his hands on it he killed one of his guards, J. W. Bell. Moments later, as Robert Ollinger, the other guard, rushed across the street, he heard his name called. Looking up he saw Billy sitting in the window of the jail, Ollinger's shotgun in his hands. It was the last thing he saw; cold-bloodedly, Billy fired both barrels and cut him down. Almost casually he escaped, only to die two months later at Garrett's hand.

The violence, however, continued, and included a number of racially orientated disputes. But with the death of Chisum in 1884, and Dolan's departure from the area, the war was effectively over.

SHEEP VERSUS CATTLE

Arizona, bordering on New Mexico, witnessed much of the troubles of its near neighbor, but it also had feuds of its own, perhaps the most notorious being the Graham–Tewksbury feud (1886–92). This feud is memorable for its passion rather than politics or greed. Yet that aspect has long been overshadowed by the belief that it was a battle for survival between cattlemen and sheepmen. The cattle–sheep dispute triggered the war but prejudice and hatred fanned the flames that kept it alive. It was a hatred that passed from generation to generation even though the majority of the combatants were long dead.

The Tewksburys and the Grahams settled in the ironically named Pleasant Valley in the Tonto Basin. Both families initially got on well together and their sons rode for neighboring outfits. The quarrel developed over cattle and there were rumors that both families were stealing strays from other ranchers, splitting up the cattle and applying their own brands. It was also alleged that one of the Grahams actually registered a brand in his own name without consulting his partners, the Tewksburys. Members of both families were

Above: *Tom Pickett was born in Texas and first became involved in rustling aged seventeen. He joined the Kid in 1880, and was later involved in the Graham–Tewksbury feud. He died at Pinetop, Arizona, in 1934.*

arrested and charged with cattle-stealing. Soon both factions were bitter enemies, which was not helped when the Grahams became more involved with their neighbors to the exclusion of the Tewksburys. Understandably, they became bitter, and in 1886, when the foreman of a local rancher accused Edward Tewksbury of horse-theft, Ed promptly shot him. Then, to add insult to injury, the Tewksburys introduced sheep into the Tonto Basin which until then had been exclusively cattle country. This aroused bitter feeling, especially among those who resented the fact that the Tewksburys had Indian blood in their veins, making them half-breeds.

In the early stages of the dispute, cattlemen confined their violence to sheep-killing, their activities held in check by Thomas Graham who was against man-killing. But when a Navajo shepherd was brutally murdered in February 1887, both sides were faced with the grim reality that their feud was not only out of hand, but others were now involved as well. In *Arizona's Dark and Bloody Ground*, Earle R. Forrest came down upon the side of the Tewksburys and told the author that he had reached that conclusion from talks he had had with surviving participants and from an exam-

ination of available documentation. In more recent years, however, researchers have discovered that the real villains were the Tewksburys. In an article published in the *Journal of Arizona History* in its Spring 1977 issue, it was alleged that 'an important pioneer settler never before associated with the killing had been exposed as the leader of the vigilantes who quenched the last embers of the feud by hanging the survivors. One obvious choice for such a role was the Blevins family, who were shadowy figures flitting in and out of the story. They arrived in the valley in 1884 and established a cattle ranch on the boundary of Graham land. Once the ill-feeling between the Grahams and the Tewksburys developed into a full-blown feud, it was impossible not to take sides, and the close proximity of the Blevins to the Grahams left them no choice but to align themselves with the Grahams.

One of Old Man Blevins' sons, Andrew, or Andy Cooper as he liked to call himself, was a hard case. He was wanted in Oklahoma Territory for selling whiskey to the Indians and in Texas for rustling and perhaps murder. Soon the Grahams had an assortment of 'hands' who seemed more at home with a gun than a rope or a branding iron. Andy, meanwhile, had per-

Left: *The Tewksbury cabin, scene of the shoot-out on 2 September 1887. The hogs feeding in the yard are probably those alleged to have chewed at the bodies of John Tewksbury and William Jacobs.*

Above: *Thomas Graham, leader of the Graham faction who tried to keep the feud from becoming a bloodbath. His own murder in 1892 heralded the end of the war in the inaptly named 'Pleasant Valley'.*

Above: *Anne Melton Graham, the long-suffering wife of Thomas Graham who was to testify that Ed Tewksbury and John Rhodes murdered her husband. In court she shoved a gun into Rhodes' back but it misfired!*

Above: *The old Graham ranch in Pleasant Valley as it looked at about the time of the feud. Few if any of these places bore any resemblance to the palatial Hollywood-style version of later depiction.*

Below: *John Tewksbury, the handsome victim (along with William Jacobs) of Andy Cooper's ambush. His death only intensified the hatred and anguish that soon boiled over and led to further bloodshed and misery.*

Right: *Commodore Perry Owens in a pose reminiscent of an earlier era. He wears his hair 'frontier style' and his double cartridge belt for rifle and pistol ammunition supports a reverse draw holster.*

suaded some of his Texas friends to hire on as hands with the Aztec Land & Cattle Company, better known as the Hashknife Outfit on account of the shape of its brand. Formed in 1883, the Hashknife Outfit covered a wide area, and led to a mutual contact with the local ranchers. The Hashknife Outfit was never part of the feud, but some of its riders joined forces with the Graham–Blevins group. Mr Forrest noted that many of these men were 'as wild and lawless a bunch as ever rode for one brand. Always looking for trouble, they simply could not keep out of a good fight.'

The Grahams had driven the sheep out by the summer of 1887 and many thought that the cattlemen had won, but beneath the surface tempers simmered and it would not take much to provoke a fight. On 10 August Hampton Blevins, accompanied by five men, some riders for the Hashknife, apparently had a verbal run-in with Jim Tewksbury who is alleged to have taken a shot at them as they rode away. The cowboys later claimed that the attack was unprovoked, but Tewksbury claimed they had drawn their pistols on him. But as more detail came to light, it was obvious that things were

now becoming very serious. It appears that Blevins and John Paine and the cowboys had ridden up to the Tewksbury ranch and invited themselves for supper. Jim Tewksbury told them he did not keep a boarding house, 'especially for the likes of you'. There then followed a frenzied gunfight, the first major battle of the war. No one inside the place was hurt, but Hampton Blevins and Paine were both killed. Both sides now realized that there was no turning back.

Thomas Graham, however, continued to do what he could to keep the lid on the feud, despite his own growing exasperation and anger. And when one of his men tried to track down Jim Tewksbury and was killed in the attempt, everyone knew it was just a matter of time before things got out of hand.

Beneath the façade of feuding families there lurked what historians now regard as the real reason for all the bloodshed – horse-stealing on a grand scale. Though it now seems evident that the Graham family were not directly involved, many of their partisans were, and no amount of denial on the family's part could convince folks otherwise. On 17 August, only days

after the killing of Hampton Blevins and Paine, eighteen-year-old Billy Graham was murdered by James D. Houck, a deputy sheriff of Apache County, as he returned home from a dance. Houck, however, claimed self-defense as the boy had drawn on him. Billy's death brought the Blevins and the Graham families even closer together.

On 2 September 1887, Andy Cooper and some unidentified companions ambushed John Tewksbury and William Jacobs as they were rounding up some horses within sight of their ranch. Both men died without any chance to defend themselves. Inside the house were Edwin and James and their father John D. Tewksbury, together with Jim Roberts, a neighbor who had joined them. Cooper and his friends kept the family pinned down until the next day, leaving the bodies of the murdered men in the yard where wild hogs started to chew at them. It is a part of folklore that John's wife Eva begged permission to bury them to prevent further desecration by the hogs, and it was agreed to cease firing while she dug shallow graves. In reality, the bodies lay where they fell, while Cooper and his band kept up a siege until the law finally arrived. Only then were the bodies buried.

Andy Cooper met his end only days later at the hands of Commodore Perry Owens, sheriff of Apache County, on 4 September 1887. Owens was after him on a matter quite unrelated to the Tewksbury affair, but knowing his man, he prepared for the worst. Following the siege, Cooper fled to Holbrook where he stayed at his brother John's home. John saw Owens arrive and warned his brother. Owens, carrying his Winchester rifle and with a holstered pistol on his hip, strolled toward the house and climbed the porch. He looked through a window and saw Cooper and three others. He ordered Cooper to come out. Moments later, the door opened slowly. Andy was using his left hand. In his right was a pistol – aimed dead center on Owens. At that moment, Johnny Blevins emerged from a side door, so that Owens was now in the middle. With great coolness, he told the rustler that he had a warrant for him on charges of theft. In reply Andy fired, as did Owens, both shots sounding as one. Andy missed but Owens did not. With Andy dead, Mose Roberts, the third man in the house, joined in and was also shot dead. Johnny Blevins took a shot at the sheriff but missed. Again Owens' Winchester cracked and the bullet smashed his shoulder. At that moment his younger brother, Samuel Houston Blevins (aged about sixteen), grabbed a pistol and leapt into the street and aimed it at Owens. He fired once again and the boy fell, dying in his hysterical mother's arms.

The feud itself dragged on until the final survivors were Thomas Graham and Edward Tewksbury. At first it seemed that they had buried the hatchet, but in 1892, Tom was murdered, some claimed by Ed Tewksbury and John Rhodes. Tewksbury was tried for murder but acquitted on a technicality. Ironically, he ended his days as a lawman at Globe, Arizona, where he died in 1904 from tuberculosis. Jim Roberts, who was to emerge as the strong man of the feud, outlived all of them, and was known as 'the last man of the Pleasant Valley war'.

CATTLEMEN AND 'NESTERS'

Sheep and cattle may have inspired feuds and wars but the eternal fight between cattle barons and homesteaders (known as 'nesters' if they settled illegally on alleged cattle land, or 'sodbusters' if they claimed land under the Homestead Act) probably accounted for more disputes and sudden deaths than the former, for the acquisition of land and water rights proved a crucial factor in the ongoing battle for supremacy or survival. Such a situation arose with the outbreak of the much publicised Johnson County cattle war of 1892.

No Western movie or novel is complete without some reference to cattle barons or 'kings' and the rustlers who plagued them. Johnson County, situated some 250 miles north-west of Cheyenne, was ideal for cattle-raising. It became so popular that many of the cowboys quit working for the big outfits and set up on their own, establishing small herds on a homestead. They claimed the right under the 1860 Homestead Act which allowed individuals to claim public land up to 160 acres; after working it for five years, they could register it and claim title. Should a man wish to claim title prior to that date, after a minimum of six months from date of possession he could do so by paying $1.25 an acre and receive title to it. But even those rights might not be enough to protect him if he took up land in the middle of a cattle empire.

The large cattle outfits claimed that many of the so-called homesteaders were too handy with a long rope and a branding iron to have worked long and hard to build up a herd. Rather, they stole cattle from their former employers and rebranded them. But proving it was something else, and even with the courts on the side of the cattlemen, evidence of theft was not easy to find. Another thing was the general dislike of the absentee barons who either never showed up at all or only occasionally surveyed their domains. This had a great affect upon juries who, despite the legality of the charge, were inclined to support the homesteaders. So began a reign of terror caused by the 'detectives' hired by the ranchers to spy on their neighbors and, where possible, catch would-be rustlers in the act.

Until 1886, most of the large cattle outfits had profited from the cattle business, and some (although they might not admit it) had also indulged in the same practises that they now accused their small-time rivals of doing. But in 1886 came disaster. The ranges were overstocked; there was a widespread drought, and many of the cowboys found themselves out of work. Then, to add to their misery, came the great blizzard of 1886–7, one of the worst in Western history. It killed an estimated three quarters of Wyoming's cattle and when it was over the cattlemen realized that to survive they would need to stock the lands with only enough cattle to make the best use of available space, and to make provision for winter feeding. They were then faced by another problem: sodbusters, large numbers of whom had moved in to claim what had previously been open range. Resentment boiled over and the cattle men protested to the powerful Wyoming Stock Growers' Association whose one hundred members included wealthy cattle

Above: *Frank Canton (Joseph Horner), former rustler, bank robber and latter-day deputy U.S. marshal who also achieved status in high places. Today he would probably be called a 'gangster' or 'racketeer'.*

barons and high-powered politicians. They invoked the 'maverick law' which allowed every unbranded calf found upon a member's land to become his property. Ostensibly, they claimed that this was to prevent rustling, but many of the mavericks were later sold at prices too high for the average homesteader or small-time cattleman to afford. This tactic

also helped pay the wages of the high-priced gunfighters who acted as detectives and who could command $250 for every rustler they caught and who was convicted.

The chief of this unsavory bunch was the notorious Frank Canton, whose real name was Joseph Horner. In his earlier years he had been a bank robber, rustler and had indulged in other nefarious pursuits. He changed his name to Frank Canton upon his appointment as field inspector for the Wyoming Stock Growers' Association in the late 1870s. His subsequent career included being elected sheriff of Johnson County (1882–6), following which he returned to the Association where he again joined the fight against rustlers. It is also reported that he was commissioned a deputy U.S. marshal. In the years following the conflict, he was to climb higher up the social and political scales and eventually achieved an enviable reputation as a scourge of outlaws and rustlers!

Perhaps one incident more than any other led to the Johnson County cattle war: the lynching of Ella Watson (known as 'Cattle Kate') and James Averill. Kate, a Canadian by birth, was reported by the cattle faction to be a noted prostitute who ran a bawdy house in Sweetwater, Wyoming Territory, where she soon established a rapport with the local cowboys. In return for her favors they paid her with beef. As an extra, she also laundered clothes for them. James Averill, a justice of the peace, and her friend and alleged partner in a thriving cattle-rustling business, was himself unpopular with the cattlemen because of his outspoken views. On 7 April 1889, the Casper *Weekly Mail* carried a comment by him to the effect that he regarded the cattlemen as speculators and land grabbers. This remark particularly angered Albert Bothwell, a cattle

Above: *Ella Watson, better known as 'Cattle Kate'. Her features appear quite plain, but she evidently had other charms that endeared her to many – except the men who decided to lynch her for alleged rustling.*

Above: *James Averill who, along with Cattle Kate, shared a fate that aroused much anger. Albert Bothwell, who lynched the pair, escaped prosecution; but not the anger and loathing of the homesteaders.*

baron who had laid claim to the land upon which Kate's and Averill's properties lay. In July, Bothwell and some friends decided to take the law into their own hands and dragged Kate and Jim from their homes and hanged them from the same tree, alleging that they were rustlers. Since no attempt was made to prosecute or even question these high-handed actions, anger erupted and matters came to a head – war was declared between the cattlemen and the homesteaders.

The cattlemen then drew up plans to invade the county and wipe out the nesters and cattle-rustlers once and for all. A list of suspects was drawn up and members of the Association were invited to nominate those they thought should be included. It was later alleged that most of the names on the final list were fugitives from justice anyway and that they were wanted in several states, but why it was thought that they were masquerading as homesteaders was never explained. Neither was it explained who organized a meeting of a large number of known gunfighters at Paris, Texas, with the promise of monetary reward if they would volunteer their services as 'Regulators' in Johnson County.

On 5 April 1892, forty-six of these so-called 'Regulators' or 'invaders' (some preferred 'vigilantes') assembled at Cheyenne. Fully armed and well provisioned, they (and their horses) were then entrained and headed for Casper. This motley crew was under the command of Canton and Major Frank Wolcott, a pompous individual who saw himself as the leader of an army of retribution. At Casper the force detrained and prepared for action. They had soon located two of the men on their 'list,' both of whom were killed. But by this time word was out, and they soon became the hunted rather than the hunters. Before they

Above: *Major Frank Wolcott, a pompous martinet who imagined himself above the law. When his army of 'Regulators' invaded Johnson County, Wyoming, they found that they themselves were the hunted.*

were intercepted, the invaders had laid siege to a cabin in which were two of the alleged suspects, Nick Ray and Nate Champion. Ray was killed early on but Champion continued to fight. Eventually, when it was decided to burn him out, Nate made a break from the cabin, somehow managing to get fifty yards before being riddled with bullets. After his death, a

document came to light which was alleged to have been written by him during the siege, in which he had noted the names of some of his attackers, among them Canton. The whereabouts of that document (if it still exists) is unknown today.

When word reached Casper that the invaders had killed Ray and Champion, the sheriff organized a posse and set off in pursuit. He caught up with the band at a ranch some thirteen miles south of Buffalo and surrounded them. At the state capital, Cheyenne, the acting governor was appraised of the situation and promptly ordered the cavalry to intercede before any further bloodshed could make the situation worse. It was demanded that Wolcott and his men should face trial at Buffalo, but instead the cavalry escorted them to Cheyenne. Here, with the help of some high-powered lawyers, they were freed at their trial in January 1893 when no one appeared against them. Rumors were rife that anyone foolish to offer testimony would simply 'disappear'.

The outcome of that trial split the state for years, but it did break the power of the barons, many of whom were bankrupted both by the cost of the invasion and legal fees. The Federal government, anxious to contain the situation still further, sent in deputy U.S. marshals to tackle the rustlers and eventually a semblance of peace was restored. But resentment and distrust continued to simmer on both sides for years.

Ironically, it was Nate Champion, alleged rustler who withstood a twelve-hour siege against nearly fifty gunmen, who is remembered by people with respect and admiration. As for Wolcott and Canton, the architects of the whole fiasco, they were regarded as craven cowards.

Above: *A rare view of some of the so-called 'Regulators' who embarked upon a reign of terror among the homesteaders. Prominent among the group is Frank Canton (No. 34) who led the group into action.*

Right: *Nate Champion (in the light coat) stares impassively at the camera. His courage and subsequent death when besieged by the Regulators is now a part of Wyoming's folklore.*

COLTS FROM THE SHOULDER

Westerners throughout the nineteenth century favored a wide variety of shoulder arms. The trapper's Hawken rifle, the buffalo hunter's Sharps, the soldier's Springfield, and everyone's favorite the Winchester, all saw heavy use. Miscellaneous other manufacturers added a variety of patented actions and other features to the mix and all had their proponents.

Prior to the American Civil War, Samuel Colt had included revolving cylinder rifles, carbines and shotguns in the company's line-up. Many of these were not practical, however, and it was not until the proliferation of metallic cartridges after the war that Colt began to develop and produce more successful shoulder arms. Single-shot military rifles sold world-wide helped to keep the firm in business through tough economic times. Hammer shotguns and rifles in the late 1870s gave way to the 1883 hammerless double-barrel shotgun and the Burgess lever-action rifle. In 1884, the first slide-action Lightning rifles were shipped and until just after 1900 Colt tried to compete with the more successful rifles manufactured by Winchester. The Burgess lever-action .44-40 was introduced in 1883 to compete with Winchester's 1873 and 1876 models, who countered with several prototypes for revolvers, thus forcing Colt to abandon this line. Westerners did use Colt shoulder arms and they became important additions to the armaments of law officers, outlaws and performers.

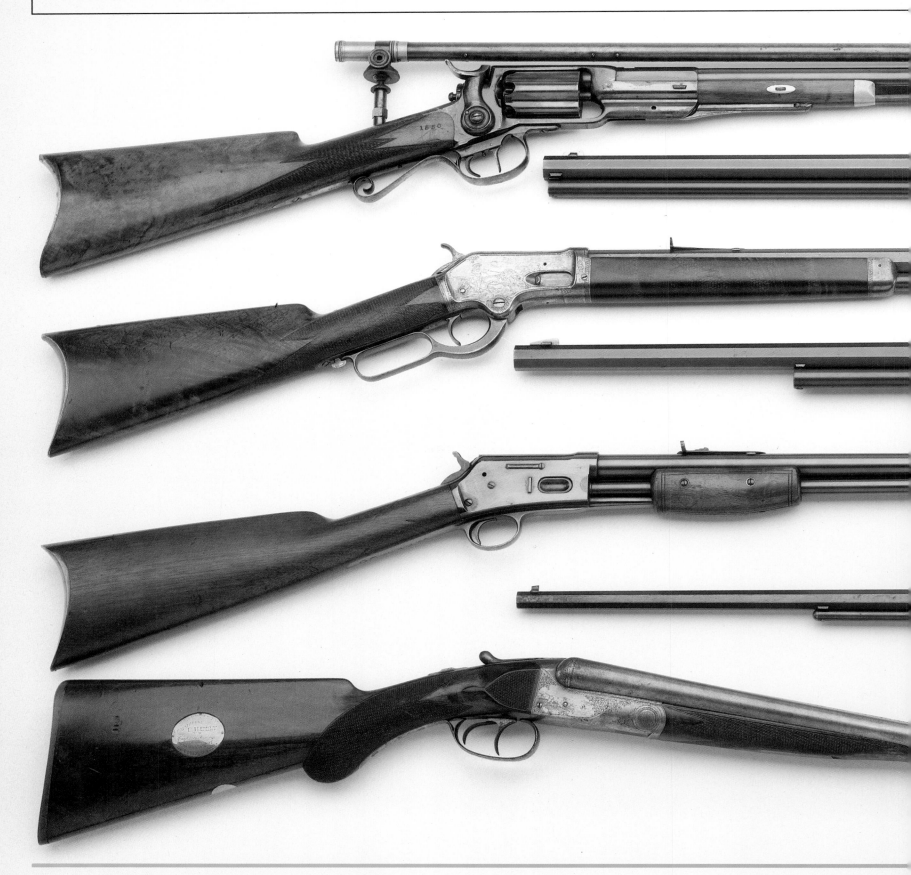

1. This half-stock Colt revolving sporting rifle of the Model 1855 is equipped with a sighting scope and has special finish and set triggers. It was the top of the Colt company's rifle line at the time.

2. Lever-action .44 caliber Colt Burgess rifle, manufactured between 1883 and 1885. Fewer than 7,000 were made.

3. Colt Burgess, deluxe engraved, inlaid with gold, presentation enscribed from the Colt factory to William F. 'Buffalo Bill' Cody in 1883, the first year his famed Wild West show traveled to the East.

4. Lightning slide-action rifle, large frame, caliber .40-60-260, half magazine, peep sight.

5. Lightning slide-action rifle, medium frame, .44-40 caliber, purchased about 1898 for the San Francisco Police Department.

6. Lightning slide-action rifle, small frame, .22 caliber, 1890.

7. This hammerless model 1883 Colt shotgun was a presentation from Samuel Colt's son Caldwell in about 1891.

(Artifacts courtesy of Gene Autry Western Heritage Museum, Los Angeles, California.)

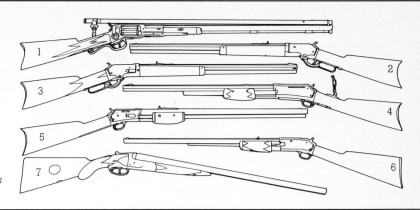

THE BLOOD FEUD

The range feud may command more publicity and lend itself to folklore but family and personal disputes that became feuds were every bit as dangerous and damaging both to individuals and communities alike. In his classic *I'll Die Before I Run*, C. L. Sonnichsen pointed out that 'feuds' took all manner of forms from 'blood' to 'vendettas' among rivals. They often started over trifling misunderstandings or over something really serious like a killing. And as generation followed generation, the reasons were often forgotten, but the 'feud' existed simply because it was a tradition.

Texas was a hotbed of 'feudists' and their activities can be traced back as far as the time white folks settled into the region in the 1820s. But it was in later years that the more memorable clashes took place. In the 1840s there was a particularly vicious encounter between Charles W. Jackson and Joseph Goodbread, in the hills along the Sabine River. Dr Sonnichsen noted that the region had long been a no-man's land where innumerable counterfeiters, horse-thieves, 'nigger-stealers' and others congregated and prospered. Jackson determined to expose this den of thieves and when he killed Goodbread the deceased's friends decided to take action. Jackson promptly organized a band of 'Regulators' who set to work on the transgressors with a vengeance. They were so successful that the outlaws organized a band of 'Moderators' in opposition. For four years both sides hounded each other; crops were ruined, families bereaved and in general it was mayhem. Finally, Sam Houston himself put a stop to it. The aging president of the Republic of Texas called in the militia and with their backing forced the warring factions to surrender and disperse.

Closer to the typical 'Wild West' feud beloved of novelists and filmmakers was Texas's classic interfamily fracas between the Suttons and the Taylors. It is made more interesting because John Wesley Hardin, the most homicidal of Texas's gunfighters, took an active part on the side of the Taylors. DeWitt County, the center of the Sutton–Taylor feud, was situated about halfway between San Antonio and the Gulf Coast, its predominant economy centered upon cattle. The abundance of cattle following the end of the Civil War and a shortage of labor led to difficulties with the erstwhile Negro slaves, who were largely unemployed and in the habit of meandering aimlessly about. When asked to work they were inclined to demand rates far higher than the norm. Worse, many of them were armed, dangerous and 'insulting their former masters'. And the Union army did not help. They tended to take the sides of the blacks, which did not endear them to the white population, especially when they also liked to disarm anyone they fancied regardless of their reasons for carrying weapons. However, a crop failure and an abundance of cattle inspired rustling and many of those animals found themselves on the long march to the Kansas cowtowns.

The Sutton–Taylor feud got off to a blazing start when Billy Sutton killed a horse-thief named Charles Taylor whom, the Taylors later protested, 'weren't no kin of ourn'. But later, in

Above: *John Wesley Hardin from a photograph believed circa the mid-1870s. The print is an excellent version of this famous plate. Wes's arrogant expression suggests that he was even then ready for a fight.*

1880, it was grudgingly admitted that he had been a 'distant relative'. There then occurred another and much more provocative incident: Buck Taylor, the son of William R. Taylor, was killed. Many considered him the leader of his particular part of the clan and feared the worst.

Buck's demise came about on Christmas Eve 1868 when a large party was planned at Clinton. During the evening there were sounds of shots and, as people rushed into the area near the courthouse, men were seen streaming out of a saloon. Word spread that the fight started because Buck had accused Billy Sutton of being involved with some recently stolen stock. When Billy suggested that they step in to the street and settle it, Buck readily agreed and stalked out of the saloon where ambushers opened up on him from the darkness. Hearing the shots, Dick Chisholm, an innocent bystander, rushed from the saloon and was also cut down in the crossfire.

Later reports claimed that the feud started long before both families even ventured into the area, but they were dismissed as hearsay. By 1874, however, the killings were mounting and attracting statewide attention. When John Wesley Hardin aligned himself with the Taylors, things really hotted up. In July 1873, Wes had a run in with Jack Helm, sheriff of DeWitt County, and believed by most people to be a shining light in the Sutton faction. Hardin claimed that Helm's gang, which included Bill

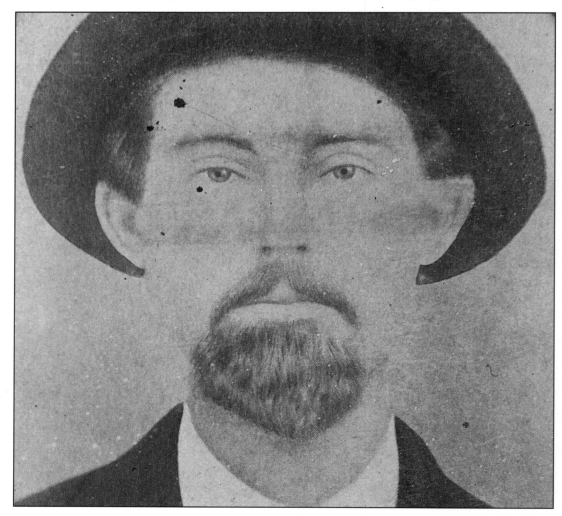

Above: *Philip Taylor, known as 'Doboy'. A veteran of the Texas Revolution of the 1840s, he was very active during the early days of the Sutton–Taylor feud. The son of Creed Taylor, he was murdered in 1871.*

Right: *James ('Jim') Taylor, Wes Hardin's cohort during the Sutton–Taylor feud. It was Jim who shot dead Bill Sutton as he and his wife boarded a steamer. He was killed by the Sutton faction in December 1875.*

Sutton, had murdered a number of men. Helm had also made an enemy of Hardin. When Helm tried to shoot Jim Taylor, he reckoned without Wes, who promptly blasted him with a shotgun. Jim Taylor then finished him off with his six-shooter. Wes, adept at finding excuses for his actions, wrote that 'I received many letters of thanks from the widows of the men whom he had cruelly put to death. Many of the best citizens of Gonzales and DeWitt counties patted me on the back and told me that was the best act of my life.' Hardin's role in the feud is not easily defined, but some claim that a large number of his alleged 'forty notches' were for killings in the feud. As it was, he was related to the Taylors by marriage, which would explain a lot.

In his autobiography, Hardin devotes a lot of space to the Sutton–Taylor feud, and imparts the impression that he masterminded some of the action. In April 1874, Bill Sutton prepared a herd for market at Wichita, and planned on setting out by rail to await its arrival. 'We had often tried to catch him, but he was so wily that he always eluded us,' Wes recalled. 'Jim Taylor had shot him and broken his arm in a saloon in Cuero. He had a horse killed under him in a fight on the prairie below Cuero and he had another killed while crossing the river below there. He was looked upon as hard to catch, and I had made futile efforts to get him myself. I had even gone down to his home at Victoria, but did not get him.'

Hardin informed his brothers and friends that 'Bill Sutton was my deadly enemy' and advised them that he understood he was to go to Kansas via New Orleans, but if they could get to him before he left Indianola, 'I could tell Jim Taylor to go at once to Indianola to kill him, as it was a life or death case whenever either I or Jim Taylor met him.' Word filtered back that Sutton, his wife and one Gabe Slaughter had boarded the steamer *Clinton*, and close behind them were Jim and Billy Taylor. Within minutes the shooting had started. Jim Taylor shot Sutton through the head, while Billy took care of Gage. In the middle of the confusion, the pair ran down the gangplank and headed for the cattle pens where friends had horses waiting for them. Minutes later they were riding hard for Cuero, which was about sixty miles from Indianola. Mrs Sutton, who was pregnant, took charge of Bill's body and had it shipped home to Victoria, where she gave birth to her child, raised it and survived to a very great age, embittered not only by her husband's violent death but by the fact that she and other innocents had been as much a victim as the feudists themselves.

The Sutton–Taylor feud persisted long after Hardin's involvement ceased, and by the time it was generally agreed to be over (some thirty years later), most of the original participants were long dead. As time passes such blood feuds as this dissolve into insignificance, but their importance on the broad canvas of the West cannot be discounted.

Those who lived either among feudists or were indirectly affected by their activities must have existed in a nightmare world, never knowing if or when they would become embroiled in the conflict. Indeed, if nothing else, it was a time for silence – better a silence of the tongue than the grave.

THREE

COWBOYS AND COWTOWN CHAOS

'. . . overall was the ever-present odor of cattle, bellowing their protests as they were driven from pen to freight car, and the shriek of locomotive whistles and the eternal crash of shunting cattle trucks moving into or out of the yards. Only when darkness fell did other noises replace the daylight din.'

Right: *View of Abilene, looking south from 3rd and Cedar Street, about 1882.*

Below: *Colt's first model 'House Pistol'; .41 caliber with a brass frame, circa 1871–6.*

THE COWTOWN ERA

The end of the Civil War and the period before Reconstruction, when the Union army would impose itself upon the defeated South, witnessed a depression. In the north, where its machine-orientated economy had dictated the outcome of the late war and where thousands had been employed in the war effort, there was a sudden halt. Manufacturers found themselves with a surplus of war goods, and even the government had difficulty in disposing of them. Unemployment was rife, while in the south many faced starvation. It was then that eyes turned toward Texas, where before the war she had already embarked upon a thriving cattle-raising and marketing business.

Andalusian cattle were introduced into the New World by Cortez and by the early nineteenth century their descendants were spread all over what was to become Texas and parts of Mexico. Cortez also introduced the horse in 1540 and they too abounded. The Spanish influence was to continue, and with it the traditional *vaquero*, or cowboy. The influx of white settlers into Texas in the 1820s who brought with them cattle and other livestock led to inter-breeding, so that by the time the Alamo fell in 1836 there were an estimated 100,000 head of cattle which ran wild during the battles that led to independence from Mexico.

Although the 'Texians' were to acquire the knowledge and skills associated with the cattle business, they grudgingly admitted that they learned much of it from the 'Mexican greasers' who in turn lost no time in reminding the 'gringos' that they had been there first. The origin of the word 'cowboy' is disputed. Some

Above: *Charles Goodnight who, in 1866 in partnership with Oliver Loving, blazed the Goodnight–Loving Trail to Fort Sumner and on to Colorado. Goodnight's tough, almost aristocratic features say it all.*

claim that it can be traced back to the American Revolution when loyalist or Tory guerrillas in New York's Westchester County stole Rebel or Patriot cows. It has even been suggested that the notorious Stamp Act and Anti-Rent Rebellion in 1766 fostered the term when Dutch colonists called their rebellious tenants 'cow-boys'.

Early pre-war drives took cattle to as far away as New York state, where their meat was considered inferior to existing local stock. Some herds were driven west to California, and others due north to Missouri. The existence of 'Texas fever', caused by a tick carried by the longhorn cattle, aroused much concern. The Texas cattle were immune to it, but domestic cattle which came in contact with the herds were at risk. In 1868, the English scientist John Gamgee was persuaded to come to the United States, where he diagnosed the problem and suggested a solution, by which time a number of Texans had suffered at the hands of ex-guerrillas and Jayhawkers in reprisal for the loss of stock.

By the outbreak of the Civil War, which brought the drives to a halt, the Texans had established the Shawnee Trail to Kansas City. In 1866 the drives were resumed as far as Baxter Springs, Kansas, on the border with Missouri, or on to Sedalia, where the Missouri Pacific Railroad could transport them east. But trouble with Indians, ex-Jayhawkers and others brought this venture to a halt. That same year, Charles Goodnight and Oliver Loving managed to get a herd as far as Fort Sumner and on to Colorado. Loving died soon afterward following infection from a wound caused when he was jumped by Comanches, but

Goodnight survived to become one of the richest of all cattlemen. Tired of Indian attacks and local disputes, the Texas cattlemen reckoned that a direct route north with a railroad link to the east would be their salvation. So began the era of the cowtowns.

The cowtown has a mystique all of its own. The word conjures up a vision of dusty streets, false fronted buildings, hitching posts, cattle pens, railroad tracks and innumerable mounted cowboys. Purists will argue that the correct term was 'cattle town'. In *The Cattle Towns*, Robert Dykstra made the point that no self-respecting shipping point would call itself a 'cowtown' – a somewhat derogatory term that appeared in the mid-1880s. But cowtown has a romanticism that the more formal 'cattle town' lacks, which may explain why cowtown prevails.

Early in 1867, Joseph G. McCoy, a partner in the firm of William K. McCoy and brothers, conceived the idea of establishing a cattle trade with the Texans. He had learned of the large herds running wild in Texas from Charles Gross, a former Union army telegrapher who had seen them personally. The problem was how to get them to market. It is a matter of history that, following a number of setbacks with the presidents of various railroads, McCoy finally persuaded the Union Pacific Railway Company (Eastern Division) building west across Kansas to construct a

switch or siding at a little place called Abilene. He then purchased land and built huge shipping and holding pens. Word was then sent down the trail to Texas to drive the herds north to the railhead at Abilene.

Although Kansas had a quarantine law in force, there were so few settlers in the region that there was little opposition to the trade, especially when it was learned that McCoy had convinced the governor of the state that the trade would be good for the economy. Handbills were printed and distributed and a route was decided upon. This followed a trail established between Texas and Wichita by a half-blood trader named Jesse Chisholm. The 'Chisholm trail' ran from the tip of Texas right up through Austin, Waco, and on to the Nations or Indian Territory, which is now Oklahoma, and on to Wichita, where it ended officially. From there the trail to Abilene was known either as 'McCoy's Extension' or the 'Abilene Trail'. The first herd of cattle reached Abilene late in August, and on 5 September a twenty-car train loaded with longhorns left for Chicago. Abilene, the first of the Kansas cowtowns was in business, and for four years it would be the focus of attention and the scene of cowboy violence.

Many of the men who drove the cattle up the trails from Texas in the immediate post-war years were inexperienced. Among them were returned veterans of the late war, some totally

Left: *This photograph of the cattle shipping pens at Abilene is dated about 1869–70. The 'KPRW' painted on the sides of the cars (for Kansas Pacific Railway) first appeared in 1869. Note the ramps.*

Above: *The Kansas Pacific Railway issued several editions of this guide to the Texas cattle trails in which they included detailed and vital information on grass and water locations, and a map of the trail.*

Below: *Jesse Chisholm, photographed shortly before his death. The original was a tintype which was copied by the Leavenworth photographer E.E. Henry. Jesse's trail is legendary.*

COWBOY GUNMEN 1870s–1880s

It is not difficult to picture cowboys riding in from the trail, celebrating their opportunity to relax, and firing their revolvers jubilantly into the air. The fact is that many cowboys did carry revolvers for a variety of purposes. They were used to put injured animals out of their misery, but they were rarely used in range wars and other conflicts. Revolvers were handy for dealing with snakes and rabid animals, and with a really lucky shot could help to put meat on the dinner table. Revolvers were also worn for reasons of status, but the truth is that they were also heavy and got in the way. Many cowboys kept their guns in saddle bags or in the chuck wagon, bringing them out as they needed or maybe just for the chance to go to town and to wear while having a picture taken. Down on their luck and out of a job, some cowboys joined the ranks of the lawless, resorting to violence and use of the gun.

Low wages kept most cowboys from having really fancy equipment. They were not without their pride, however, and fancy silver mounted bits and spurs were not uncommon. A Colt revolver with ivory and pearl grips might compliment such an outfit along with nicely stitched boots and a particularly fine shirt and hat. This was rare and it is not surprising that Dakota cowboys thought rancher Theodore Roosevelt a bit of a dude. He ultimately proved himself and earned their respect, later writing articles and books which showed his respect for them in turn.

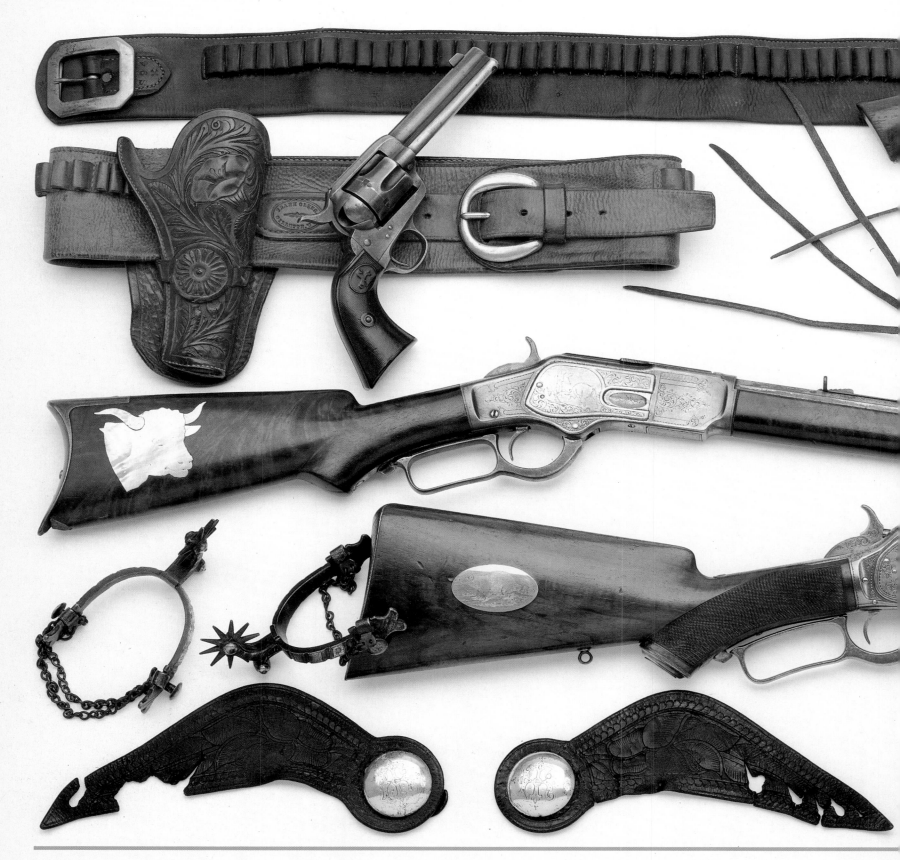

1. Hand-tooled holster and cartridge belt which doubles as a money belt, c. 1900, used by George Gardiner, a working cowboy.
2. Colt-single action, .38-40 caliber, carried by George Gardiner in the above holster.
3. Typical holster of about 1880, made by R.E. Rice, Dodge City.
4. Colt .44-40 Frontier single-action revolver of about 1885.
5. Rawhide hand-braided *riata*, late 1800s.
6. Factory engraved and pearl inlaid Winchester rifle model 1873, owned by Charles Goodnight.
7. California-style silver mounted spurs used by Theodore Roosevelt.
8. Spur straps with engraved 'TR' conchos, probably made by J.S. Collins in Cheyenne, Wyoming, and used by Roosevelt in the Dakotas, late 1880s.
9. Roosevelt's Winchester model 1876 carbine.
10. Engraved six-shooter with carved ivory grips carried in the West by Roosevelt. It represents his vision of the typical cowboy revolver but does not quite fit the bill.
11. Cheyenne made holster, fitted to TR's revolver in about 1886.

(Artifacts courtesy of Gene Autry Western Heritage Museum, Los Angeles, California.)

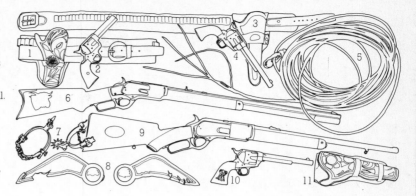

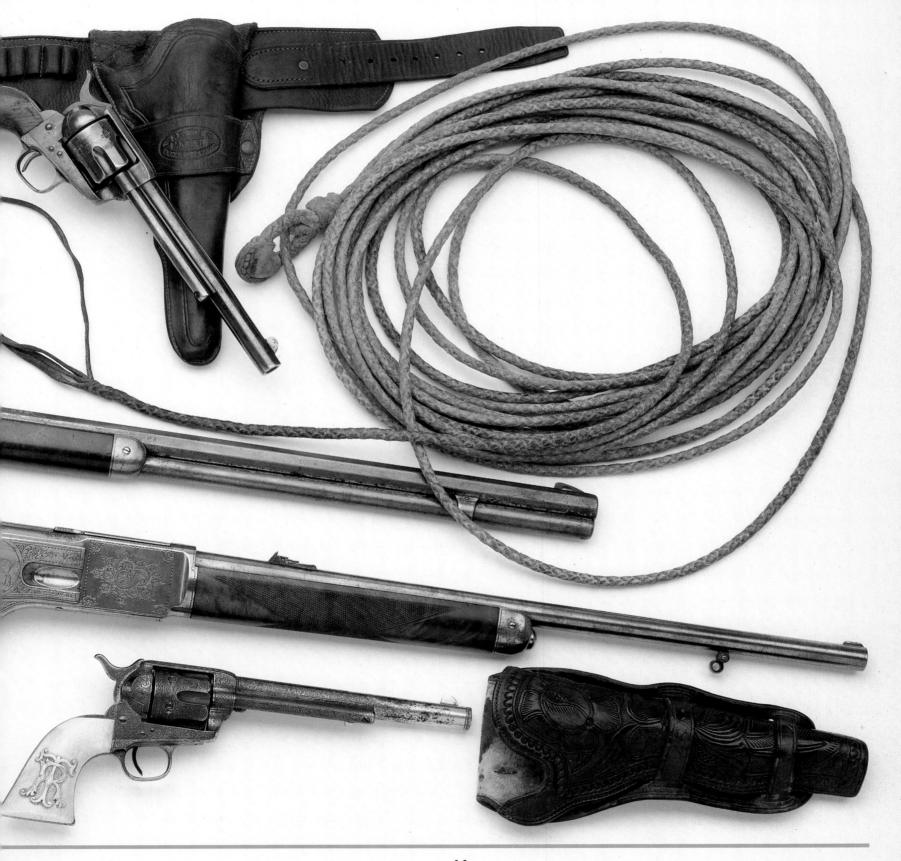

'unreconstructed' in their attitudes. *The Kansas Daily Commonwealth* of 15 August 1871 described the typical cowboy as 'unlearned and illiterate, with few wants and meager ambition', who seemed content to live on a 'diet of Navy plug and whisky'. His principal vice was gambling, and wherever he went he sported a pair of revolvers 'which he will use with as little hesitation on a man as on a wild animal. Such a character is dangerous and desperate, and each one generally has killed his man. There are good and even honorable men among them, but run-away boys and men who find it too hot for them even in Texas join the cattle drovers and constitute a large pro-portion of them. They drink, swear, and fight, and life with them is a round of boisterous gaiety and indulgence in sensual pleasure.'

It was this view of the cowboy that remained uppermost in the minds of the public. To them he was a ne'er do well. And as late as 1896, the cowboy's penchant for the pistol was noted in an amusing comment in the Oberlin, Kansas, *Herald* of 5 March which reported that cow-boys in Arizona, on waking in the morning, in-variably shot at each other to 'increase the cir-culation of the blood'. However, one of them, it was noted, 'shot himself in the foot'. Similarly, the cowboy had his own lingo as explained by the Garden City, Kansas, *Finney County Democrat* of 26 March 1887:

The cowboys have a language intelligible only to the initiated. They call a horse herder a 'horse wrangler', and a horse-breaker a 'broncho buster'. Their steed is often a 'cayuse', and to dress well is to 'rag proper'. When a cowboy goes out on the prairie he 'hits the flat'. Whisky is 'family disturbance', and to eat is to 'chew'. His hat is a 'cady', his whip a 'quirt', his rubber coat a 'slicker', his leather overalls are 'chaps' or 'chapperals', and his revolver is a '.45'. Bacon is 'overland trout' and unbranded cattle are 'mavericks'.

COWBOYS AND COWTOWN CHAOS

The growth of the cattle industry following the Civil War proved to be the salvation of the Southern states. It also led to a massive expansion in meat products, and with the introduction of refrigeration, to exports of American beef to places as far off as England, where by the 1880s tons of beef were being shipped into the ports of London and Liverpool.

We have noted in the text how the trails sprang up, following existing routes (such as Chisholm's trail up from Texas to Wichita) or were blazed in the direction of a known location. But it was the railroads that proved to be the key factor, supplying direct routes east and west.

When the Kansas Pacific Railway began issuing maps to potential trail drivers, they included a detailed account of the trail. Here, for example, is how they described the route from Cox's Crossing to North Fork on Bluff Creek:

Trail from head of Pond Creek bears a little west of north to Cox's Crossing of Bluff Creek, about a quarter of a mile west of mouth of north fork. This is the best crossing on Bluff Creek, and is the only place where wagons can cross for several miles up and down the creek. C. H. Stone's store will be located here. Drovers should lay in supplies here as there is no other store or settlement until Ellinwood is reached. Good camping grounds on north and south side of creek; plenty of weed and water. Take wood here for five or six days' use.

▬ Chisholm Trail
▬ Abilene Trail or McCoy's Extension
▬ Abilene–Waterville Trail
▬ Texas Cattle Trail
▬ Western Trail
▬ Goodnight–Loving Trail
▬ Shawnee Trail
▬ Wichita–Newton Trail
╁ Railroads

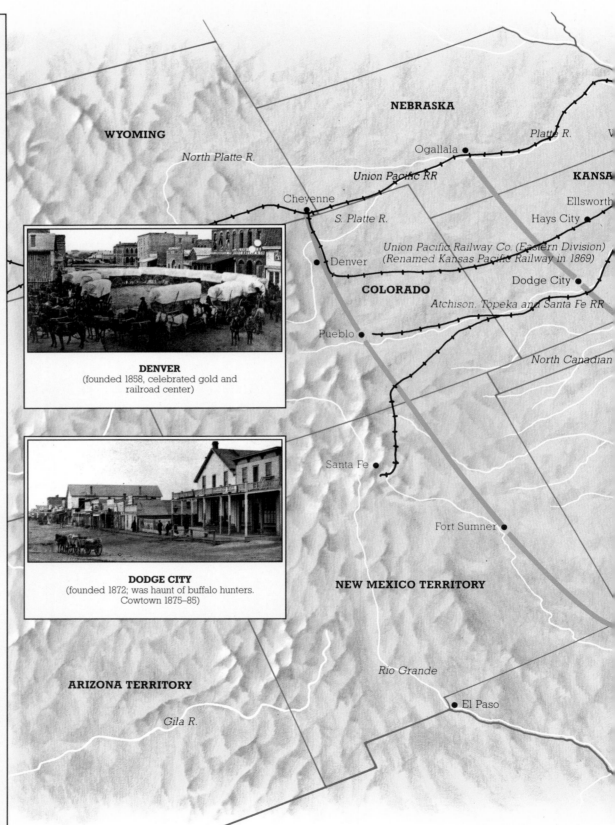

NEBRASKA

WYOMING

North Platte R.

Platte R.

Ogallala

Union Pacific RR

Cheyenne

S. Platte R.

KANSAS

Ellsworth

Hays City

Denver

Union Pacific Railway Co. (Eastern Division)
(Renamed Kansas Pacific Railway in 1869)

Dodge City

COLORADO

Atchison, Topeka and Santa Fe RR

Pueblo

North Canadian

Santa Fe

DENVER
(founded 1858, celebrated gold and
railroad center)

Fort Sumner

DODGE CITY
(founded 1872; was haunt of buffalo hunters.
Cowtown 1875–85)

NEW MEXICO TERRITORY

ARIZONA TERRITORY

Rio Grande

Gila R.

El Paso

Anti-cowboy feeling was by no means confined to Kansas. Back in Texas, the editor of the Denton *Monitor* had pointed out that the addition of Mexican spurs, six-shooters and pipes only inspired the young men toward a career of thievery, when they should be encouraged to stay home and learn a trade. As it turned out, they did learn the hard way how to handle half-wild and totally unpredictable longhorn cattle. As for those who had survived the horrors of the late war, the indignity and shame of defeat made them understandably resentful of the so-called northern or 'Yankee' involvement in the cattle business. Yet they accepted their lot in much the same manner as they had survived

the long years of war when food was scarce, clothing became rags and only a blind faith in the fight for 'Southern rights' kept them going. Ironically, in their new role they fared little better. Poor food and all-weather existence for an average wage of $30 a month only added to their frustration. Many of them also succumbed to disease and suffered from rheumatic problems. In later life, hernias and slipped discs were common. One old-time cowboy told this writer that 'hanging three pounds of loaded Colt and a belt full of cartridges around my hips did not help much either!' So much for the romantic outdoor life of the cowboy on the trail.

On the trail itself, most of the Texans managed to control their prejudices against the Mexicans and the blacks who also rode the cattle trails. Philip C. Durham and Everett L. Jones state in their book *The Negro Cowboys* that according to available figures an estimated 35,000 cowboys followed the herds north between 1868 and 1895, and 'about one-third were negroes and Mexicans'. They concluded that the Mexicans, although better *vaqueros*, were bitterly prejudiced against the Texans, few of whom spoke Spanish, whereas the blacks proved more adaptable. And besides, abolitionist feelings still ran high in the cattle states. The Texans regarded the

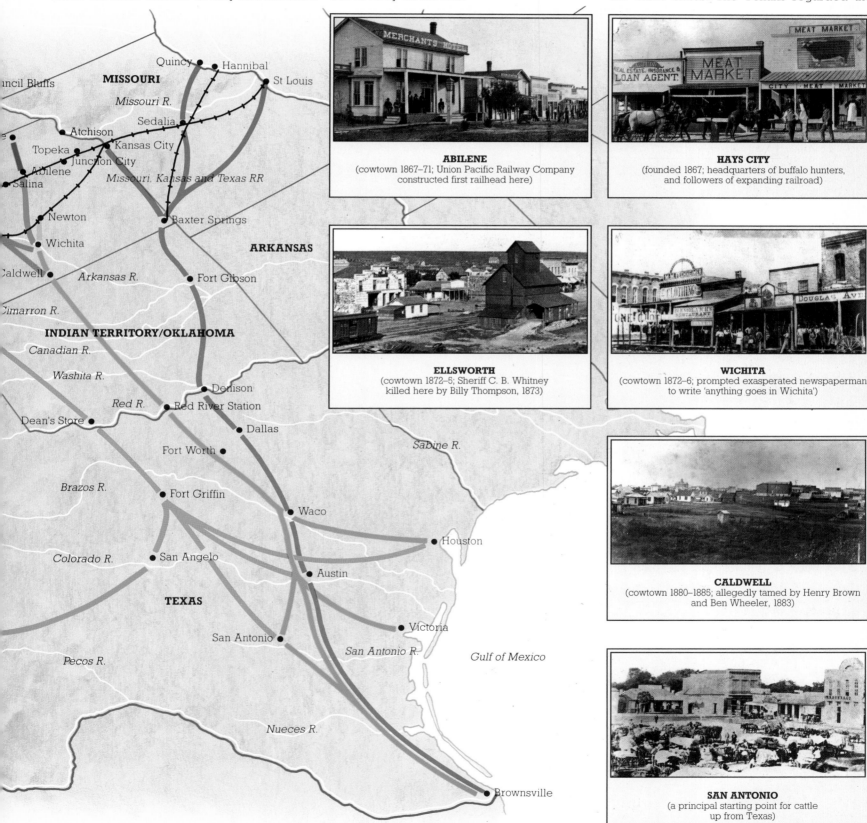

ABILENE
(cowtown 1867–71; Union Pacific Railway Company constructed first railhead here)

HAYS CITY
(founded 1867; headquarters of buffalo hunters, and followers of expanding railroad)

ELLSWORTH
(cowtown 1872–6; Sheriff C. B. Whitney killed here by Billy Thompson, 1873)

WICHITA
(cowtown 1872–6; prompted exasperated newspaperman to write 'anything goes in Wichita')

CALDWELL
(cowtown 1880–1885; allegedly tamed by Henry Brown and Ben Wheeler, 1883)

SAN ANTONIO
(a principal starting point for cattle up from Texas)

MISSOURI
Quincy
Hannibal
Council Bluffs
St Louis
Missouri R.
Sedalia
Atchison
Kansas City
Topeka
Junction City
Abilene
Missouri, Kansas and Texas RR
Salina
Newton
Baxter Springs
Wichita
ARKANSAS
Caldwell
Arkansas R.
Fort Gibson
Cimarron R.
INDIAN TERRITORY/OKLAHOMA
Canadian R.
Washita R.
Denison
Red R.
Red River Station
Dean's Store
Dallas
Fort Worth
Sabine R.
Brazos R.
Fort Griffin
Waco
Houston
Colorado R.
San Angelo
Austin
TEXAS
San Antonio
Victoria
San Antonio R.
Pecos R.
Gulf of Mexico
Nueces R.
Brownsville

Above: *Abilene in 1879. Its rip-roaring cattle-driving days behind it, the place had now settled into a peaceful existence, farmers and others having replaced the cowboys, gunfighters and other frontier 'types'.*

Mexicans as foreigners and treated them as outcasts. A number of blacks achieved status on the trail, a few were even employed as trail bosses, but they were the exceptions. In later years, however, when the encroachment of settlement, quarantine laws and the introduction of barbed wire severely curtailed the routes, many blacks replaced the whites on the trail drives.

In the immediate post-war years, however, young 'unreconstructed rebels' made no secret of their dislike for blacks. But trouble, when it did occur, was usually directed against other whites or the Mexicans. Typical of those who sought confrontation with either race was John Wesley Hardin. When, in 1871, he came up the trail to Abilene as trail boss with Columbus Carroll's outfit (perhaps one of the youngest ever to hold that position), he killed eight men, most of them Mexicans. In his

posthumously published autobiography, Hardin claimed that his herd came into contact with one driven by Mexicans. When he protested that they were in danger of mixing, there was a row. The boss Mexican then took a shot at him with a rifle from 100 yards (knocking off his hat, so Hardin alleged), and then made the mistake of walking toward him, firing his six-shooter. Hardin shot him dead. Other Texans then rushed to join Wes and the fight ended with six Mexicans dead, five of whom were claimed by Hardin himself. Wes' contemptuous attitude toward Mexicans was typical of many who rode the cattle trails, and accounted for much of the trouble that broke out in the early years of the drives.

Abilene was the first true cowtown. Although Sedalia, Baxter Springs and perhaps Kansas City had a prior claim as shipping points, Abilene was the first of such places to

be developed solely for the purpose. Named after the Biblical city 'The Tetrarch of Abilene' or 'City of the Plains', it started life in the early 1860s as a stagecoach stop, and by 1867 it also boasted a couple of log huts and a saloon. However, once McCoy began building his shipping pens on 250 acres of land on the northeastern side of the village, more people arrived. Soon other structures sprang up, including an hotel. This was the celebrated three-story Drover's Cottage (which was demolished later and moved to Ellsworth). Later still, a bank, stores and more saloons were built on either side of the railroad tracks

Above: *This woodcut originally appeared in Joseph G. McCoy's book on the cattle trade, and depicts Abilene in its early years. The Drover's Cottage hotel was later dismantled and moved to Ellsworth.*

Below: *Bader & Laubner's saloon at Dodge City in later years. Gone is the ramshackle rough flooring and green wood effects of earlier times. In its place is cleanliness and comparative opulence.*

which ran east–west. Texas Street initially housed the saloons and some business premises, while to the north a collection of shacks were the province of dance halls and brothels.

Abilene was a typical Western town of the period. It was dominated by the railroad, and a person's social standing depended upon which side of the tracks he resided. Most of the buildings and the sidewalks were constructed of wood, much of the timber was still green and affected by changes in the weather. The ankle-deep dust of summer gave way to a muddy mire by the fall and winter. Unwary pedestrians who failed to watch their step sometimes tripped over warped planks and stretched their length in the dust or mud. The few permanent residents were mostly storekeepers or the owners or licensees of various saloons or businesses. During the cattle season, however, the population exploded,

boosted by Texans and an army of pimps, prostitutes, gamblers and others anxious to relieve the cattlemen of their hard-earned cash. And overall was the ever-present odor of cattle, bellowing their protests as they were driven from pen to freight car, and the shriek of locomotive whistles and the eternal crash of shunting cattle trucks moving into or out of the yards. Only when darkness fell did other noises replace the daylight din.

The saloons were open most of the day, but really only came into their own at night, when they were rivalled by dance halls and brothels. Abilene's most prestigious saloon was the Alamo, which prided itself on a forty-foot frontage on Cedar Street. Inside there was an impressive mirror extending along its bar. There were also a number of paintings depicting Venetian Renaissance nudes. Its counterpart was the Gold Room at Newton which was

not quite so palatial but did have a large mirror which was bordered by an impressive display of liquor bottles. Gambling took precedence in the Alamo, and a number of tables were placed just inside the main doorway, which were covered in green baize. Similar establishments were found in other places, notably Dodge City which had the Long Branch Saloon – although in appearance and amenities it was inferior to its Abilene or Newton rivals.

During the day, most of the cowtowns appeared almost sleepy. Visitors might be misled into thinking that perhaps the stories of unruly Texans and licentious living were figments of a fevered newsman's imagination, but the permanent residents knew better and dreaded nightfall. In Abilene, which survived two years without any real law and order, the residents grew tired of the cowboy chaos that interrupted their lives or ruined business.

VOLCANIC RIFLES

The so-called Volcanic magazine rifles and pistols were really a development of earlier pistols produced by Smith & Wesson in the early 1850s. These .30 and .38 caliber pistols (and a few very rarely encountered arms in .44) were unique. They were cartridge weapons at a time when the percussion system was in general use. Unfortunately, the cartridge, which consisted of a hollow-nosed bullet that contained its own propellent, was not reliable; it was later replaced by an improved rimfire version. By that time, Smith & Wesson had incorporated the company into Volcanic Arms, and concentrated upon other ventures.

As for the Volcanic pistols and rifles, they enjoyed a limited popularity and in 1857 Col. Charles Hay, in command of the British Army's School of Musketry at Hythe, put the Volcanic through some severe tests. An expert shot, using the long-barreled version with a stock he was able to hit an 8 inch bull's eye at 300 yards, placing nine bullets into the ring and two into the bull's eye. And firing off hand at 100 yards he had also hit the bull's eye with a pistol. At the time that Col. Hay was experimenting with the Volcanic, Oliver Winchester purchased the company and renamed it the New Haven Arms Company. He appointed B. Tyler Henry to manage it and his modifications to the mechanism and the ammunition culminated in the Henry rifle. But the Volcanic rifles were viewed as milestones in arms manufacture.

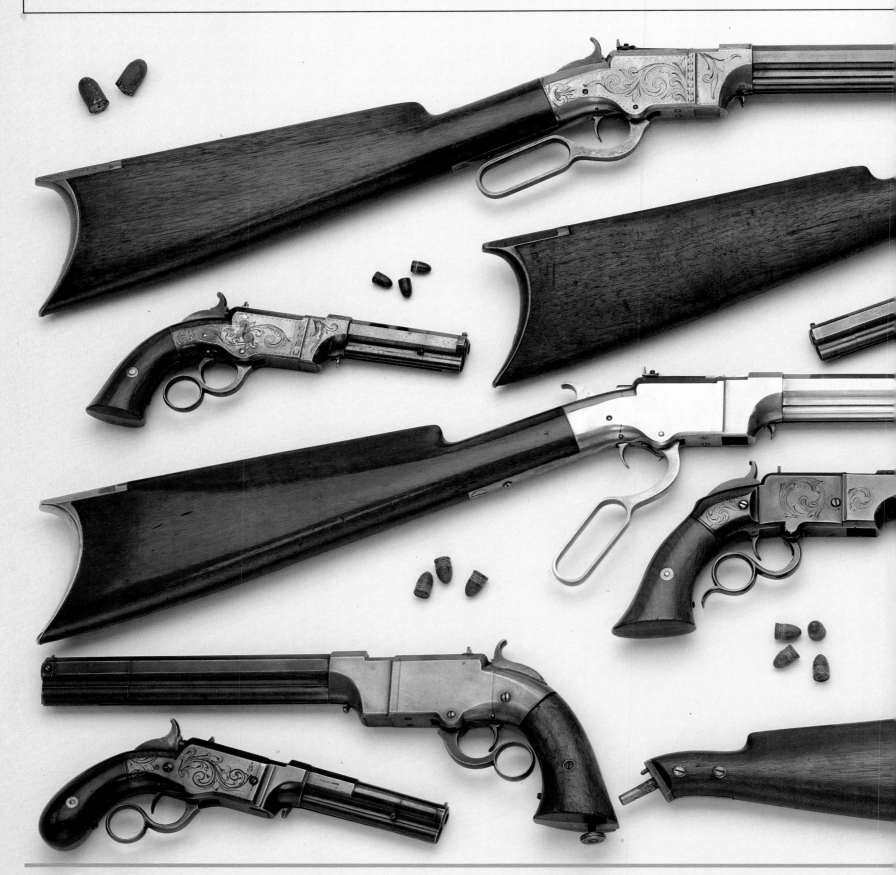

1. Pair of Hunt's patented caliber .54 'rocket balls'.
2. Volcanic caliber .38 (.41 cartridge), 30 shot carbine (s.n. 88).
3. Trio of Volcanic No. 2 (caliber .41) bullets.
4. Volcanic caliber .30 (.31 cartridge), 6 shot pistol (s.n. 1340).
5. Volcanic caliber .38 (.41 cartridge), 25 shot carbine (s.n. 82).
6. Volcanic caliber .38 (.41 cartridge), 10 shot pistol-carbine (s.n. 1342).
7. Smith & Wesson caliber .30 (.31 cartridge), 6 shot pistol (s.n. 44).
8. Volcanic caliber .38 (.41 cartridge), 20 shot carbine (s.n. 1).
9. Volcanic caliber .30 (.31 cartridge), 6 shot pistol (s.n. 1868).
10. Volcanic caliber .38 (.41 cartridge), 10 shot pistol (s.n. 1159).
11. Smith & Wesson caliber .38 (.41 cartridge), 10 shot pistol.
12. Box of 200 No. 2 (caliber .41) Volcanic cartridges.
13. Volcanic caliber .30 (.31 cartridge), 10 shot target pistol (s.n. 1999).
14. Volcanic caliber .38 (.41 cartridge), 10 shot pistol (s.n. 1528).
15. Volcanic caliber .38 (.41 cartridge), 10 shot pistol (s.n. 1161).
16. Volcanic caliber .38 (.41 cartridge), 8 shot pistol (s.n. 822).

(Artifacts courtesy of Buffalo Bill Historical Center, Cody, Wyoming.)

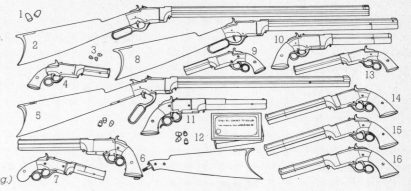

PISTOLIFEROUS PRANKS

Theophilus Little, an early resident and businessman, recalled that during the early part of the day when the Texans came to town it was quiet enough; but when it came time to leave and they were liquored up everybody feared the worst. 'The signal for leaving town at about 3 p.m. was a few pistol shots into the air, their ponies mounted, a general fusilade all along the line, every pony on the dead run and as they passed my office, it was crack, bang, boom of fifty or a hundred six shooters into the air. The air, blue with smoke as it curled upward into spiral wreaths . . .'

A similar view was shared by old-timer John B. Edwards who noted that the Texan of the 1860s and 1870s invariably got 'too much tanglefoot aboard', and was 'liable under the least provocation to use his navies [six-shooters], of which not less than one or two were always hanging to their belts. In fact, if their fancy told them to shoot they did so, in the air, at anything they saw and a plug hat would bring a volley at any time from them, drunk or sober.'

Skillfull though he might be with the pistol, like most people the Texan was probably more adept with a rifle. After the war, many cowboys had (illegally) hung on to their service issue weapons (which under the terms of the surrender at Appomatox should have been confiscated), or simply acquired others. These consisted of an assortment of Colt Navy or Army revolvers; Remington Army or Navy pistols, and some copied by Confederate arsenals. Their longarms were a mixture of single-shot percussion or early breech-loading weapons, some of them Sharps or even the Spencer seven-shot repeaters admired by the Union cavalry. And others might have been fortunate to acquire a Henry 16-shot lever-action .44 rim-fire repeater.

Christopher Miner Spencer was born in 1833 and died in 1922. During his long life he invented a number of things, but he is best remembered for his firearms, in particular the range of seven-shot repeaters that saw service in the Civil War and were adapted for cavalry use during the Indian wars that followed. B. Tyler Henry was chosen by Oliver F. Winchester to manage the newly formed New Haven Arms Company in 1857, which took over the original Volcanic Repeating Arms Company that had manufactured a lever-operated weapon based upon a system created by Smith & Wesson for pistols. Henry redesigned the ammunition for the Volcanic and also improved the action. The result was the Henry rifle, a weapon infinitely superior and one which saw service during and following the Civil War and one that was much coveted by troops and plainsmen alike. The redesigned rim-fire cartridge and action and the fact that the weapon could hold sixteen cartridges in the tubular magazine set beneath the barrel gave the Henry rifle added importance. It proved its worth on a number of occasions, most notably in August 1866 when troops and civilians, armed with .58 caliber Allin-converted Springfield single-shot rifles and Henrys managed to repel an assault of Red Cloud's Sioux at Piney Island until reinforcements arrived with cannon.

Above: *The tall figure in the dark shirt armed with a Sharps buffalo gun is William ('Bill') Tilghman, who looks remarkably like the late movie star Joel McCrea. Bill carries his Colt in a reverse draw flap holster, and the cartridges for his rifle are clearly seen. The photograph dates from the early 1870s when buffalo hunting was a profitable business, both for their hides and their bones. With him is James Elder.*

Above: *A number of noted gunfighters, among them Hickok, Earp and Masterson, at one time or another hunted buffalo. Here hunters armed with Sharps rifles have set up camp near Sheridan, Kansas.*

Below: *Oliver F. Winchester, from a painting by G.S. Hopkinson. His name is now a legend, but few people know much about the former shirt manufacturer who realized cartridges not cuffs were 'in'.*

Above: *William ('Billy') Dixon (center front) was a noted shot. It is reported that at the Adobe Walls fight against the Comanches in 1874 he shot a warrior from his horse a thousand yards away.*

The colorful yet inaccurate claim that the Winchester rifle was the 'Gun that Won the West' may have been untrue, but it contributed greatly to its popularity. By the time the trail-drivers were headed for Abilene, Oliver Winchester had redesigned the Henry rifle and the Winchester Model of 1866, the first to bear his name, became the plainsman's favored rifle. Basically similar in appearance to the Henry rifle, the new Winchester included improvements to the action and the means of loading. To load the Henry one had to push the cartridges directly into the tubular magazine. Winchester incorporated a loading slot on the side of the receiver which was retained in later models. Like the Henry, the new Winchester retained a brass frame which earned it the name 'Yellow Boy'. By 1873, however, Winchester had introduced a modified version with an iron frame and receiver chambered for the .44 caliber center-fire cartridge which held forty grains of powder.

The riders who came up the trail armed with the latest weapons were also aware that the cattle trade would bring prosperity both to Texas and for those connected with it. But the combination of firearms, arrogance and defiance in the face of authority could no longer be tolerated. By 1869 Abilene was determined to put a stop to the violence. On 3 September, a deputation of citizens appeared before Cyrus Kilgore, probate judge of Dickinson County, and presented a petition requesting the incorporation of Abilene. The judge granted the request and Abilene became a third-class city empowered to hold elections. A board of trustees was chosen to act pending an election, and in 1870 the position of town marshal was created. Ellsworth, which would succeed Abilene as a cowtown in 1872, had been incorporated since 1867, and by the time the Texans arrived, a police force awaited them. The same happened with Newton, Wichita and Dodge City. In later years when the trail moved on to Caldwell, the place had long been under the influence of the law.

THE HENRY RIFLE

The Henry rifle was a derivative of the Smith & Wesson/Volcanic arms. Henry's modification of the action and improved cartridge revolutionized the concept. It consisted of a brass casing with the propellent in its base and a 216-grain bullet and 25 grains of powder. This 'rimfire' proved successful and was modified several times. Ordnance tests were encouraging and it was claimed that at 400 yards the bullet could embed itself 5 inches into a wooden target.

The U.S. government was tardy in accepting the Henry rifle, but by 1863 a large number of them had been issued to volunteer and State troops. Kansas in particular took to the Henry. It was reported in 1863 that Gen. James Blunt's bodyguards were to be armed with 'Henry's Volcanic repeating rifles and two revolvers and will be mounted on picked horses'. The Henry was fitted with a tubular magazine that could hold sixteen rounds. Its only drawback was its price: in October 1862 it was listed at $42, the ammunition at $10 per thousand. Even the dealers failed to get a good discount but demand was sufficient to keep the company busy. A major weakness was its exposed magazine spring which necessitated loading it from the muzzle end. In 1866 this was rectified by placing a slot in the side of the receiver and spring pressure from the muzzle end. Too late for the Henry, it was incorporated instead in its successor, the Winchester model 1866.

1. An early brass frame Henry rifle (s.n. 14).
2. Iron frame Henry rifle, levered for loading.
3. Iron frame Henry rifle (s.n. 155).
4. Early production (rounded butt) brass framed, engraved Henry rifle (s.n. 172).
5. Box of early caliber .44 Henry rimfire cartridges.
6. Early production brass frame, silver plated Henry (s.n. 2115).
7. Box of post-Civil War

caliber .44 Henry rimfire cartridges.
8. Early production brass frame, silver plated, engraved Henry rifle.
9. Early production brass frame Henry military rifle (s.n. 2928).
10. Four-piece wooden cleaning rod stored in the butt trap of Henry rifles.
11. Later production (crescent butt) brass frame Henry military rifle (s.n. 6734).
12. Later production silver

plated Henry military rifle (s.n. 7001).
13. Leather sling for Henry military rifle.
14. Later production brass frame Henry military rifle (s.n. 9120).
15. Later production brass frame Henry military rifle (s.n. 12832).
16. Quartet of caliber .44 Henry flat nosed cartridges.

(Artifacts courtesy of Buffalo Bill Historical Center, Cody, Wyoming.)

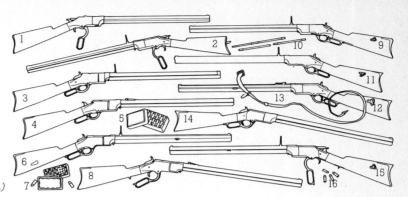

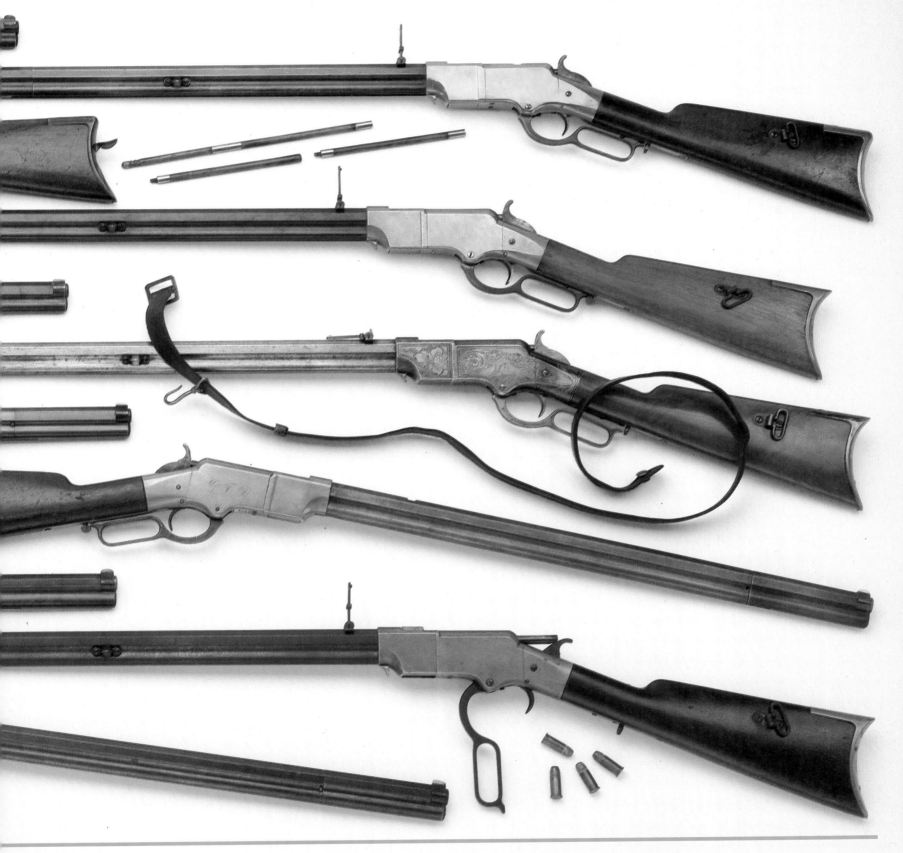

PISTOLS, POKER, PIMPS AND PERDITION

Firearms and their use within city limits were a constant problem. The Texans felt undressed without a pistol or pistols adorning their waistbelts, and the idea that they should disarm was abhorrent. It was by no means a new situation, for although the *Kansas Statutes* of 1868 decreed that if former Confederate soldiers and others who had been in rebellion were found carrying 'a pistol, bowie-knife, dirk or other deadly weapon', they would be fined a maximum of one hundred dollars and face a jail sentence of three months, there were few attempts to enforce the unenforceable. However, the law remained on the statute books for some years, and formed the basis for local legislation. In April 1870, Ellsworth's city council passed 'Ordinance No. 1' which made it an offense to discharge a firearm within city limits, or to be exact: 'On the North Bank of the Smoky Hill River East of the Round House on West of a point 600 yards of the East of the Rail Road switch in the eastern part of the town, and south of the North line of the town which is about 100 yards from the foot of the Hills.' Failure to obey that ruling could be punished with a ten dollar fine, and to discharge a pistol in the center of the city meant a twenty dollar fine. Enforcing such a law, however, proved difficult and dangerous.

By 1871, Abilene's city council had also decided that it was time for the Texans to disarm. On 8 June the *Chronicle* published the following editorial comment:

> *Fire Arms.* – The Chief of Police [James B. Hickok] has posted up printed notices, informing all persons that the ordinance against carrying fire arms or other weapons in Abilene, will be enforced. That's right. There's no bravery in carrying revolvers in a civilized community. Such a practice is well enough and perhaps necessary when among Indians or other barbarians, but among white people it ought to be discountenanced.

Some chose to ignore that warning, but there were fewer incidences of gunplay in the suc-

Above: *Wichita in 1870, when the 'corner of Main and Douglas Avenue' was mere tufts of prairie grass. Within weeks, shacks and tents had sprung up, soon to be replaced by permanent structures, many of them saloons.*

ceeding months, some claim simply because the Texans feared a confrontation with Hickok and his 'posse'.

In 1872, Wichita was only too well aware of its growing reputation as a 'wild and woolly' town, and the fear was that the cattle trade and the violence associated with it would prove a deterrent. 'Wichita desires law and order,' declared the editor of the *Eagle* on 7 June, 'with their consequent peace and security, and not bloodshed and a name that will cause a thrill of horror whenever mentioned and which will effectually deter the most desirable class of people from coming among us. Right speedily will the latter follow if the former are not maintained.' Unfortunately, his words fell upon deaf ears. The city council then tried what they thought was a smart move: they approached the owners of the privately owned Chisholm Trail bridge (which crossed the Arkansas River and linked the city with Delano), who agreed that their tollkeepers should be sworn in as special policemen. This empowered them to disarm all those who

crossed the bridge. In exchange for their pistols, people received a metal token. This proved to be a failure. A year later, notices were put up which stated: LEAVE YOUR REVOLVERS AT POLICE HEADQUARTERS AND GET A CHECK. Similar tactics were tried at Dodge City and other cowtowns with little success. Consequently, the police always wore their pistols prominently displayed, a state of affairs that many citizens, with some justification, found objectionable.

The antics of cowboys and others when drunk were alarming and occasionally led to fatalities. However, there were few instances of total domination by 'armed transients'. Rather, most places were prepared to back their police forces if need be by citizen participation if things got out of hand. The Kansas State Code empowered mayors to order all male citizens aged between eighteen and fifty to arm themselves and help enforce the law should the alarm be rung (the fire station bell or some other means). It was rare, however, for this to be enforced.

Below: *By the fall of 1872, Newton was making great strides. Typically railroad tracks ran through the middle of the town. Social status often depended upon 'which side of the tracks' one resided'.*

Probably the most serious near-riot that afflicted any cowtown was the so-called 'Newton General Massacre'. Its cause was deep-rooted but its effect deadly. It began innocently enough, with the citizens of Newton voting, on 11 August 1871, on a proposal to issue twenty thousand dollars' worth of county bonds to aid the building of the Wichita & Southwestern Railroad. Michael McCluskie (sometimes spelled McCluskey), a former night policeman employed by the railroad, was commissioned as a special policeman for the election. He was known as a troublemaker and it came as no surprise when he and another policeman similarly hired, a Texas gambler named Wilson (alias Billy Bailey), rowed over cards. They then pulled pistols and Wilson died the next day. His infuriated Texan friends set out to find McCluskie who decided to slip out of town. On 19 August, however, he foolishly returned. As it was a Saturday, he spent the evening in Perry Tuttle's dance hall. Word soon got around that McCluskie was back and a number of Texans made their way to Tuttle's place. The Emporia

Below: *William Smith served as marshal of Wichita and later as county sheriff. Born in England, he emigrated to the United States at an early age. He was rated a good officer and was highly regarded.*

Above: *Scots-born photographer Alexander Gardner visited Fort Harker in fall 1867. This interesting group of employees of the Quartermaster's Dept has been joined (far left) by Wild Bill Hickok.*

News of 25 August described the scene of carnage as the Texans wreaked their revenge. Led by one Bill Anderson they advanced on McCluskie and opened fire. Hit in the neck, he staggered to his feet and shot Anderson through the thigh. 'The shooting then became general,' reported the editor. 'McCluskie was shot in three places and died in a couple of hours. John Martin, a herd boss, was shot through the jugular vein and died.' Bill Anderson's brother John was 'shot through the right arm and lungs. Garrett was shot through the lungs and has since died. Patrick Lee, a railroad employee, was shot through the loins and has since died. He was in no way a party to the difficulty . . .' Other innocent people were shot, some of whom died later, and it was also reported that a consumptive youngster named Riley, who had been befriended by McCluskie, appeared in the midst of the shoot-out and killed several of the Texans before disappearing. Anderson was arrested and a coroner's jury decided that he fired the first shot and was guilty of manslaughter. He never went on trial.

Instead, his father came up from Texas and took him home. The 'massacre' caused outrage and state-wide condemnation, and the *Kansas Daily Commonwealth* on the 22nd described the affair as 'worse than "Tim Finnegan's Wake"'. Further cries for a better police force and legislation against firearms were to no avail: the pistol still ruled.

Texans, it seemed, continued to cause, and attract, trouble. The *Eagle* of 20 and 27 August described the murder of a Texan by two Mexicans following a gambling dispute. Friends of the deceased pursued the pair and both were shot and killed 'in an attempt to resist an arrest, that at least is what they call it in these parts'. It was only one of several incidents that occurred in Wichita that summer and fall. On 13 November 1873, the *Eagle* pinpointed the basic prejudices of the races when it reported that 'a dozen Mexican greasers, camped upon the other side of the river, last night attacked Constable Prentiss and beat him with their revolvers most inhumanly. Sherriff [William] Smith is out with a posse this morning and we have no doubt of their arrest and punishment. Some of the people of this city have been laboring under the impression that there was an ordinance in force prohibiting the carrying of firearms within the city. From the number of revolvers flourishing upon our streets in the last two weeks, we conclude that it was only an impression.'

Ellsworth experienced similar problems. On 7 March 1868, the Junction City *Union* reported that one 'Chaves', described as a 'Mexican bummer' formerly of Kansas City, and accompanied by other Mexicans, entered a saloon and announced that 'Americans did not like Mexicans'. Drawing his pistol he opened fire, shooting a man in the arm. Despite the shock of his wound, the man drew his own pistol and shot Chaves dead. The unpopularity of the Mexicans was voiced by the Leavenworth *Daily Commercial* of 7 July 1872, when it noted that society at Ellsworth was 'of

Below: *Ellsworth in 1872. Founded in 1867, the place was desperate for respectability; when the Thompson brothers 'treed' the town following the Whitney shooting, many recalled its past.*

Above: *This excellent sketch of a Mexican bandido was painted by Edward Borein in 1910. In dress he resembles the haughty Mexican vaquero who rode the cattle trails to Kansas in the early days.*

the roughest kind, boiled down. The Greasers are rougher, and the soiled doves [prostitutes] are roughest.' The writer described a 'genuine greaser' lounging in a saloon, who was 'dressed in a buckskin suit, Mexican spurs, Navy revolvers, bowie knife, and long hair. Across opposite was a Texan similarly dressed.' Most of the Mexicans, however, preferred the knife to the pistol, and proved to be very dextrous in its use.

In the middle of chaos there lurked one diversion that on the one hand provided a social escape and on the other was a direct cause of violence: the saloon. The focal point in any Western movie or novel, the saloon is where strangers are 'put upon' to prove their courage, or where the villain and the hero exchange words before the inevitable gunfight. In reality, its social attraction counted far more than the occasional violence. It was a place where men could relax, drink, have a meal, play cards or, if the proprietor catered for it, listen to music. In most camps or settlements the saloon or beer tent was among the first places to be erected. During the railroad boom, tented saloons followed the tracks from place to place, and they were often accompanied by companion tents that housed gamblers and prostitutes. Once a place was settled, however, the saloon took on a distinct life of its own. Later, perhaps, the owner might include 'entertainment' in the shape of a 'singer' who was usually a practising prostitute, backed by either a piano player, a banjoist, violinist or, rarely, a three- or four-piece orchestra. The whole was contained in an area that rarely exceeded sixty feet by thirty, much of that taken up by the bar, so it was a compact community that endured the aroma of body sweat, liquor and tobacco smoke.

The fare provided by the average Western saloon varied. Abilene's Alamo saloon boasted fine liquors and a selection was displayed along the back bar. In Newton, the Gold Room displayed rows of barrels, each containing beer or selected wines, surmounted by a bar

that displayed 'clusters of decanters daintily arranged and polished until their shimmer is like that of diamonds', noted the Topeka *Daily Commonwealth* of 17 September 1871. Prices were usually clearly marked, and some idea of the wares available can be gleaned from the following taken from the account book of George M. Hoover, proprietor of a wholesale liquor store at Dodge City: High Mucky Much (a soft drink); Energy; Fire Fly; Orinoco; Ginger Ale, per cask $20. British Bass Ale and Irish 'Guinness Stout' were also available for $20 per cask. As for American-brewed beers such as Anhauser, they were $2.50 per case. Jamaica Rum was $5.50 per gallon. Port and sherry

Below: *The St James' saloon, Dodge City, is typical of the time – long bar and a narrow room. The posed look of the place suggests that everyone was on their best behavior despite the boots on the table.*

Above: *A typical saloon of the 1880s. This one was located at Caldwell, which was much advanced in building techniques and other refinements by the time it received the cattle trade and experienced its 'evils'.*

averaged between one and five dollars a gallon; but Western brandy was $20 per case. Gin, surprisingly, was only $1.50 per gallon. Perhaps the most popular drink was whiskey, home-brewed or imported. This averaged two to four dollars a gallon. Saloon beer prices fluctuated but on average cost two glasses for twenty-five cents. Indeed, it was a dispute over the price of beer that led to the famous shoot-out between Tom Nixon and Mysterious Dave Mather, which is discussed elsewhere.

For those who demanded entertainment with their drinking, the *Times* of 3 November 1877 recommended the Saratoga in Dodge City. An additional attraction was its stove. It

was not a '"grass valley" stove, but the largest stove in town, reaching nearly to the ceiling and shedding its warmth to the remotest corner of the large room. It was shipped from St Louis especially for the Saratoga.' The proprietors, Chalkley ('Chalk') Beeson and W. H. Harris, had provided a 'first class' place and did everything they could to make their customers welcome. 'The bar, under the charge of Mr Adam Jackson, furnishes the finest wines, liquors and cigars that can be found in any market. Mr Jackson is favorably known, and is cordial and polite.' An added attraction was the fact that Beeson was an accomplished musician and saw to it that his clientele enjoyed good entertainment, a feature noted by the *Times* on 29 September. A particular favorite among those of Irish descent was 'The Lakes of Killarney', which always drew 'crowds of attentive listeners'.

Other aspects of saloon life, however, were not so pleasant. The 'facilities' in some places were primitive in the extreme, sometimes a rope, a blanket and bucket were all that was provided. Others, however, ensured that provision was adequate. Unfortunately, there were those to whom the niceties of social behavior meant little. On 14 July 1879, nine citizens despatched the following petition to the Mayor and members of the council of Wichita:

Gentlemen –
We the undersigned petitioners would most respectfully represent that we are seriously annoyed and our health is greatly endangered by the stench that arises from the filth deposited in the rear of the 'Star

Below: *An unusual photograph of 'Chalk' Beeson (left, with watch chain behind his belt buckle) and friend. 'Chalk' was not known for his violence, suggesting that he posed for this photograph.*

Saloon' and adjoining buildings and also the rear of Whitworths Block – in some of the following ways – viz: – The *filthy* condition and positions of the swill barrel of the 'Eating Saloon' – the careless manner in which slops of various kinds are thrown into the alley & backyards of above named buildings. Also the conversion of the corner at the rear of the 'Star Saloon' into a place where all the frequenters of Said Saloon & Eating House accustomed, habitually, to *urinate* – would respectfully ask your honorable body to take immediate steps for the removal of said nuisances and prevent any or all repetitions of a like character . . .

Rivalling the saloons in the Old West were the gambling places and houses of prostitution. If anything, gambling was the biggest attraction, for it promised more than a 'taste-bud tickle' or a 'ten second spine tingle'. For gambling as a pastime and a passion was common to all the frontier regions. The end of track railroad 'tent cities' attracted gamblers, as did the mining boom towns such as Denver, Deadwood, and other places that sprang up during the latter part of the last century. They all followed the pattern of initial capitulation to the pasteboard pirates who flocked there; but time and the inevitable establishment of local ordinances and taxes redressed the balance. Although historians quite rightly have been criticised for spending too much time in 'peering into the smoke-filled saloons of the Kansas cowtowns' when assessing the rise and fall of the gambling elite, the fact remains that it was the era of the cowtown that added the color and romance usually attributed to the deftly digited denizens who haunted the baize-covered gaming tables. And also it was the cowtown experience that best explains, from surviving records, how the 'politics of economics' overcame the resistance to change.

THE PASTEBOARD PIRATES

If violence was a problem in the early cow-towns, the addition of gambling and prostitution only made matters worse. The frontier gambler is as familiar to most Western fans as the cowboy and the gunfighter, and he is often depicted as a combination of all three characters. His origins, however, can be traced back many years before he made his presence felt in the cowcamps, railheads and anywhere that a turn of a card could reap riches or despair. Perhaps the earliest, and certainly most prosperous era of the Western gambler was the halcyon days of the steamboat. Romantics tend to think of the low-lying high-stacked river boats, with their huge side or rear paddle wheels flashing through the waters of the Mississippi or Missouri rivers, as the golden age of travel. Reality was different. When Charles Dickens ventured upon an American steamboat in the early 1840s he recalled that one tried to find accommodation aft, because the boilers were liable to burst forward. Underwater snares, sandbanks and the occasional burst boiler were daily hazards, but it was a relatively inexpensive means of travel, provided one kept clear of the harpies, pimps, and the gamblers who plied the river.

The gambler has for long had a bad reputation. Steamboat gamblers were particularly well versed in tricks and schemes to divest the dudes and tenderfeet from their dollars. Even

the stockists of warlike implements lost no time in advertising the fact that gamblers were an endangered species. The *Philadelphia Mirror* of 10 October 1836 published a 'NOTICE TO GAMBLERS AND OTHER SPORTSMEN – Bowie knives and tomahawks sold here.' Pistols and knives were the favored weapons. The revolver was not yet available, but Henry Deringer's .41 and .45 caliber pocket pistols certainly were, and the demand was such that they were widely copied. Produced in several sizes, the most popular was the .41 caliber pistol that was just five inches long. Loaded with loose black powder, a lead ball and fired by means of a percussion cap, it was deadly at

close range. Carried in waistcoat pockets, coat sleeves, boot tops or indeed anywhere convenient, secret but accessible to the user, its presence, or at least that of some kind of weapon, was comforting, and the other players invariably were also 'heeled'. In later years, as a gesture of good faith, it was common for members of such games to disarm or at least place a token pistol on the table. What was hidden away, of course, only came to light in a crisis.

By the mid-1860s, with the movement West, the cattle drives, gold fever and the advancing railroads, the gambling elite moved with it. Mining camps were popular because the

Below: *Virginia City, Montana, in the early 1860s. The streets are unpaved, sidewalks non-existent, and the whole place has the look of hasty erection. But for the lone figure in the rear, it looks totally deserted.*

Above: *Bodie, California, in its later years following the establishment of the gold and silver mines, and as this photograph shows, a good transport system. The Concord stagecoaches plied all over the West.*

Right: *'The Fight at the Roundup saloon' by William Gollings graphically depicts the violence that erupted after dark in many cowtowns. Some said the gunfire made it light enough to read a newspaper.*

prospect of large amounts of gold 'dust' lured many 'sports' or 'genteel loafers' to such places. And the more that arrived the greater the prosperity, particularly among the saloon and brothel set where most of them congregated. Bodie, California, was a fine example. Gold was first discovered there in 1859 by W. S. Bodey, who was a member of a party led by Terence Brodigan. According to the *Bodie Chronicle* of 3 November 1879, his find was accidental, following a run-in with some warlike Paiute Indians. Forced to take a different route, the party found a likely looking valley and Bodey dug a prospect hole. When he turned up evidence of gold everyone joined in. But it was 1877 before the real bonanza strike was made, and eventually an estimated $20 million worth of gold and silver was mined from the area. In the years between the discovery and the strike of 1877, the place simply ticked over, with a population that rarely exceeded fifty. Back in the early 1860s, J. Ross Brown stumbled on the place, and in his *Adventures in the Apache Country* he recalled that when he arrived at Bodie he found only two married miners, the remainder being without women. But instead of misery, he claimed that these 'jolly miners were the happiest set of bachelors imaginable', spending their time perfecting all the arts and crafts usually performed by women, thereby 'proving by the most direct positive evidence that woman is an unnecessary and expensive in-

stitution which ought to be abolished by law'.

By the 1870s and until the place peaked as a mining town, perhaps only ten per cent of the population of Bodie were women, and many of those were prostitutes. Its rival, Aurora, was founded in 1860, and for a time boasted among its inhabitants Samuel L. Clemens, known to history as Mark Twain. Like Bodie, Aurora had its share of violence, saloons, gamblers and the inevitable prostitutes. In general, the violence and eventual taming, civilizing and growth in population experienced by the mining camps was very similar to the cattle towns. Although the demise of the mining camp was often total, the cowtown prospered. There was, of course, one other major difference: the cowboy. Tough, hard-bitten and interesting they may have been, but the old-time miners lacked the glamor associated with the cowboy – exemplified by his colorful dress, nomadic life-style and, of course, his horse. That, combined with the danger met daily when branding, driving and generally tending the awesome and totally unpredictable Texas longhorn, inspired an adulation that goes far to explain why the cowtowns receive more than their share of attention.

The cattle shipping points were obvious targets for the 'pasteboard pirates' and the 'locusts of lechery'. Abilene's launch into the cattle trade in 1867 did not start an immediate invasion of gamblers and others, but by 1870 they were well entrenched. The city council in

1871 imposed fines for gamblers and exacted license fees from those who provided accommodation. It was a situation that existed in all the cowtowns. Newton's gamblers were well publicised. On 17 September 1871, the Topeka *Daily Commonwealth* noted that:

There is a mania for gambling in Newton. The heart of every man who has been here long enough to dig down a little to the substrata of life, nestles the germ of this passion. In some it has bloomed into a full blown flower. These latter are mostly professionals, who sit on the percent side of the table. Most of them are well known all over the extreme west. Listen to their chat as they sit together after dinner or supper smoking their cigars and re-counting bygone experiences, and you will discover that they are well traveled, earnest men – thinkers in a rough sort of way, and invariably readers of human nature.

The editor of the Abilene *Chronicle*, however, found no reason to romanticize about gamblers. Rather, he sought to warn his readers of the dangers of gambling and the wicked element that promoted it. On 1 June 1871, he published an exchange item headed simply 'Gambling' which listed some of the more common tricks. The article explained the games of roulette, rouge et noir, vingt et un, and poker. The tricks employed to cheat

DERINGERS 1845-60

The traditional 'hide-out' pistol favored by gamblers, gunfighters or indeed anyone who feared being caught unawares was usually single-shot and less than six inches in length. Henry Deringer introduced his famous range of large caliber pocket pistols in the early 1840s (the second 'r' in 'derringer' is believed to have crept in when a reporter covering Lincoln's assassination misspelled the weapon used by John Wilkes Booth).

1. Henry Deringer's pocket pistols were the 'Rolls Royces' of their day. This is the medium size pocket pistol with ramrod.
2. Deringer small size pistol.
3. German silver was used for triggerguards and as stock decoration.
4. Typical powder flask.
5. The percussion lock was a boon to Deringer and others.
6. Deringer's pistols all followed the same graceful lines. Smaller ones, however, could be hidden in the palm of a hand.
7. Engraving on deringer pistols is mostly confined to the lock plate.
8. A tin of American-made percussion caps.
9. A small size pistol – compare the sizes.
10. A medium size pistol complete with ramrod.
11. 'Baby' of the family, and probably the most famous version. John Wilkes Booth used one of these in .41 caliber to kill Lincoln.
12. Eley Brothers of London supplied millions of percussion caps to American makers (Colt notably).
13. Although clearly marked, Deringer's pistols were widely copied, some even bearing his name.
14. The sights on a deringer were basic, and consisted of a blade front sight and a 'V' cut into a plate behind the nipple housing. Most users ignored the sights and fired point-blank.
15. Checkering was common to most deringer stocks.
16. A handsome pistol of the larger size minus its ramrod.
17. Ethan Allen's bar hammer pistol that rivaled the deringer.
18. This version of the Allen bar hammer pistol was not as

popular as that shown at (17).

19. Typical playing cards of the period.
20. Pair of ivory dice.
21. Another Allen-type pistol but with a conventional center hammer.
22. Powder flasks of this type are often found with Colt's pistols as well as makers of deringer-type arms.
23. A Blunt & Syms side hammer pocket pistol.
24. Unmarked 7 mm pin-fire single-shot pocket pistol.
25. Removable screw-on barrels were common in Europe, but not within the United States.
26. English pocket pistol converted from flintlock to percussion.
27. Lindsay two-shot belt pistol with brass frame.
28. Bacon & Co. single-shot ring trigger pistol.
29. Allen bar hammer pistol. The mechanism of these arms was of the self-cocking type.
30. Massachusetts Arms Co. single-shot pocket pistol fitted with Maynard's tape primer mechanism.
31. Roll of Maynard's tape primers.
32. Lindsay two-shot belt pistol.
33. Unmarked .28 caliber single-shot breech-loading pocket pistol.

(Artifacts courtesy of Buffalo Bill Historical Center, Cody, Wyoming.)

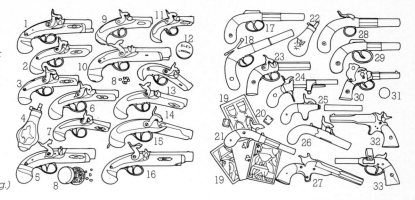

addicts (the 'suckers') by the professional cardsharps ranged from simple to ingenious. Marked cards (that is with notches on the edge or other indications of their face value) and fixed roulette wheels abounded. Some cheats had small knee mirrors to 'reflect' upon their opponent's hand during dealing. And the superstitious souls who liked to sit in certain places, particularly with their backs against a wall, were often the victims of their own obsession. Instead of a real wall to lean against, it was sometimes a cunningly concealed partition behind which lurked an accomplice. A peephole enabled him to see that victim's cards, and by means of a prearranged signal (either a loose board upon which the gambler's foot rested or a wire tied to a foot) the hand was read and cheating commenced.

Many of the well-known cowtown figures gambled, some professionally. Benjamin ('Ben') Thompson gambled professionally for much of his life. He was born at Knottingley, Yorkshire, England, on 2 November, 1843, and was the son of a mariner. His family, which included his younger brother Billy, emigrated to the United States in the early 1850s where he was brought up in Texas, later achieving a reputation as a gunfighter and gambler.

Wyatt Earp, whose best remembered exploit was the gunfight at the O. K. Corral, was involved in gambling from the early 1870s. In the 1880s at Tombstone, Arizona, he acquired an interest in the flourishing Oriental saloon. He later owned a couple of saloons in Idaho and was involved in mining ventures. In the wake of the Klondyke gold rush, Earp was active in the saloon business in Nome, Alaska. Earp was also accused in later life of being mixed up in various confidence games but the evidence is not very clear. What is certain,

however, is that gambling and the saloon business were passions of his.

Probably the best known of the gunfighters to become involved in the saloon and gambling business was Luke Short, whose 'war' with Dodge City received nationwide publicity. It all began with the 'wet' and 'dry' debate in Kansas, following the Kansas State Legislature's decision in 1880 to change the

Above: *William Barclay Masterson, one of the Dodge City 'Gang', in a business-like pose that shows not hint of his gunfighting–gambling exploits. Rather, a sober citizen staring into posterity.*

constitution so that it would seriously affect the drinking habits of the saloon set. Dodge City became the center of attention when the town council decided to implement some of the proposed reforms. Rival factions sprang up composed of pro-saloon men (keepers and gamblers) generally called 'the Gang', and the 'Reformers', composed of anti-liquor councilmen and, surprisingly, several saloon owners. These were more concerned with their public image in a political sense than any moral scruples.

The 'Gang' included Bat Masterson, W. H. Harris and the likes of Luke Short, whereas the 'Reformers' counted among their membership the erstwhile mayor, Alonzo B. Webster, Mayor Lawrence E. Deger, and Mike Sutton, a lawyer. The 'Reformers' alleged that the gang members were con men who were up to all manner of tricks and schemes. Their activities in effect deterred settlement. Webster had been elected mayor in 1881, and is reported to have put a stop to many of the so-called rackets, imposing certain quasi-moral restrictions. His successor Deger, elected in April 1883, was thought by some to be his 'creature' and still guided by Webster.

Luke went into partnership with W. H. Harris in the Long Branch saloon and within days was confronted by a new ordinance against prostitution – his 'singer' was arrested and charged with soliciting. A run-in with a local policeman, during which shots were fired but no one was hurt, led to Luke's arrest and within days he was told to leave town. This he did, but he headed for Topeka where he spoke to the press and had an audience with the governor. Word also spread to the west that 'Luke Short is in trouble' and a number of his friends announced that they would come to his assist-

Below: *Tombstone's Oriental saloon attracted Wyatt Earp, who invested in it. Here the bartender takes just pride in the highly polished bar and maintains the high standards expected by patrons.*

Below: *Lawrence E. Deger, an early day marshal of Dodge City and, in 1883, its mayor. He took over from Alonzo Webster who had introduced many 'reforms'; some regarded Larry as Webster's 'creature'.*

ance. The press had a field day! Dire warnings were given on what might happen if Wyatt Earp, Bat Masterson, Doc Holliday, Charlie Bassett, Rowdy Joe Lowe, Shotgun Collins and others appeared on the city's streets. As it turned out, the city fathers capitulated when some of those characters showed up, and Luke was reinstated. But, had things gone badly for the council, the governor had been prepared to send in troops to restore order! In honor of the occasion, Luke and friends were photographed and the picture was quickly dubbed 'The Dodge City Peace Commission'. In 1884, Luke tried to sue the city of Dodge for throwing him out the previous year. It was settled out of court, and Luke departed satisfied.

Bartholomew ('Bat') Masterson (he later changed his name to William Barclay Master-son), the Canadian-born gambler, saloon owner and prizefight enthusiast who became a newspaperman, served as a county sheriff in Kansas and later as a deputy U.S. marshal. He, too, enjoyed gambling and became an expert in both its tricks and potential. In later years he was to write at length on the characters who turned a card as easily as they pulled a trigger. But according to Arthur Chapman, writing in the New York *Herald-Tribune* of 3 January 1930, on one occasion Bat himself was accused of cheating and came near having to prove his skill with a gun as well as his sleight of hand. Bat and his friend, one 'Conk' Jones, fell out when Jones claimed that he had taken advantage of a young fellow with more money than sense. Mr Chapman's informant was John L. Amos who had been sharing an hotel room with Masterson and Jones:

> He and Bat had come to a showdown in a poker game. The rest of the table had dropped out, Jones among them. Bat raked in the pot without showing his hand. The young fellow started to protest and then thought better of it. The play may have been alright, but it did not suit Jones. Conk leaned over and said, 'Bat, don't ever make a play like that again when I'm around.' I knew from the sound of Jones' voice and the look in his eyes, that he was trying to force Bat into a fight right there. Bat laughed it off and Conk walked away, and apparently forgot the incident as the men remained on a friendly footing. Someone spoke about it afterwards, but Bat poo-poohed the idea of any trouble between Jones and himself. But knowing Jones as I did, I am certain the stage was set for a gun battle between experts for a few seconds that night . . .

Even James Butler ('Wild Bill') Hickok is reputed to have run a gambling place. This was described in the press as a 'hell' at Junction City during the late 1860s. He also built a saloon at Hays City, but soon disposed of it, having

Above: *The 'Dodge City Peace Commission' of 1883. Back (left to right): Harris, Short, Masterson, W.F. Petillon (champion pie eater of Dodge). Front: C.E. Bassett, Earp, M.F. Mclain and Neil Brown.*

Below: *The Long Branch saloon (center, showing exterior) is almost as famous as Dodge City itself. But it bears little resemblance to the version that appeared regularly in Hollywood's 'Gunsmoke'.*

SHARPS COMPETITORS

Christian Sharps (1811–74) established a tradition of excellence; his firearms were sturdy, accurate, well-made and much admired both by the military and civilians alike. His many rivals sought to surpass him but few did. By the late 1860s and early 1870s (when Sharps himself was no longer involved in rifle manufacture), a number of rival makers produced arms that appealed to the civilian market, in particular the buffalo hunters who were busy exterminating the Lords of the Plains in droves. Remington, Ballard and others vied for the lucrative market. Ballard in particular produced a number of 'hunting' rifles in calibers ranging from .32 to .44 which met with some success. But it was the Remington sporting and hunting rifles that proved to be Sharps' biggest rivals. Their calibers ranged from .40 to .50 with a powerful cartridge to match, ideal for hunting buffalo and other big game.

No matter who the makers were, hunting or buffalo rifles were expensive. They averaged between $100 and $300 depending upon the maker and the quality of the weapon. Also the addition of special sights or telescopic sights was an important factor. Ammunition aroused as much controversy as the weapons themselves. Hunters 'loaded their own' most of the time and paid special attention to the black powder used. The American powders tended to burn 'hot and dry' and cake up the bore, whereas the English version made by Curtis & Harvey burned 'moist'.

1. Maynard .50 caliber rifle in fitted case with reloading tools, powder flask and cartridges. Note second barrel. These were normally supplied in different calibers from .32 to .44 rim- or centerfire.
2. Cartridge box for the Maynard rifle.
3. Sturdy breech-loader by the Brown Mfg Co.
4. Remington No. 1 Rolling Block sporting rifle. It was chambered for various calibers from .40 to .50; popular with hunters and plainsmen alike.
5. Remington-Hepburn rifle with pistol grip.
6. Fine example of Frank Wesson's two-trigger rifle.
7. The outside hammer Peabody hunting rifle appeared in calibers .44 to .45.
8. Remington Rolling Block short-range rifle in the 'Light Baby Carbine' model.
9. Winchester single-shot rifle Model 1885 with a 20-inch round barrel.
10. Similar weapon fitted with 30-inch octagonal barrel. Both weapons have adjustable rear sights.
11. Fine Marlin-Ballard No. 2 sporting rifle in .38 centerfire.
12. .38 centerfire 'shells' for the Marlin-Ballard.

(Artifacts courtesy of Buffalo Bill Historical Center, Cody, Wyoming.)

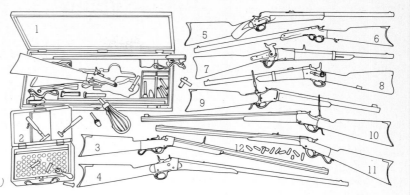

little interest in the problems that went into owning and running such places. In Abilene he indulged in the pastime in between his duties as city marshal, as he had done at Hays City when acting sheriff of Ellis County in 1869. Once his gunfighting days were behind him, Wild Bill concentrated upon gambling, and it was when playing poker at Deadwood in 1876 that he was murdered while holding a hand which comprised the ace of spades, the ace of clubs, the eight of clubs, the eight of spades and a queen or jack of diamonds 'kicker', today remembered as 'the Deadman's Hand'. In later years some claimed that Hickok was a poor gambler, but others believe that he was as canny as the next man when faced by would-be cheats. There is a story long in circulation that best explains Hickok's *modus operandi*. This version comes from the *Ellis County Free Press* of 5 January 1887, and was copied from the Chicago *News*. Headed 'A Good Hand at Poker' it stated:

'Did you ever hear of Wild Bill's ace full?' asked a local manipulator of the cardboards. 'The story may be old, but it's true . . . Wild Bill had a weakness for poker, and knew no more about it than a baby. The consequence was he was a picnic for the sports, and they fleeced him right and left. He was repeatedly warned that he was being robbed, but he always replied that he was able to take care of himself.

'One night he sat down to play with a fellow named McDonald, a fine-worker and expert. McDonald did as he pleased, and the scout found his pile getting smaller and smaller as the game progressed. As he lost he began to drink, and midnight found him in a state of intense but repressed excitement – a condition that made him one of the most dangerous men in the West. It was at this juncture that McDonald, smart gambler as he was, made his mistake. He should have quit. However, Wild Bill's apparent coolness deceived him.

'Finally, the scout seemed to get an unusual hand, and began to bet high and heavy. McDonald raised him back every time, until the top of the table was about out of sight. At last there was a call.

'"I've got three jacks," said McDonald, throwing down his hand.

'"I have an ace full on sixes," said Bill.

'"Ace full on sixes is good," said McDonald, coolly turning over his opponent's cards, "but I see only two aces and a six."

'"Here is the other six!" suddenly roared Bill, whipping out a Navy revolver, "and here" – drawing a bowie knife – "is the one spot."

'"That hand is good," said McDonald, blandly, arising. "Take the pot."'

Some gamblers were extremely dangerous people, and among the genuine 'good bad men' of the gambling fraternity was Joseph

Right: *Wild Bill Hickok, photographed at Rolla, Missouri, 1864–5. His dandified dress seems out of place for a Civil War contract scout, but since he was paid $5 a day, he could afford good clothing.*

('Rowdy Joe') Lowe, one of the most interesting of the many lurid characters who ever turned a card, or pulled a pint behind the bar of a saloon. Born in New York state in 1845, Joe grew up in Illinois and Missouri from where, in February 1865, he enlisted in Battery B of the Second (New) Missouri Regiment of Light Artillery. The Civil War was over before he really heard a shot fired in anger, but he remained in the regiment until December of that year, by which time he had served in the Powder River Indian Expedition that took him to Montana and back through Nebraska and Missouri. He appeared at Ellsworth in 1867 and was a typical roustabout and hanger-on. By 1869, however, he was involved in the saloon business and remained in it (and the lucrative dance hall trade) for most of his life. With his common-law wife Kate ('Rowdy Kate') Lowe, whose real name and origin have so far eluded us, he ran gambling halls and 'houses of ill-

Below: *N.C. Wyeth's painting of Wild Bill Hickok unmasking a card cheat has a great sense of drama heightened by the use of shadow. Wyeth is reported to have found Hickok an interesting subject for his talents.*

fame' in Ellsworth, Newton, Wichita, and places in Texas and later in Colorado. He had shoot-outs with several individuals, but it was his feud with Edward T. ('Red') Beard at Delano, across the river from Wichita, that is best remembered.

The pair were rival saloon owners and occupied space within yards of each other. On 27 October 1873, Red looked through the window of his dance house and as Joe appeared at the window of his, Red took a shot at him with his Navy revolver. Red was drunk at the time, otherwise his aim might had been better. As it was, the slug grazed Joe's neck. Furious, Joe rushed over to complain. The pair had a slanging match and then both fired at each other. Red's shot went wild, but Joe's missed Red and passed across the bridge of bartender Billy Anderson's nose. This blinded him and robbed him of his sense of smell. Red and Joe then began stalking each other taking pot-

Left: *Joseph 'Rowdy Joe' Lowe in later years when he became almost respectable. Joe was known as a 'character' all over the West. As was his one-time 'partner' the redoubtable 'Rowdy Kate'. The pair parted in 1876.*

shots before retreating to reload. Beard, in his drunken state, also shot one of his 'girls' in the stomach which did not endear him to his employees.

Shortly afterwards, as Red was creeping about near the Chisholm Trail bridge, there came the thunderous report of a shotgun and Red was found with one arm shattered and a ball in his hip. Lowe soon afterwards gave himself up to Marshal Mike Meagher, later claiming that he remembered little of the fight since he, too, was drunk at the time. Joe was cleared of the killing, but skipped the state rather than go on trial for his wounding of Anderson. Ironically, on 11 February 1899, Joe Lowe died unarmed and with his boots on following a row with a former policeman who shot him without allowing him any chance to defend himself.

Whatever the attitudes to gambling – and they varied considerably – the obsession with gambling was a major source of revenue in the cowtowns and other places. Stuart Henry noted that luck in all things was paramount, and especially the 'chuminess' between people who regarded luck as their guide. Few felt that it was sacrilegious to gamble. The gamblers who frequented the cattle towns did so only during the trail-driving season (May to October), moving on elsewhere for the winter months. Mining towns or those with more perennial activities could claim resident or itinerant gamblers. Of the more permanent characters, the Ellsworth *Reporter* of 3 October 1872 noted that the few Texans who

Above: *Abilene in 1879. The corner building, constructed of brick and with architectural embellishments, compares with the earlier style wooden, false-fronted buildings further down the street.*

Below: *Ellsworth in 1879, looking very peaceful, having by then rid itself of the cattle trade. Those who had demanded the streets be made safer were the first to feel nostalgic for the old days.*

stayed over when the season ended were subject to 'the off-season doldrums': 'Just at present his stock in trade is light. His bank roll, which last summer he flashed up on every occasion, now scarce ever sees the light of day . . . He makes no reckless bets, nor does he indulge in games whereof he does not understand . . . at the recollection of those past flush times he sighs and says, "d—n such a country as this, the Black Hills is the place for me." But after a second thought he takes it all back and concludes to wait for the cattle trade [to return].'

Gambling, whether it was at cards, wagers or the risks involved in driving cattle to market, represented status and a place in society, and to some it suggested power. Joseph G. McCoy, however, made it plain that bankruptcy could easily stare one in the face, and he should have known. For his founding of Abilene as the first direct shipping point of cattle east had been based upon an oral arrangement with the Union Pacific Railway Company, Eastern Division, for a return of five dollars per carload of cattle shipped. When the company changed its name to the Kansas Pacific Railway in March 1869, they reneged on the deal. Despite winning a lengthy court battle, McCoy was a broken man.

In his *Human Life* articles Bat Masterson recalled that 'gambling was not only the principal and best-paying industry of the town at the time, but it was also reckoned among its most respectable and . . . the elements of chance played a part, an important part . . . it was also reckoned . . . [to be] . . . respectable.' Respectable or not, the potential for taxation was enormous. Gary L. Cunningham noted that the legal heritage of this action can be traced back to the city of New Orleans in 1823, when the law allowed the city to license six gaming establishments at the rate of five thousand dollars apiece. It was eventually repealed, but not before municipal income had benefited. Abilene, however, imposed no such sum, preferring fees that worked in the form of fines. Individuals paid between five and ten dollars, plus costs, whereas proprietors of gambling establishments could expect to pay an average of $20 or as much as $75 per month. Further fines were imposed if the gambler got drunk or committed another misdemeanor, such as being caught carrying a 'concealed weapon' in contravention of the State Statutes; if proved, this always resulted in a fine.

In 1873, Wichita looked with a jaundiced eye on gambling, and imposed severe penalties within the city itself. The council curtailed both the gambling and saloon-keeping fraternity's activities. The rot had begun to set in the previous year when it was reported that income from the gambling houses and places of prostitution had proved very lucrative. One irate gambler, Isaac Thayer, a former sheriff of Ellis County and a veteran of the Battle of Beecher Island, addressed a note of complaint to the city council in which he alleged that, having paid fifty dollars per month for permission to run a gambling establishment, he was now being asked to pay a further twenty-five dollars. Thayer requested that the money be returned or offset against his next monthly payment. The outcome of that exchange is not known, but by August 1873, the *City Eagle* reported on the 14th that 'All gambling houses in the city have been closed. Quite a number had taken their tables and fixings and gone to the other side of the river where no fines will be imposed on them nor "police!" arrest them . . .' Across the river was Delano which was not yet a part of the city, and therefore apart from county taxes was immune from city taxes.

Abilene's demise as a cattle town and the reforms that smote it months before the final season ended was not lost either on the press or the patrons of the gambling dens. In his *Chronicle* of 27 July 1871, V. P. Wilson described gamblers as 'licentious and stealing characters who . . . crawled into this place in violation of the laws of the State and ordinances of the Town'. He forgot to mention the lucrative fines and license fees exacted by McCoy's administration, probably because he and the mayor were at loggerheads over the rights and wrongs of the cattle trade and the money it brought to the region.

SISTERS IN SIN

Like the gamblers, saloon keepers and the other flotsam and jetsam of the cowtowns, prostitutes also played their part in creating a thriving community. The morally inclined may well have detested the harlots, but in an almost totally male dominated society they performed a role that if nothing else sated passions in an atmosphere that always remained potentially violent.

While some towns accepted, willingly or otherwise, the existence of prostitution in their midst, others did not. In May 1870, the Board of Trustees of Abilene passed an ordinance authorizing the removal of brothel owners and 'lewd women' from within corporate limits. By September most of them had moved to St Louis, Kansas City, even faraway Baxter Springs. But when the cattle season opened again in May the following year, they came flooding back in even greater numbers than before. Texas Street now housed all the ingredients that made a cowboy's life even bearable. Ultimately, however, the permanent residents of Abilene made a stand and Mayor McCoy ordered Marshal Hickok to supervise the removal of all the brothels to an area southeast of the city, known as 'McCoy's Addition', much to the Mayor's annoyance. By September 1871, fed up to the back teeth with heavy fines and other abuses which affected their lives (such as the revoking of licenses to run dance halls and to sell whiskey and brandy), and mindful of the fact that the cattle season was once more at an end, the inmates of McCoy's Addition finally moved on to pastures new.

James B. Hickok was one of a number of cowtown lawmen who had affairs or lived with known prostitutes. Other well-known figures also formed associations. Bat Masterson had several cowtown affairs, as did others, includ-

Above: *'Squirrel-tooth Alice', one of Dodge City's better-known prostitutes. Dressed very respectably, she perhaps reflects the far-reaching changes taking place within the city itself.*

Below: *The Pearl saloon at Abilene in the early days before paved roads and sidewalks replaced the wooden shacks; by the end of the 1880s, the kerosene lamps were replaced by gas or electric light.*

ing the Earps. In their case, they went further than most: in Wichita in 1874 two of their women were charged with soliciting. According to the police court records, Bessie Earp, the wife of James, was fined for soliciting in May, and a similar charge was made against Sallie Earp, whose relationship to the brothers has not been clarified. Both Bessie and Sallie Earp were fined eight dollars and two dollars court costs.

Wyatt Earp's involvement with women (he was married three times) has not received the same scrutiny as have his alleged gunfighting exploits, but one encounter with the notorious Frankie Bell, a well-known denizen of Dodge City's red light district in July 1877 reached the ears of the press. According to the *Times* of the 21st, she had heaped 'epithets upon the unoffending head of Mr Earp [who was at that time on the police force] to such an extent as to provoke a slap . . . besides creating a disturbance of the quiet and dignity of the city, for which she received a night's lodging in the dog house and a reception at the police court next morning, the expense of which was about $20. Wyatt Earp was assessed the lowest limit of the law, one dollar.

With time and the declining cattle trade, the encroachment of so-called civilization, and other restrictions, social changes in cowtowns and mining camps were marked. Gambling, saloons and prostitution still flourished, but their activities were much more low key or pointedly ignored by the 'better class of citizen' who rarely came into contact with such people. The late Lucile Stevens, who was born in Wichita just before the turn of the century, told this writer that as a small child she knew many of the old-timers who had founded the place and witnessed its growth into a respectable community. But the 'other side of the tracks' and those who inhabited the place were never discussed. She then recalled that

one Sunday, about 1905, she was returning from church with her mother and an aunt. For some reason they took the wrong turning and their buggy passed a place outside of which sat a number of desperate looking women, in various stages of dress, who stared at them in amazement as they drove past. When, in all innocence, she asked her father who they were, he was furious. 'Only years later,' she recalled, 'did I learn that those poor women were dance hall girls and prostitutes.'

Mrs Stevens also explained why documentation about the early days in the cowtowns was lacking. Local fires (a common problem) were only partially responsible. The real culprits were the people who destroyed records, for whatever reason, who did not wish their early participation in the founding of the city to be known. 'They were more concerned with what it had become than what it had once been. People of that time were more concerned with what was happening in Washington or your Queen Victoria's court, and its social significance than the whereabouts of old city records and lurid stories about cowboys and gunfighters.'

This was true, of course. George L. Cushman, the author of the first in-depth account of Abilene's period as a cowtown, told this writer that in the early 1930s he had reason to visit the local fire station, and was just in time to rescue many of the old city records for the period from the department's incinerator. Someone had decided that they were no longer needed. Similar horror stories have been circulated concerning other places. Fortunately, a large number of such records have survived. They indicate how cowtowns and mining camps grew from tents, shacks and muddy streets strewn with dung and debris, the inevitable saloons, dance halls and brothels to the stores and other civilised enterprises that are part of its respectability and its life.

Above: *'Timberline', a noted Dodge City prostitute, still shows some of the good looks she had before dissipation, drink and disease ruined her and many other such 'soiled doves'.*

Below: *It is hard to believe that this is Front Street at Dodge City at about the turn of the century. All gone are the false fronts, hitching racks and other signs of the cowboy era; bricks replaced bullets and Bowie knives.*

FOUR

LAW AND ORDER: FROM GUNS TO GAVEL

'The "Gunfight at the OK Corral" lasted about thirty seconds, and an estimated seventeen shots were fired. At the end, of the eight men who were involved three were dead, three were badly wounded . . . Tombstone's relief when the Earps quit Arizona was reflected nationwide.'

Right: *Pinkerton detective Bill Sayles, during pursuit of the 'Wild Bunch'.*

Below: *Colt single-action Army revolver, with 7½ in. barrel, .45 caliber.*

LAW AND ORDER

The eternal struggle between good and evil – religious belief versus paganism, honor, integrity and morality versus anarchy, dissipation and other sins of the flesh – or corruption of morality set against a Western background has stirred passions for generations. The personal conflict between the 'good' gunfighter and the 'bad' gunman is a particular attraction, but the reality of the West was not a simple 'good guys' and 'bad guys' scenario. Rather, it was human endeavor to better itself in a harsh, sometimes hostile environment. It is a curious fact that, despite innumerable accounts of the lawlessness of the West, there is also the underlying belief that justice and law and order would eventually triumph.

By contemporary standards, it is daunting to consider a society where everyone might be armed, yet the West of the early and middle nineteenth century was such a society and also a contradiction in terms. Parts of it were populated and civilized, while other regions were regarded as near barbaric and hazardous. Consequently, it was accepted that those who lived in the less populated regions were armed more for defense than offense. Another factor, before the arrival of the railroads, was the sheer distance between settlements or cities. Places sprang up simply because they were on the route of a well-known overland trail or because of the railroad, and well ahead of the advance of settlement.

People moving West also created some of the conditions that favored the lawless ele-

ment. Individuals reserved the right to settle disputes among themselves; problems with Indians, who naturally resisted white encroachment upon their lands, led to frequent disputes, and the U.S. Army had the thankless task of establishing lonely forts or posts simply to keep both sides apart. That this frequently failed is a matter of history, as is the fact that people resented interference by government (they still do), so the establishment of law and order often lagged far behind settlement. Would-be emigrants naturally assumed that the law would ultimately follow on after them, and with it social, economic and political developments to enhance their livelihood. Vigilantes were expedient but not the answer to the problem, and neither were squatters' rights associations which had been formed to

protect claims or embryonic settlements, for their sometimes overzealous reactions failed to protect the bona fide claimants, which caused resentment. Therefore, the basic need of the ordinary folk was established community law and not anarchy. With time, territorial, district and state courts took care of the problems, but mostly the individual fended for himself.

Responsible for building forts and posts across the country to protect both red and white man, the army was also initially responsible for bringing law and order to the West. Sometimes martial law was all that stood between civilization and anarchy. The government established Indian agencies at many of these posts, appointing agents to keep Indians and whites from each other's throats. Keeping

the peace on the frontier was essential, not only for the present but the future. The Indian suspected it, and the government knew it for a fact: whites would one day rule the roost and if this could be achieved peaceably so much the better.

The law, like government, followed in the wake of emigration and this resulted in sparsely populated areas relying to a lesser or greater extent upon individual policing. Even when territories were established, or granted statehood, the lack of railroads, proper trails or other means of communication meant that communities or individuals took care of their own problems. The vigilantes of California and Montana were extremes dictated by demand at a time when the law was just not functioning or established. Vigilantes in other areas, such

as those that influenced the running of Hays City, Kansas, in 1869, were more concerned with political power than maintaining law and order, so it is useful to understand how the American legal system of the time worked to appreciate its benefits and shortcomings.

Law and order within the United States was based upon the old English legal system; despite numerous changes since, many features remain especially in regard to officials. The sheriff and marshal still exist. In the United States, the sheriff would be an elected officer of a county responsible for maintaining peace and keeping order, attending court, guarding prisoners, serving processes and executing judgments. A sheriff need not have any legal experience, his appointment being more political than professional. However, his

Above: *Charles Behrer, a prominent member of the Montana vigilantes who broke up the notorious Plummer gang and was very active in the clearing-up operation that put paid to the likes of George Ives.*

Below: *Alexander Davis, the celebrated 'miners' judge' who on one occasion issued a warrant for the arrest of Jack Slade for upsetting a milk wagon. Slade, however persuaded him to drop the charge.*

Left: *A rare photograph of Judge Roy Bean (with watch chain), 'the Law West of the Pecos', outside his saloon at Langtry, Texas. His verdicts were very controversial and often delivered humorously.*

salary would be paid by the county and, depending upon how much he was paid, dictated both the number of deputies he had and how much they were paid. His immediate subordinate was the under-sheriff (a term rarely used today), and a couple of deputies, one of whom acted as jailer. During troubled times it was not unusual for extra deputies to be sworn in and dismissed when no longer needed. Crime committed within the county came within his jurisdiction and although he could invoke his authority within city limits he usually left that to the town police force.

The city council elected its own police force. The term 'marshal' was still in use until recent years but, even in the period of this present study, it was often coupled with the more grandiose title of 'chief of police'. The 'marshal' in turn hired 'constables' or 'assistant marshals' at the discretion of the city council. Usually only two men were hired but in most cowtowns as many as five men might be taken on during the cattle season. The marshal was sworn to uphold the state laws, implement local ordinances and generally keep the peace. They were rarely well paid. Tom Smith, Abilene's first marshal or chief of police (and one of the earliest recipients of the title in the cowtown era) was initially paid $150 per month, later raised to $225. Smith's immediate successor (following his murder in November 1870) was paid $150 to act in a caretaker capacity until a new man was chosen. Other places were not so generous. During the height of the cattle season a marshal might be paid $100 or more a month but once the season ended he took a salary cut down to $75 or perhaps $50. Since the county sheriff and his deputies were paid a fixed rate by the county, if a city council paid below the norm then a marshal's deputies fared even worse. This is rather ironic because it cost a council nothing to pay the police force whose salaries came out of monies extracted from fines or taxes imposed upon the gambling, saloon-keeping and

LAW AND ORDER

The gunfighter was ubiquitous: he was to be found in most parts of the West. Elsewhere we have noted the terrain best suited to the lawless element anxious to escape any kind of civilization. But for the lawmen, the closer they were to established procedures the better. The mid-West of the 1870s–80s underwent the transition from lawlessness to law-abiding much quicker than some of the outlying regions.

Early day peace officers experienced frustration when dealing with the ungodly. Lack of organized law and great distances across hostile territory proved a bonus for the outlaws and a chore for the men who wore the star.

Folks who lived on the cattle trails or in the cowtowns or mining camps were used to the sight of such as Hickok, Earp, Masterson and others meandering around with a pair of pistols prominently displayed. Some felt that so long as such men were around upholding the law, there was an element of safety. Others, however, were anti-firearms and were vociferous in their opinions. It became increasingly obvious by the late 1870s that the day of the 'pistoleer' was drawing to a close. Man-killers were facing a changing world. The gun was giving way to the gavel: where once a squeeze of the trigger settled an argument, the emphasis was now on the courts. Soon, the exploits of the James gang, the Daltons, Youngers and others would be history. As also would be the deeds of the lawmen who faced or pursued them. Police forces, both civil and Federal, co-operated in the fight against crime, which meant that the traditional peace officer exemplified by such as Hickok, Masterson or Tilghman would be obsolete. Communities no longer needed to rely upon noted individuals to keep the peace.

During the period 1860–1900, the gunfighter, whether on the side of the law or against it, had made his mark on a nation. But that was about to change. Now it was the turn of the courts. The gun abdicated in favor of the gavel.

W.F. CODY
(1846–1917)
Frontiersman

DAVE MATHER
(1851–1886?)
New Mexico, Kansas

WYATT EARP
(1848–1929)
Kansas, Arizona

'DOC' HOLLIDAY
(1842–87)
New Mexico, Arizona

TOM NIXON
(1834?–80)
Kansas

VIRGIL EARP
(1843–1905)
Kansas, Arizona

TOMBSTONE
(founded 1877, scene of O.K. Corral shoot-out)

MORGAN EARP
(1857–82)
Kansas, Arizona

WYOMING

Deadwood

Casper

North Platte R.

S. Platte R.

Union Pacific RR

COLORADO

Glenwood Springs

Colorado R.

Pueblo

NEBRAS[K]

Santa Fe
Las Vegas

NEW MEXICO TERRITORY

Socorro

Rio Grande

ARIZONA TERRITORY

Gila R.

Tucson

Tombstone

bawdy house 'trade'. Worse, the city fathers even begrudged the amount spent on ammunition for the police force. A typical example can be found at Wichita where in 1871, according to city records, a measly $6 was allocated for each policeman. Seventy-five cents was allowed either for a box of six paper or foil cartridges for a .36 or .44 caliber pistol, and a box of caps cost twenty cents. For powder, shot and cartridges, $1.35 was admissible. One can only assume that they were expected to make every shot count or be personally liable for unauthorized discharges! Considering the restrictions placed upon the police, one can only wonder how the Texans could afford their all too frequent bouts of cowboy chaos.

Most town councils insisted that their police should conduct themselves properly. The previously mentioned Ellsworth 'Ordinance No. 1' passed in April 1870 decreed that members of the police force found in brothels, or gambling and drinking on duty would be fired. Other places had similar rules, for there was always the danger (so they thought) of their policemen being corrupted or bribed by the inmates, a situation that has not changed! Then there was the question of firearms in the hands of the police. Contrary to popular belief, police forces seldom shot it out with criminals then carried on as if nothing had happened. Rather, an officer might be hauled before a coroner's court and statements taken from the officer and from witnesses. Sometimes, of course, the coroner's court convened to examine the events that led to a policeman's death; this was accepted as a hazard of the job by those who undertook the task of policing a sometimes unpredictable population made up of large numbers of transients with scant regard for the law.

State police, as existed in Texas and other southern states following the Civil War, were more politically expedient than constitutional and were eventually replaced by local organizations – in the case of Texas by the reinstatement of the Texas Rangers in 1874.

WILD BILL HICKOK
(1837–76)
Missouri, Kansas

TOM SMITH
(1840–70)
Wyoming, Kansas

BEN THOMPSON
(1843–84)
Texas, Kansas

JUDGE ISAAC PARKER
(1839–96)
Arkansas, Indian Territory

HECK THOMAS
(1850–1912)
Texas, Indian Territory

TEXAS RANGERS
(Indian fighters, lawmen 1823–61; reinstated 1874, and to present time)

THE UNITED STATES MARSHALS

The U.S. marshal dominated local and county police forces. Created in 1789, the U.S. marshal was a presidential appointment ratified by Congress. Between 1840 and 1900 he was elected to cover 'districts', which could be states or territories. His main brief was to uphold the Federal code of laws. Some of the larger states might have two marshals covering districts described as 'Northern' or 'Southern', but in most cases the appointment covered one state or territory. Some old-time (and more modern) marshals had policing experience but that was not essential. In fact, the idea of a U.S. marshal pursuing evil-doers personally would probably horrify members of the judiciary. In the old days, however, some of them did get actively involved but most of the actual field-work was delegated to the deputies.

Each marshal had an office deputy who took care of the paper work. He in turn issued orders to the field deputies who were sworn in as 'posse comitatus' (the word 'posse' suggests a crowd, but in fact it could be one man). Before 1896, when the U.S. Government issued official commissions and paid a salary, only the office deputies were salaried; the others were sworn in and, in return for serving subpoenas, warrants and arresting individuals charged with federal crimes (robbing the mails, desertion from the army or the navy, stealing government stock, or murdering Indians on or off the reservation), they were paid a fee, plus mileage. This was $2 per day and the mileage was worked out at about six or ten cents a mile while on active duty. The marshal himself received no salary – his reward was the office itself – but he did receive a proportion of the fees allowed against his deputies' claims.

Before 1896 deputy U.S. marshals were eligible for State or Territorial rewards; not so the marshal or his salaried office deputy. In 1869, for instance, Wild Bill Hickok arrested two Negro deserters from the Tenth Cavalry and lodged them in the jail at Fort Hays. He later received the reward for their capture. In some instances, however, promised rewards were withdrawn on a technicality or the recipient might have to share it with his assistants. The term 'bounty-hunter' was more aptly termed 'man-hunter' in the old days. Those individuals who set out on man-hunts were invariably either commissioned police officers or employees of railroads, express agencies or well-known organizations such as Pinkerton. An exception, perhaps, was the 'Nations' or Indian Territory – present-day Oklahoma.

In Indian Territory, law was aligned with tribal law of incumbent tribes. These laws applied only to individuals belonging to the Nation or tribe where the alleged offense took place. It could be complicated and the Indians had their own ideas about how justice should be carried out. Judge Isaac Parker, whose United States Court for the Western District of Arkansas until the late 1880s included the Indian Territory in its jurisdiction, employed a large number of deputy U.S. marshals, many of them blacks or Indians. In his interesting book *Black, Red, and Deadly*, Art T. Burton has told their (much neglected) story and emphasized the role such people as Baz ('Bass') Reeves, a

Above: *His Honor Judge Isaac Charles Parker, the 'hanging judge' of Fort Smith, Arkansas. His jurisdiction included Indian Territory. Some eighty-eight men were hanged outside his courtroom.*

Above: *Baz ('Bass') N. Reeves, one of a number of black lawmen who worked for Parker. The judge also employed Indians as deputy U.S. marshals. Some sixty-five black, red and white marshals died in the territory.*

Above: *Crawford Goldsby, better known as 'Cherokee Bill'. 'Bill' was part Cherokee, part Mexican, part Negro and part white – a dangerous mixture. He killed a number of men and was hanged at Parker's court in 1896.*

Above: *Henry Andrew ('Heck') Thomas, one of the 'Three Guardsmen' (the other two were Bill Tilghman and Chris Madsen) who helped establish law and order in early day Oklahoma.*

Above: *Ben Daniels, whose checkered career included a jail sentence for mule theft, service as a policeman at Dodge City, and as one of Teddy Roosevelt's Rough Riders.*

Above: *Louis C. Hartman, the City Clerk of Dodge City in 1883 (who was also on the police force), who fell foul of Luke Short when he arrested Luke's 'singer'. Luke shot at him twice and missed each time!*

Above: *Christian Madsen another of the 'Three Guardsmen'. Born in Denmark he served in the Danish army before emigrating to the United States, where he served in the Fifth Cavalry and later as a lawman.*

Negro lawman, played in establishing law and order in the region. Both black, white and red marshals faced some of the roughest and toughest criminals on the continent, and if Parker's reputation as the 'hanging judge' is anything to go by, they were all remarkably effective.

In other areas, however, local interpretation of the law depended very much upon the prevailing situation. The cowtowns largely concerned themselves more with state rather than federal laws since they were of prior concern. Boosted by local ordinances, they generally worked. Yet even here there seems to be a belief that cowtowns were without law, doubtless a reference to a Wichita editor's exasperated comment that 'anything goes in Wichita!'

When counties were established and cities were granted the right to elect their own government, the election or appointment of local police forces became commonplace. In essence, a town marshal or chief of police had no jurisdiction outside town limits; that was the province of the county sheriff. Since both were responsible for civil rather than federal crimes, the U.S. marshal for the state or territory took over that responsibility. He did not normally interfere in the matter of civil crime, but if asked could provide deputies to assist.

The emphasis upon 'frontier justice' as seen from the muzzle of a six-shooter is understandable. In the early days the lack of jails, and intimidation by the lawless to impede justice, did emphasize the role that the gun played in bringing law and order to the frontier. As each place was founded, or gold and silver deposits encouraged mass migration and the birth of yet more 'boom towns', attempts to bring law to such places proved difficult. Vigilante groups, regulators and other 'sin sifters' played a part, but it was not justice in a legal sense: hotheaded prejudice was no substitute for cold logic based upon established principals. In general, lawlessness in the West was as much

a result of a lack of law as a reaction by those opposed to it. The tradition of the lone avenger – righter of wrongs, a combination of the duelist and an executioner – has little place in reality, yet the role of the individual in establishing, implementing or supervising the carrying out of legal requirements did play a part in the fight to bring calm out of chaos. Nowhere is that tradition better exemplified than in the years immediately following the Civil War, when unreconstructed rebels, disillusioned ex-guerrillas, and those sworn to uphold the law clashed head on. In its wake came the myths and fables that today inspire stories about the gunfighting lawmen whose exploits have thrilled generations.

Town marshals, or chiefs of police, were provided with deputies whose numbers were increased or decreased at the whim of the city council. During winter months it was not unusual for the marshal to be on his own, whereas once the cattle season started he could have as many as five deputies, some full-time, others taken on to assist during a particularly busy period. The cowtowns had populations (in the 1870s) of perhaps one thousand permanent residents, but during the cattle season this number could treble. Theophilus Little recalled in 1910 that at Abilene in April 1871 there were about five hundred people, but by 1 June there were about seven thousand of them sleeping in tents, filling hotels and boarding houses or simply 'under blankets spread upon the prairie'. Controlling such a mass of people required firmness and tact. Fortunately, the majority of them were well aware of their transient nature and were only concerned with enjoying themselves in the many saloons, gambling houses and other places of entertainment.

Town marshals were also responsible for street-cleaning as well as patrolling, although it is unlikely that they attended to these tasks themselves. They were also supposed to keep

an eye out for blocked chimneys and other public nuisances, particularly stray dogs. At Abilene, the council allowed Marshal Hickok fifty cents for each stray dog he shot. History does not record if he personally carried out that task or assigned it to a deputy. On one occasion, however, he was called upon to shoot a maddened Texas longhorn that had escaped the pens and was careering along Texas Street. This writer has examined the set of horns from the animal which are now on view at the Dickinson County Museum at Abilene, where they were placed by J. B. Edwards in 1940, shortly before his death.

Town police were also responsible for seeing that places of entertainment were properly supervised and trouble free. In the cattle towns and mining camps, however, this had its problems. Street patrols, spot checks and the occasional arrest of a troublesome drunk were the norm. Only when things really got out of hand did the police call for assistance from the public. Usually, however, the presence of the police on the street kept things in check, and proved comforting for those citizens who appreciated the economic advantage of the cattle trade, but abhorred its evils.

In attempting to contain the violence and establish some form of law and order, city councils were faced with a problem. There were few so-called professional policemen available, so much reliance was placed upon men of reputation whose standing in the community inspired trust simply because they could quell the mob. As McCoy expressed it in what was thought to be a reference to Hickok: 'no quiet-turned man could or would care to take the office of marshal, which jeopardized his life; hence the necessity of employing a desperado – one who feared nothing and would as soon shoot an offending subject as to look at him.' It was far from ideal, but it was better than nothing. So began the era of the gunfighting town marshal.

WINCHESTERS '66–'73

The legendary Winchester rifle owed its origin to the early Smith & Wesson and later Volcanic arms. But by the mid-1860s it was a much improved version. The Model of 1866 (called the 'Yellow Boy' on account of its brass receiver) could be loaded with fifteen cartridges. By far the most popular model was the standard rifle with a 24-inch octagonal barrel (the carbine had a 20-inch round barrel). Early adverts for the Model 1866 made much of the fact that an expert shot could empty the magazine in fifteen seconds – if loaded at that speed sixty shots a minute was possible. By the late 1860s, however, rimfire ammunition for rifles and other large arms was in decline. With the centerfire cartridge came a new and improved Winchester – the legendary Model of 1873.

Winchester improved the mechanism, and replaced the brass receiver with an iron one. The new .44-40 cartridge (.44 caliber backed by forty grains of powder) was a great improvement, but it did not impress the Ordnance. For it was a pistol round and the army wanted a much more powerful cartridge. The civilian market, however, welcomed the new cartridge, and in 1878 Colt chambered some of their Peacemakers and double-action Army pistols in .44-40 which were marked 'Frontier Six-Shooter'. Despite a lack of military orders, the Model 1873 enjoyed a popularity that kept it in production until 1919.

1. A fine Winchester Model 1866, .44 caliber, with 24-inch octagonal barrel and sling swivels.
2. Carbine version with a saddle ring and a round 20-inch barrel.
3. Some Model '66 rifles were made with round barrels on request.
4. Fine hand-carved leather scabbards were prized.
5. This Model 1866 was once Indian-owned – note the typical brass tack design.
6. Model 1866, with broken stock repaired with wet rawhide strips.
7. An original box of 50 .44-100 rifle cartridges.
8. Cleaning rod for the '73 shown in (17).
9. The cocking action of the Winchester – note how the breech-pin cocks the hammer as the lever drops.
10. Spent cartridges.
11. Some original 'shells' for Winchester '73.
12. Two-part cleaning rod.
13. Typical 1873 carbine with the round barrel and saddle ring.
14. A '73 with a round barrel and fitted with a shortened magazine.
15. Fine '73 carbine.
16. Typical saddle scabbard for a Winchester rifle.
17. Fine example of the Winchester target rifle with additional sights set behind the hammer.

(Artifacts courtesy of Buffalo Bill Historial Center, Cody, Wyoming.)

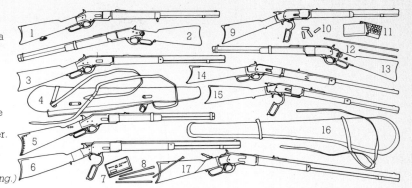

THE PEACEMAKERS

The man with a gun served to mar or motivate, and we have seen how the cowboy influenced or deterred growth. Now it was the turn of the peacekeepers, the men who more than any others inspired the legend of the gunfighter.

The lone man facing down a mob of drunken Texas cowboys by sheer force of character, or by the threat of his reputation as a killer, is the dominant image of the gunfighting lawman. The visual impact of Gary Cooper's almost single-handed fight against a band of killers in *High Noon* was good cinema but it was not based upon fact. Any suggestion that the mob would overwhelm the police force would result in a rush of citizens anxious to help. Fortunately, that rarely happened, for citizens relied upon their police force to do the job they were paid for and most of the time they succeeded.

Abilene's experience with violence from 1867 to 1870 has already been mentioned, but with the appointment of Thomas J. ('Bear River') Smith as her first marshal (or chief of police), aided by a couple of deputies, the lawless element soon realized that they had someone to contend with. Tom Smith proved to be an effective and courageous officer. In 1904, following the dedication of a memorial to him, Theodore C. Henry (elder brother of Stuart), the man who hired Smith, recalled that he

Below: *Thomas James ('Bear River') Smith, who led the Union Pacific workers' riot at Bear River, W. T., in 1868. He is said to have served as a policeman in New York before coming West and later to Abilene.*

would wade into a crowd of unruly cowboys using his fists to disarm them. Perhaps he did on occasion but Smith, like his successor Wild Bill, wore his pistols prominently displayed at all times. Sober, a Texas cowboy was liable to do as he was told; with drink inside him he was prone to react violently to authority. Stuart Henry noted that Smith and Hickok 'feared this in cowboys more than anything. To guard against it Marshal Tom Smith rode or walked in the middle of Texas Street and Marshal Wild Bill kept his back to some wall.'

Tom Smith proved so effective that his services were sometimes asked for by the county sheriff, Joseph A. Cramer, who appointed him a deputy. It has also been reported (but not verified) that the then United States marshal for the District of Kansas, Dana W. Houston, appointed him a deputy U.S. marshal. It was while acting on the behalf of Sheriff Cramer (who was terminally ill) that Tom Smith met his tragic end. He and a deputy, James H. McDonald, went to arrest a homesteader named Andrew McConnell, charged with murdering a man named John Shea. First reports had indicated that McConnell killed Shea in self-defense in a dispute over cattle on his land, but it later transpired that the shooting was cold-blooded murder. Leaving McDonald with the horses, Smith advanced alone to the cabin where he told McConnell that he was under arrest. McConnell promptly drew a pistol and shot the marshal through his right lung. Smith fired back, and grappled with him. Then Moses Miles, a near neighbor and McConnell's original alibi for the defense story, rushed up and struck Smith with a gun, knocking him to the ground. He then grabbed an ax and almost decapitated Smith.

Alerted by the shots, McDonald rushed toward the cabin but was beaten back by a fusilade of shots from both men. He returned fire and managed to wound Miles, shooting two of his fingers off. A bullet removed his hat, then he felt a hard blow to his chest and assumed he had been shot. It was later discovered that the ball had lodged in his pocket book! The two men then made good their escape on the officers' horses. McDonald raised the alarm and a furious posse set off in pursuit. The pair were eventually captured and put on trial. To the disgust of Abilene's citizens, they received only long-term prison sentences instead of the rope that many believed they deserved. Thirty-four years later the citizens dedicated a monument to Tom Smith, describing him as 'A Fearless Hero of Frontier Days Who in Cowboy Chaos Established the Supremacy of Law.'

Patrick Hand, a gunsmith, was appointed to succeed Smith and he in turn was replaced by James McDonald, who was to prove himself a good officer and later achieve a good reputation at Newton. But despite his heroic attempt to apprehend Smith's murderers, McDonald was shunned by some of the citizens who believed that he had deserted Tom in his hour of need. They ignored the fact that Smith was in part responsible for his own downfall. Had he ordered McDonald to accompany him to the cabin instead of waiting by the horses (a precaution any thinking officer would have taken) it is likely that he would have arrested McConnell without any trouble.

'A TERROR TO EVILDOERS'

At Abilene's first municipal election on 3 April 1871 Joseph G. McCoy was elected mayor. One of his first tasks was to reorganize the police force and prepare the city for the imminent arrival of the first Texas herds of the season. His own personal dislike of McDonald ruled him out as a contender for the job as marshal (although he would remain on the force), and, since there were no others anxious for the job, McCoy sought an outsider. John B. Edwards in later years claimed that Wild Bill Hickok himself applied for the position, while Charles Gross asserted that it was at his suggestion that McCoy approach Hickok who was at the time living at Junction City, filling in his time as a deputy U.S. marshal or gambling. In any event, Hickok arrived in Abilene about 11 April and on McCoy's personal recommendation the council 'unanimously confirmed' the mayor's choice; on 15 April Hickok was appointed marshal, or chief of police of Abilene.

For most people, Hickok epitomizes the breed of gunfighting lawmen. What he may have lacked in professional expertise in such matters, he more than made up for it in presence and reputation. It was his reputation that counted for much during the eight months that he administered law and order at Abilene. Once news of his appointment got around, writers all across the West either extolled his reputation as a scout and 'pistoleer' or invented numerous accounts of the 'hundreds' of bad men he had killed either in the line of duty or in personal combat. The fact that by the time he became Abilene's marshal, Wild Bill's tally amounted to five known victims meant little to the press and public. As a result, during the eight months that he ruled the roost, Wild Bill had little trouble with the Texans. The townspeople never really got to know him except by reputation, yet most of them felt safe with him around, whereas the Texans found themselves outclassed and preferred to leave well alone. Nevertheless, Hickok never took any chances and made sure he kept clear of dark alleyways or other places where a would-be assassin could lurk.

Stuart Henry had made it clear that neither Smith nor Hickok trusted the Texans, and some are convinced that Hickok did not understand them, which may account for his reported animosity toward them. Certainly, he stood no nonsense and there is a legendary account of him wading into a crowd of drunken cowboys and thrashing its leader. What may have some bearing on that yarn is a report published in the *Kansas City Journal of Commerce* on 13 August 1871, that alleged that he had hit a Texan over the head with the butt of his revolver, and 'stamped him in the face with his boot heel, inflicting a severe wound'. The other Texans then informed Wild Bill that he would not be safe overnight, but they 'mistook their man', as "Wild Bill" is the last man to be driven away by such threats. At last accounts he was still there and unharmed. Such a marshal might do for such a place as Abilene, but for Kansas City we don't want him.' The writer obviously did not understand the frontier tradition of 'marking' an enemy and neither was it made clear why Hickok attacked the Texan in the first place.

The council took full advantage of Hickok's presence. On their orders he arrested vagrants, closed down illicit gambling games and, in the height of summer, following complaints from a large number of respectable ladies, he supervised the removal of the dance halls and brothels from Texas Street. Such a move, we have noted, was viewed with delight by the occupants. Even when it came to a complete shutdown in the September, Hickok and his deputies received little resistance, if any at all, from the denizens of the so-called 'McCoy's Addition'.

Below: *Wild Bill Hickok photographed by A. P. Trott of Junction City in 1871. His presence in Abilene caused quite a stir, and he was considered to be one of the 'sights' at the end of the trail.*

Tourists who had visited Abilene during the summer of 1871 simply to meet Wild Bill, 'the hero of *Harper's Monthly*', were disappointed to find that he did not 'have a man for breakfast' in true frontier tradition, but was generally courteous, self-effacing and quietly spoken. His presence, aided by a number of policemen, deterred most of the troublemakers and it was October before he was finally compelled to use the pistols that had earned him such an awesome reputation.

On 5 October, a large number of Texans were in town, some of whom had remained to visit a local fair, others enjoying a final fling before returning home. As the excitement mounted and the Texans grew more lubricated and began massing on the streets carrying pistols, Hickok confronted them and advised them to disarm. He went into the

Alamo saloon and minutes later a shot was heard on the street. Hickok had been standing at the bar with Michael Williams, a former Kansas City bartender who had acted as a part-time jailer in the summer and later as a 'special policeman' hired by the Novelty Theater. When the shot came he told Williams to stay where he was and headed for the front door. Outside he was confronted by about fifty armed Texans led by Phil Coe, a gambler and owner of the Bull's Head Tavern. Coe is reported to have had a grudge against Wild Bill; he told him that he had fired at a stray dog. But he still had his pistol in his hand, and it is claimed that he made a movement or a remark that prompted Hickok to draw his own pistols 'as quick as thought'. Both men were only eight feet apart. Coe fired twice; his first shot went through Hickok's coat tails and the second hit the ground between his legs. Hickok also fired twice, both shots hitting Coe in the stomach. He was then conscious of a figure rushing at him from the shadows, gun in hand . . . He fired twice more. Surrounded by a howling mob of drunken and armed Texans, their shadows dancing in the light of the spluttering glare of kerosene lamps, he roared to them to back off. Only then did he see that the second man was Williams.

Old-timers (and some of the press) claimed that Hickok was visibly moved when he realized what had happened. He holstered his pistols, gently picked up his friend and carried him into the Alamo and laid him on a billiard table. Then, with tears streaming down his face, he charged from the place and began pushing and shoving the crowd, ordering it to disperse. Within half an hour the place was deserted. Williams' death had a great effect upon Wild Bill and it was widely reported that he paid for the funeral. As for Coe, he lingered for three days in great agony. It was even claimed that he was visited by a preacher sent by Wild Bill to 'pray with him and for him'. Coe's body was shipped home to Texas for burial and it was reported that Hickok's name was much vilified and that threats were made against his life.

Editor Wilson, who in the past had criticised the city council and its police force, decided that Hickok's actions during that night of chaos were commendable. He believed that Coe deserved what he got and warned other would-be trouble-makers that 'there is no use in trying to override Wild Bill, the Marshal. His arrangements for policing the city are complete, and attempts to kill police officers or in any way create disturbance, must result in the loss of life on the part of violators of the law. We hope that all, strangers as well as citizens, will aid by word and deed in maintaining peace and quietness.'

Charles Gross, who got to know Wild Bill better than most, recalled late in life that when he was advised of the threats made against him, Hickok procured a shotgun which he adapted to his needs: the barrel was shortened to twelve inches and it was loaded with heavy shot. A strap enabled it to be concealed beneath a coat. But Hickok never carried the weapon outside city limits.

Late in November, during a train ride to Topeka, five Texans tried to attack Hickok, but he 'circumvented' the parties and at pistol point ordered them to remain on the train when it left for Kansas City. On 25 November the Topeka *Commonwealth* published an account of the event under the heading 'Attempt to Kill Marshal Hickok', which was copied verbatim by the *Chronicle* on the 30th.

Below: *The main street at Ellsworth early in 1872. The famous Drover's Cottage had just been erected following its removal from Abilene. The railroad was making provision for large cattle shipments.*

Hickok's attempts at preventing further bloodshed were considered commendable, and he deserved the thanks of all law-abiding citizens throughout the state for 'the safety of life and property at Abilene, which has been secured, more through his daring, than any other agency'.

By December, however, the council had decided that it could no longer submit to the 'evils' of the cattle trade (a public statement to that effect was issued in the following February), and neither did it have need for. Mr Hickok's expensive services. On 13 December Hickok and his deputies were dismissed, to be replaced by a temporary marshal hired for $50 a month.

Abilene's demise as a cowtown was welcomed by Newton and Ellsworth, which, together with Solomon, Salina and Brookville, had vied with each other for the lucrative cattle trade. The latter three towns, which had only received a small share of the market, are nowadays hardly remembered as cowtowns, whereas Ellsworth, Newton, Wichita, Dodge City and Caldwell share a place in folklore that ranks with Abilene.

Ellsworth had been shipping cattle by rail since 1871, when it was reported by the Topeka *Daily Commonwealth* of 16 July that an estimated thirty-five thousand head had been sent east. Founded in 1867, the place had achieved a reputation for violence that ranked with Hays City, itself only recently established and reputed to be so rough that citizens went armed all the time. By 1868, vigilante action had given way to established law and order, and with the arrival of the cattle trade proper in 1872 it took on its new role with ease. The Drover's Cottage at Abilene was dismantled and shipped to Ellsworth, where it became one of the sights and vied with the Grand Central Hotel for custom. The police force was headed by Chauncey B. Whitney, who would

Above: *Chauncey B. Whitney, the sheriff of Ellsworth County, gunned down by Billy Thompson on 15 August 1873. Whitney was one of the survivors of the Beecher Island fight in 1868 against the Indian Roman Nose.*

Below: *This Governor's Proclamation was widely distributed, but copies of it are now rare. Despite the public outcry and the efforts to detain him, Billy managed to escape justice on a technicality in 1877.*

GOVERNOR'S PROCLAMATION.

WHEREAS, C. B. Whitney, Sheriff of Ellsworth County, Kansas, was murdered in the said county of Ellsworth, on the 15th day of August, 1873, by one William Thompson, said Thompson being described as about six feet in height, 26 years of age, dark complexion, brown hair, gray eyes and erect form; and Whereas, the said William Thompson is now at large and a fugitive from justice;

NOW THEREFORE, know ye, that I, Thomas A. Osborn, Governor of the State of Kansas, in pursuance of law, do hereby offer a reward of **FIVE HUNDRED DOLLARS** for the arrest and conviction of the said William Thompson, for the crime above named.

 IN TESTIMONY WHEREOF, I have hereunto subscribed my name, and caused to be affixed the Great Seal of the State. Done at Topeka, this 22d day of August, 1873.

THOMAS A. OSBORN.

By the Governor:
W. H. SMALLWOOD, Secretary of State.

soon leave office when elected county sheriff. He was succeeded by John L. Councell, who was later fired and in turn replaced by John ('Brocky Jack') Norton, one of Hickok's deputies from Abilene whose poor reputation in Abilene had followed him to Ellsworth. Norton was later demoted but remained on the force. The new marshal, however, was Edward O. Hogue, a gutsy individual who did his job without fuss or fanfare.

Ellsworth's economy boomed during the latter part of 1872 and the early months of 1873. The saloon business in particular was a great source of income both to the proprietors and the local tax collectors so it was inevitable that the saloon would be the focus for trouble; the first real shoot-out of the cattle season occurred on 27 July 1872 when the notorious cattleman Isom Prentice ('Print') Olive was shot by James Kenedy, the son of the Texas cattleman Miflin Kenedy, in the Ellsworth billiard saloon.

The *Ellsworth Reporter* on 1 August described in graphic detail exactly what happened:

> THE FIRST SHOT
> TWO MEN WOUNDED, NO ONE KILLED
> Ellsworth, which has been remarkably quiet this season, had its first shooting affair this season last Saturday at about six o'clock, at the Ellsworth Billiard saloon. The room was full of 'money changers' at the time, busily at work, and lookers on intently watching the games. Among others I. P. Olive was seated at a table playing cards. All of a sudden a shot was heard and sooner than we can write it, four more shots were fired. Kennedy [*sic*] came into the room, went behind the bar and taking a revolver walked up in front of Olive and fired at him – telling him to 'pass in his checks'. Olive threw up his hands exclaiming 'don't shoot.' – The second, third and fourth shot took effect, one entering the groin and making a bad wound, one in the thigh and the other in the hand.
>
> Olive could not fire, though he was armed; but some one, it seems uncertain who, fired at Kennedy, hitting him in the hip, making only a flesh wound. The difficulty arose from a game of cards in the forenoon, Kennedy accusing Olive of unfair dealing. Olive replied in language that professionals cannot bear. The affair made considerable excitement. The wounded were taken in custody and cared for. Drs Duck & Fox extracted the bullet from Olive and a piece of his gold [watch] chain which was shot into the wound. It was feared that Olive would not survive, but the skill of the doctors saved him. Kennedy was removed to South Main Street and put under the charge of three policemen, but by the aid of friends he escaped during the night from the window and has not been heard of.
>
> All has been quiet since the affair and is likely to remain so.

The man who shot Kenedy in the hip was James ('Nigger Jim') Kelly, Olive's trail boss, who had been outside on the veranda when the firing commenced. He shot through the open window, then rushed in to help his

WINCHESTERS '76-'86

Faced with the military's rejection of the Model 1873 because if its ammunition, Winchester produced a modified version known as the Model of 1876. This had a receiver able to accept the pressures generated by the government's .45-70 cartridge which was 2 inches long – almost twice the length of the standard .44-40 round. In fact, the Model 1876 could accept a .45-75 cartridge with a bullet weight of 350 grains which was more powerful than the government version. The rifle never achieved the fame of the '73, but it was adopted by the Northwest Mounted Police and, like its predecessor, enjoyed a frontier reputation.

The prolific arms designer John M. Browning, whose brilliant designs would enhance Colt's and other companies' reputations, completely redesigned the Winchester rifle Model of 1886, the most powerful of them all. Chambered for .45-90 it also appeared in .50-110-300 Express, which proved to be a very popular caliber. The Browning-inspired Models of 1887, 1892 and 1894 also met with great success, and keen-eyed observers will have noted that most 'Winchesters' featured in Westerns are either 1892 or 1894 models, rather than the legendary model of '73.

Many old-time gunfighters and plainsmen carried a Winchester. The Model 1873 and the 1886, or even the Henry rifle, were used by buffalo hunters, but most hunters preferred the larger calibered rifles.

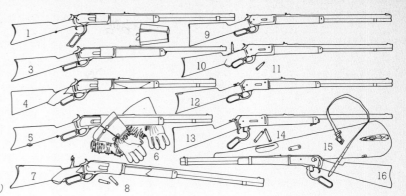

1. Superficially similar to the Model '73, the '76 has an enlarged receiver and bigger loading-slot plate.
2. Cartridges for the Model 1876.
3. Like the '73 some Model '76s were sold with short magazines.
4. Serial no. 45569 is a nice example of a Model 1876 carbine.
5. Serial no. 40330 in contrast is a fully-blued rifle.
6. A fine pair of lady's buckskin gauntlets.
7. Serial no. 10018 is a '76 equipped with a checkered pistol stock and target sights.
8. Two .45-70 cartridges for the Model 1876.
9. The Browning-designed '86 rifle: big improvement on earlier models.
10. Similar weapon, with choice wood pistol stock and target sights.
11. Note long 'shell' case.
12. 'As new' carbine version of the Model 1886 (s.n. 84841).
13. The short magazine '86 rifle (s.n. 57909).
14. High-powered cartridges for the Model 1886.
15. Silver-embossed hand-tooled rifle scabbard for the Model 1886.
16. Model '86 carbine with a ring which allows it to be slung over a saddle or shoulder.

(Artifacts courtesy of Buffalo Bill Historical Center, Cody, Wyoming.)

Above: *Isom Prentice ('Print') Olive, one of Texas's most famous cattlemen. He fought hard to build his empire which was hit by the blizzards of 1885–6. He moved to Kansas and was murdered by Joe Sparrow in 1886.*

Below: *James Masterson, the youngest of the famous brothers, whose gunfighting career surpassed Bat's. Jim was later involved in the arrest of the Doolin gang. He died from 'galloping consumption' in 1895.*

Above: *James H. Kelley, generally called 'Dog' on account of his love of the animal, was prominent in the saloon business at Dodge and later served as its mayor. A bullet meant for him killed Dora Hand.*

employer. Kenedy was the same individual who later shot and killed the dance hall girl Dora Hand at Dodge City, mistaking her for the mayor, James 'Dog' Kelley, against whom he bore a grudge.

Ellsworth's violent reputation, earned in the 1860s, dogged it all through the cowtown era. The editor of the *Reporter* expressed local concern when, on 14 August 1873, he wrote:

> We protest against so much arming by our police. It may be well enough for our marshal and his assistants to go armed, but one six-shooter is enough. It is too much to have to see double armed men walking our peaceful streets. It is not probable that any of the shotted revolvers will hurt anyone, for these are not the days of '67 and all people know it. Don't let us by too big a show of deringers, lead strangers to imagine that order is only to be maintained by the use of them. One pistol is enough and that should be concealed as much as possible.

A day later the editor had cause to reflect on his words when perhaps the most infamous killing in Ellsworth's violent history took place, one that is still hotly debated. That summer of 1873 witnessed a national panic over the economy, and in Ellsworth its effect upon the cattle business was cause for alarm. An estimated 177,000 head of cattle were held in pens or pastured some miles from town awaiting shipment east. In the saloons, cowboys, drovers and the inevitable gamblers sat and sweltered in the ninety degree heat. The police force at that time consisted of Brocky Jack Norton, the marshal, Ed Hogue and John ('Happy Jack') Morco, the latter a particularly obnoxious individual who offended fellow officers, citizens and Texans alike. The Texans and the gamblers disliked Morco particularly. He had

arrested Ben Thompson's brother Billy for alleged assault with a pistol, for which Billy was fined ten dollars plus fifteen dollars court costs.

That morning, Ben Thompson had financed a friend, John Sterling, to enable him to take part in a high stake monte game, with the promise of a percentage of any winnings and the return of his original stake. Sterling won more than a thousand dollars but was not anxious to return either the stake or advance a percentage of his winnings. This made Ben mad, and he cornered Sterling in Nick Lentz's saloon. Sterling struck Ben in the face but before Ben could retaliate, Morco forced himself between them and made Ben leave. Ben went straight to Brennan's saloon where he remained until Morco and Sterling, both heavily armed, appeared at the entrance of Brennan's and defied him to come out. Knowing what would happen if he did, he ducked out of the

back door and into Jack New's place where he had left a pistol and a Winchester rifle. Billy then arrived, armed with Ben's fine English-made double-barreled shotgun (made by George Gibbs of Bristol). Having got himself 'heeled', Ben decided to face his tormenters. Billy, who was liquored up and staggering around, jerked one of the triggers of his shotgun and discharged a barrel. The shot just missed a couple of passing Texans. The brothers then walked toward the railroad intending to continue the fight and to do so without endangering local residents.

Hearing the shot, Sheriff Chauncey B. Whitney, a friend of the Thompson brothers, hurried to defuse the situation, persuading the pair to accompany him back to Brennan's. As Ben listened to him, he moved near the door, heard someone shout a warning and turned to see Morco coming toward him, pistol in hand. Ben promptly fired at him, the ball splitting the door jamb of a local store. Morco ducked and ran inside. At that moment, Whitney and Billy rushed into the street, Billy brandishing the shotgun. He staggered, turned and fired point blank at the sheriff. Whitney's scream of agony stopped the place dead. Several men ran up and tenderly picked up the injured man and carried him to his home. While he remained conscious he repeated that it was an accident. He died in great agony on the 18th.

Following the incident, Ben turned on his brother for shooting their friend, and he feared that he might not be able to keep the equally incensed mob at bay for long. Billy turned his whiskey-sodden gaze upon his brother and is reported to have mumbled that he would have shot if it had 'been Jesus Christ'. Ben *did* hold the town at bay while his brother escaped, and only agreed to surrender if the mayor disarmed Morco and friends. This was agreed, and he then surrendered to Ed Hogue. The

Above: *William ('Billy') Thompson, the homicidal brother of Ben. Ben had saved Billy's neck several times, and it was Ben who 'treed' Wichita when Billy escaped after killing Sheriff Whitney in 1873.*

Above: *John ('King') Fisher, former rustler, cowboy, rancher and later lawman and gunfighter. In later years he became a deputy sheriff. He was with Ben Thompson when he was murdered in March 1884.*

Above: *Benjamin ('Ben') Thompson, who earned a reputation as a gunfighter and gambler. He was elected city marshal of Austin, Texas, but Ben's past and his association with gamblers finally caught up with him. His feud with Jack Harris led to a fight in which Harris was killed. Friends of Harris plotted revenge, and on 11 March 1884, he and King Fisher were murdered in The Variety theater by hidden assassins.*

disgusted mayor promptly fired the whole police force. In later years it was claimed that Wyatt Earp actually arrested Ben, but city records disprove that. In 1877, Billy Thompson was arrested and brought back to Ellsworth for trial, but escaped justice on a technicality.

Ben Thompson's devotion to his brother was legendary – he got him out of one scrape after another. Mean, vicious, vindictive and totally unpredictable, Billy's survival was remarkable. E.D. Cowan's recollection of one incident in his life was typical. Writing on the 'Happy Bad Men of the West' in the Denver *Daily News* of 23 October 1898, Cowan said:

A conspicuous example of his type was Bill Thompson, brother of that other Texas Thompson named Ben, who made considerable of a record as a pacifier at Austin before he was assassinated. Bill was 'laying off' up in Colorado, after having had to slip across the Texas border between suns, when the historic double lynching of Frodsham and Stewart occurred at Leadville. Obedient to a request more imperative than polite, several hundred thugs, footpads, lot jumpers, burglars and assassins left Leadville the following morning and colonized thirty-five miles away at Buena Vista, the new temporary terminal of the South Park Railroad. They were soon joined by their kind in numbers from every quarter of the state. Highway robbery and every other sort of robbery and murder in the first degree became the pastime of the place . . .

But there was a happy bad man in the town, and it was Bill Thompson. He was elected mayor on the quiet by a backroom oligarchy. After the Texan had punctured the anatomy of a few of the worst bad men of Buena Vista, and satisfied everybody that he really enjoyed a good stand-up-and-shoot fight, the gaiety of the select society subsided, and in a few days he was the unchallenged despot of the town.

Meanwhile robbery and crime increased . . .

Cowan then related that a certain Colonel Amos C. Babcock loaned Billy $50 when the railroad moved on and the inhabitants dispersed. Billy was penniless and needed money to return home, where he had been assured he would not be charged with any offenses. Aware of Billy's nature, the colonel made the loan anonymously, but Billy learned who he was. Later, at Austin, when the colonel was trying to get a state capital loan for a project, and he wished to involve Ben Thompson, he found it impossible to reach him, for it was concluded that those involved were 'damn Yankees'. His luck changed when he passed a saloon and bumped into a drunken Texan. It was Billy, who recognized him right away. By the next day Ben, too, was his friend, and joined in his project.

Billy Thompson's eventual demise has so far escaped the record. Ben's widow heard it said that he was killed in a confrontation down at or around Laredo, Texas, in the late 1880s. She had heard that Billy killed several Mexicans before he finally expired. Whatever the truth, few mourned him, unlike Ben, whose hearse was followed by sixty-two vehicles.

FROM GUNS TO GAVEL: THE END OF AN ERA

The gunfighter's role in settling the West was magnified by novelists, film makers and others anxious to cash in on a burgeoning myth. We have already examined the role he played on both sides of the law, and shortly we will consider his role as a latter-day duelist. First, it is important to take a closer look at the weapons of his trade, primarily the pistol. The most popular weapon of the time was the single-action pistol. The principal instrument was the Colt, but Remington, Smith & Wesson and others played a part in furthering the mystique of the gun-slingers. Colt's Navy revolvers (both the so-called 1851 and 1861 models) proved to be among the most popular during the percussion era, and were closely rivaled by Colt's New Model Army of 1860 and the several Remington Army and Navy pistols of the period. Accuracy varied, of course, and all sorts of claims have been made concerning one or the other of them, but Colt's .36 caliber 1851 Navy was probably the most accurate, even if it lacked the power of the heavy .44 models. While it amused some of the better known pistol shots to fire at targets at one hundred yards or more, they were really only concerned with their accuracy at ranges of between five and fifteen feet, which was the normal distance when they were called upon to defend or make a reputation.

The romantic attachment of later generations to various guns and their alleged part in winning the West is not reflected in contemporary attitudes. Guns were regarded as necessary tools in the business of survival. Some weapons were more popular than others but that was reflected in their practical as well as popular appeal. In an article entitled 'FRONTIER WEAPONS' that appeared in the Wichita *Daily Eagle* of 11 October 1884, it was reported that a correspondent had spent some time at El Paso, Texas, where he entered a large store that enjoyed a reputation for selling more firearms than any of its rivals. Wandering around the cases of glittering weapons, his attention was drawn to a young man of about twenty-three, whose appearance suggested that he was a cowboy. 'He was dressed in approved frontier style, sombrero it would take three days to walk around the rim of, white handkerchief tied loosely round the neck, blue shirt, pants stuck in his boots, and large Mexican spurs upon his heels, jingling as he walked. He wished to buy a "gun".'

It was then explained in the 'expressiveness and laconic tongue of the frontier' that a 'gun' was a revolver. A rifle was called by the name of the maker, whereas a sporting weapon was generally called a 'shotgun'. At this point the salesman directed the young fellow to a case containing a handsome revolver: 'How would you like this? It is the newest thing out – a double-action forty-five.' The cowboy shook his head. 'Ain't worth a row of beans. No man 'cept a tenderfoot wants that kind of thing.

Give me an old reliable all the time. Ye see a man that's used to the old style is apt to get fooled – not pull her off in time – and then he'll be laid out colder'n a wedge.'

The reporter then noted that the cowboy was handed a single-action version of the same model which he carefully examined, cocked, fired, and twirled around his forefinger, cocking and pulling the trigger as the butt returned to his hand. He decided to purchase the pistol and disappeared into the crowd. The storekeeper then claimed that few men could spin and cock a pistol with such skill – among them had been 'Curly Bill' Brocius (who had pulled that stunt on Marshal White at Tombstone), Billy the Kid, Pat Garrett and

others, but Curly Bill had been the best. He might have added that a similar trick was claimed by John Wesley Hardin to have fooled Wild Bill; but it now appears that no one heard of that incident until Wes mentioned it in his *Life*.

By this time the newspaperman was very interested in the sort of people who purchased weapons. He asked if many 'Bulldog' type pistols were sold. The storekeeper told him that they were 'chiefly bought by railroad laborers, tramps and boys'. The Bulldog owed its name to the British .450 five-shot Webley pistol of that name. Small and easily concealed, with its short barrel and heavy caliber it was both handy and deadly. The store-

Right: *'Was it something I said?'.* N. C. Wyeth's graphic *'The Gunfight'* could almost be a still from an old-time Western, a freeze-frame capturing the mood and the action of a desperate saloon showdown.

keeper, who was probably more used to the innumerable 'suicide specials' turned out in the east, damned the whole breed with faint praise: 'The bull-dog is a poor pistol, shoots wild and can't be depended upon for over fifteen feet. The great trouble with all these pistols are that they are hard on the trigger. The boys get over this by having the catch filed down. The pistol of the cowboy is as fine on the trigger as were the hair-triggers of the old dueling days.'

The storekeeper then introduced his by now fascinated listener to 'a kind of shot-gun that has a limited use' and led him to the back of the store. Here were half a dozen shotguns that had been cut down so that the barrels were only two feet long. 'These guns are prime favorites with sheriffs, deputy sheriffs, United States marshals and officers of the law generally, and when they get the drop on you with one of them it's a case of throw up your hands, no matter how much sand you may have got. They are handy, and you can stow them away under the seat of a buggy with ease. Wells-Fargo's messengers all carry them, and at a short range they beat rifles and six-shooters all to hades . . . '

Suitably impressed, the correspondent remarked that there seemed to be fewer acci-

Above: *This business-like pair of Wells Fargo 'messengers' (stagecoach guards) are equipped not only with regulation shotguns, but rifles as well. Note the heavily laden double cartridge belts.*

dents with firearms in the West than in eastern states – extraordinary when it was appreciated that every man out West went armed. The storekeeper disagreed:

'It is not. The men who are always handling fire-arms are the most careful with them. I'd like to see you point a pistol or shotgun at a cow-boy, and he'd make you drop it so quick 'twould make your head swim. There used to be a good many accidents, though, a few years ago, when the boys were in the habit of carrying the full six loads in their guns, and trusting to the safety catch to avoid any danger. Sure as the gun dropped on the ground off she went. A number got shot this way. Now nearly every fellow carries one chamber empty with the hammer resting on it when, of course, no jar can discharge it.

'Some of the cowboys,' said the dealer in conclusion, 'are regular dudes about pistols. Nothing will do them but gold and silver mounted and ivory handled weapons. Rich Mexicans are more given to this style of thing and even Americans. The truth is that nickle-plated [*sic*] and silver-plated revolvers are not the best on the plains. The reflection of the sun on the white metal surface of the barrel is fatal to accurate shooting.'

The reference to self-inflicted wounds due to carelessness reminds us that even some of the better known pistoleers had their moments.

Below: *Dodge City advises wouldbe troublemakers against carrying firearms, but advertises a favorite 'gunfight lubricant' 'Prickly Ash' – a popular alcoholic beverage made from that aromatic and bitter shrub.*

ENGRAVED COLTS

Finely engraved and embellished Colts could be ordered directly from the factory or acquired from a number of independent artists. From early days, the Colt company offered engraving, inlaid precious metals, grips of ivory, pearl, or other exotic materials, special cases, and other features for an added fee. Sam Colt began a tradition of giving such firearms as a way of encouraging business and favors; in many circles an engraved Colt marked a person of stature.

1. Third model Dragoon revolver, .44 caliber, dated about 1851, scroll engraved. The revolver features a bust of George Washington, with deluxe walnut stocks.
2. 1851 Navy revolver, featuring early vine style engraving, about 1851, with walnut grips.
3. London pocket revolver, about 1855, London style engraving, .31 caliber, special walnut grips.
4. Model 1861 Navy, .36 caliber cased revolver with checkered ivory grips, in the best engraving style of Gustave Young. This revolver was presented to banker William H. Cox by the Colt company.
5. Gold inlaid and engraved Colt double-barrel hammer rifle, serial number 33, embellished by Cuno A. Helfricht, about 1880, and known to have been used by California politician J.H. Budd.
6. Samuel Colt presentation 1851 Navy revolver with detachable canteen shoulder stock, engraved by Gustave Young. Special walnut stocks, silver plating.
7. Model 1860 Colt Army .44 caliber revolver, about 1870. This one shipped in 1877 to Kittredge and Company of Cincinnati, Ohio.
8. Gustave Young engraved 1861 Navy, conversion to cartridge, ivory grips.
9. Gold and silver plated, L.D. Nimschke engraved Colt .44 caliber rimfire open top revolver with cast plated grips, made by Tiffany and Company, New York.
10. Deluxe engraved Colt frontier .44-40 caliber revolver embellished by Cuno Helfricht, about 1880, silver plated, engraved pearl grips, shown with the engraver's business

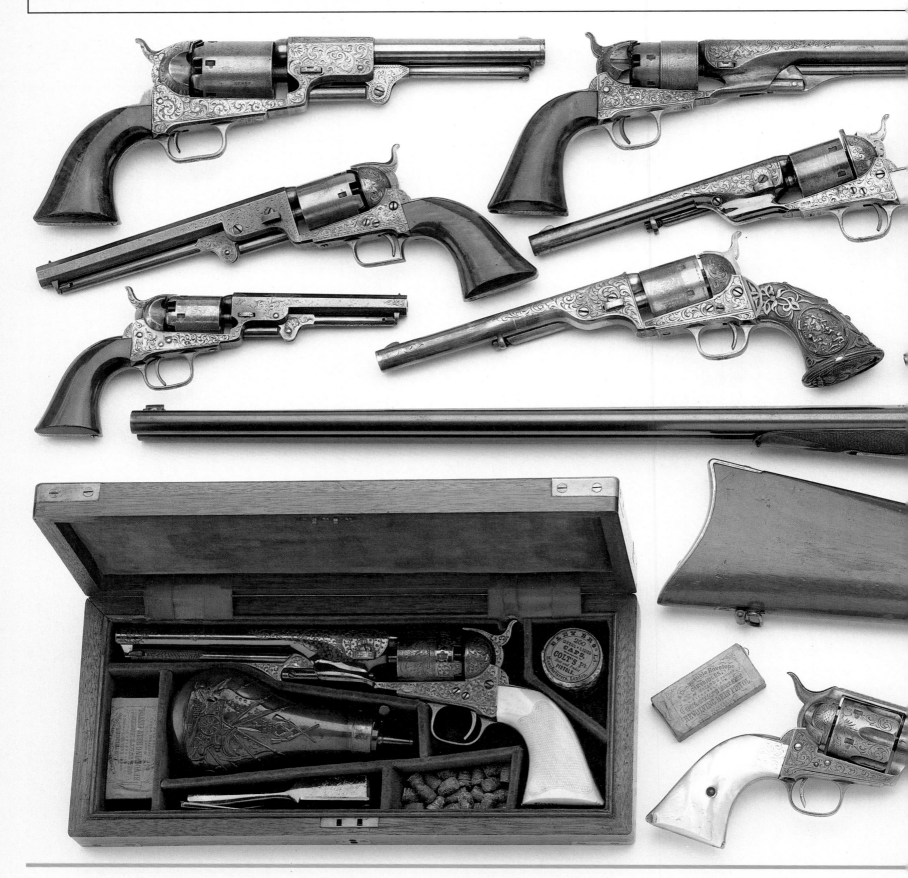

card and an example of one of his engraving tools.

11. Engraver's sample gun, third model deringer, .41 caliber. This is a pattern or sample gun made by Cuno Helfricht in the 1870s.

12. Colt single-action Army 'Sheriff's Model', scroll engraving by Cuno Helfricht, pearl grips, 1912.

13. Model 1902 automatic pistol, Cuno Helfricht

engraved, pearl grips, nickel plating, sporting version of a military pistol.

14. This .38 caliber Model 1903 New Army & Navy double-action revolver was shipped as an army shooting prize to Captain John T. Thompson in 1903. Cuno Helfricht's full floral engraving is handsomely complimented by the checkered ivory grips.

15. Cased New Police

double-action revolver, engraved by Helfricht, with ivory grips, and made about 1905.

16. Flat top target single-action army revolver engraved by William Gough, inlaid with gold and mounted with checkered ivory grips.

(Artifacts courtesy of Gene Autry Western Heritage Museum, Los Angeles, California.)

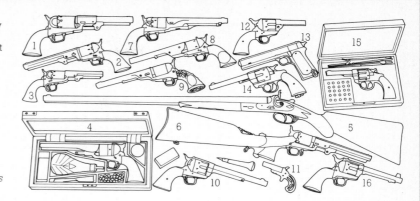

On 9 January 1876, Wyatt Earp, then a policeman on the Wichita force, was sitting in on a card game with some cronies when, according to the *Beacon* on 12 January an unusual event occurred:

Last Sunday night, while policeman Erp [*sic*] was sitting with two or three others in the back room of the Custom House saloon, his revolver slipped from its holster and in falling to the floor the hammer which was resting on the cap, is supposed to have struck the chair, causing a discharge of one of the barrels [chambers]. The ball passed through his coat, struck the north wall then glanced off and passed out through the ceiling. It was a narrow escape and the occurrence got up a lively stampede from the room. One of the demoralized was under the impression that some one had fired through the window from the outside.

Mr Earp evidently failed to heed his own alleged comments to his biographer Stuart N. Lake who reported that he only loaded five shots in a six-shooter to 'ensure against accidental discharge'. Even more embarrassing was the predicament faced by deputy marshal Daniel Jones of Caldwell one evening in September 1879. The *Post* on 25 September reported what happened when, during the course of his duties, the deputy marshal found himself in desperate need to relieve himself:

It happened at one of Caldwell's fashionable hotels, and, like all other fashionable hotels, has two small rooms – over each door is an inscription by which a person may know whether he is to be admitted or not, but it being dark, and Dan's 'business' qualifications not allowing him to stop, and read everything that is hung up entered. About this time a lady attempted to enter but was foiled by Dan turning an inside latch – the lady hastened away, but soon returned with the key – (this is not a romance) – locked, unlocked and relocked and finally left to return no more.

Now, as Dan's occupation calls him on the street he concluded that he might depart with safety, but imagine his feelings when he discovered that he had been locked in, but, as will be seen, Dan is equal to all emergencies, and began trying to extricate himself from his odorous prison. There is a seat in the room just opposite the door upon which Dan sat himself down, put his feet against the door, and with Heenan like strength pushed the door assunder, and at the same instant back went Dan's revolver down, down to the bottomless – after which a light was brought into requisition – it was fished up, a tub of water, barrel of soft soap and scrubbing-brush were readily used up and the pistol looks as natural as ever, and if the street gossip don't mention this we will never say a word about it to Dan.

One classic example of carelessness with a pistol occurred when a man from Emporia, Kansas, appeared in Newton in August 1872. The editor of the Emporia *News* noted that on the 4th one Dan Beckwith 'accidentally shot himself with a small revolver in the right arm, while showing some boys how to use the weapon. It is believed that the arm will have to be amputated. Another warning to be careful in the handling of firearms.'

The *Daily Eagle*'s correspondent, used as he was to the general sight of hip holsters worn so that the butt of the pistol faced to the rear or forward for a 'reverse' or a 'cross-draw', was intrigued to learn that there was now available another kind of holster, and the clerk was anxious to show him. 'Men who are used to the country either buy a caliber 41 or carry a 44 or 45 in a shoulder scabbard,' he remarked. On being asked to elucidate, the clerk described it as a scabbard [holster] with a strap 'passing over the right shoulder, and supports the pistol under your coat on the left side. It enables you to draw while a man is thinking that you are only looking for your handkerchief.'

The *Eagle* feature is important for several reasons: it proves that weapons were the sub-

Below: *Caldwell, Kansas, by the early 1880s was largely brick-built, but still retained the unpaved streets of most Western towns. Already known for its violence, the cattle trade enhanced it.*

ject of discussion and very much a personal choice. But one facet in particular needs clarification: the ongoing rivalry between the single-action and the double-action revolvers. Until the early 1870s the majority of American-made revolvers were single actions. The few percussion and early cartridge versions prior to that date met with little favor, mainly because their mechanisms were frail and difficult to repair. That state of affairs did not change much until the late 1880s, by which time most European countries were using well-made and designed 'double-acting, self-extracting' pistols. As early as 1851 the Englishman Robert Adams had patented a 'self-cocking' revolver, utilizing an action that had been available for some time in the numerous multi-barreled weapons generally called 'pepper-boxes'. Simply by pulling the trigger, the hammer was cocked and fired in one movement, and at the same time the cylinder was turned to bring a chamber in line with the barrel. Its Colt rivals had to be thumb-cocked for each shot. In practise, however, the Adams proved to be inferior to the Colt, and Sam Colt dismissed the Adams pistols out of hand. But in 1855, a certain Lieutenant Beaumont of the

Below: *The Meagher brothers both served the law. But it was Mike (right) who earned a peace-keeping reputation – first at Wichita and later at Caldwell, where he was killed in a gunfight on 17 December 1881.*

Royal Engineers patented a modification to the Adams pistol that enabled it to be fired either as a double- or single-action. Later, when metallic ammunition became common in Europe, various forms of 'self-extraction' were tried, the most common a device that allowed the barrel to break and as it was turned down, the cylinder pin, complete with turning ratchet, was thrust to the rear of the cylinder and the empty cartridges were ejected in one movement. The contemporary Colt pistols had to be loaded or ejected by means of a 'gate' cut in the side of the recoil shield, and a spring-loaded rod set in a tube alongside the barrel which was used to push them out.

In the middle 1870s, in response to demands from the company's London agency and a growing interest at home, Colt introduced three double-action revolvers: the .41 caliber 'Thunderer', the .38 caliber 'Lightning', and in 1878 the .45 caliber 'Double Action Army Revolver'. In each case, they basically resembled the Peacemaker in that they had loading gates and rod ejection, but instead of the familiar Colt flair to the stocks, they had a so-called 'bird's head' shape. Each of these pistols sold well, but there were many complaints about breakdowns. Billy the Kid is reputed to have owned a .41 caliber 'Thunderer' when he was killed, but the evidence is not conclusive. Although popular in some parts of the West, Colt's early double-actions did not find general favor and were not popular in Europe.

The New Model Single Action Army Revolver, first introduced in 1873, had its problems too. In essence, the Peacemaker (Colt's dealers coined the name), was a modified version of the original 1851 Navy pistol, with an enlarged solid frame that enclosed the cylinder. The government had suggested the change rather than continue the old style 'open frame' that had been popular for nearly thirty years. So instead of the original key or wedge that held the barrel to the frame, the new pistol was equipped with a screwed in barrel and generally was much stronger and more pleasing in appearance. Although the pistol found little favor in Europe, it nevertheless became a firm favorite in the United States. Adopted by the U.S. Cavalry in 1873 and issued to other branches of the service, once it became generally available after 1876, the Peacemaker soon found an admiring public. Rivaled by Remington's 1875 model (which closely resembled the Colt), Smith & Wesson's 'American' and 'Russian' models and several other makes, the Peacemaker beat them all in military trials. From then on it became the firm favorite of cowboys, peace officers and anyone who relied upon a revolver for protection or survival. With time all manner of legends have been built around it, for if any one pistol symbolized the man with the gun, deadly, a peerless marksman and gifted with phenomenal reflexes and a lightning draw, it was the Peacemaker.

COLT DERINGERS, POCKET PISTOLS

The development of Colt firearms was always characterized by the constant process of invention and improvement. Beginning in about 1869 the Colt company diversified, producing a great variety of single-shot pocket pistols, small pocket revolvers, double-action revolvers, and other products in addition to its line of shoulder arms. Small pocket pistols for self-defense were used by women and men, gamblers, gunmen and lawmen.

1. First Model Deringer pistol, about 1870, .41 rimfire, engraved, handy as iron knuckles in a fist fight.
2. Second Model Deringer pistol, .42 rimfire caliber, made 1870 to about 1890.
3. Third Model Deringer pistol, .41 caliber, manufactured about 1875–1912.
4. Open Top Pocket Model revolver, .22 caliber, 1875, seven shot cylinder.
5. New Line Pocket Model revolver, .22 caliber, nickel with pearl grips, 1876, backstrap engraved 'J.M. Foote, Jr'.
6. New Line Pocket Model revolver, .32 caliber rimfire, 1880.
7. Model revolver, for the .38 caliber rimfire New Line, unfinished and stamped M.
8. New Line revolver, .41 caliber rimfire, 1874, five shot cylinder.
9. New House model revolver .38 caliber centerfire, five shots, 1881.
10. Cloverleaf House model revolver, the first solid frame metallic cartridge revolver made by Colt. Four shots in .41 caliber, made in 1874.
11. New Police model revolver, .38 caliber centerfire with lanyard, 1882.
12. Model 1877 double-action Lightning revolver, .38 caliber, backstrap engraved 'Capt. Jack Crawford', used by this well-known scout and 'poet laureate' of the plains.
13. Model 1877 double-action Lightning revolver, .41 caliber, blue finish with pearl grips.
14. Model 1877 double-action Lightning revolver, caliber .38, engraved with ivory grips, with longer barrel and attached ejector rod.

15. Factory model gun for the Model 1878 double-action revolver, this version a flat-top target gun, serial number M.

16. .38 caliber Long Colt cartridges, popular in several different models of revolvers.

17. Frontier double-action revolver, model 1878, .45 caliber, portions cut away at the factory to demonstrate the mechanism.

18. Short barrel 'Sheriff's'

model 1878 double-action in .45 caliber, unfinished factory model gun, serial number M.

19. Hammerless model 1878 double-action, an experimental version which did not go into production. Serial number 1.

20. Standard production 1878 double-action Frontier revolver, .45 caliber, 7½ in. barrel.

21. .44 S & W cartridges.

22. Experimental

prototype double-action revolver with swingout cylinder, no serial number, patented 1884. Five years later Colt issued first production swingout cylinder revolver, a mechanism similar to many used in the West from 1889 to the present day.

(Artifacts courtesy of Gene Autry Western Heritage Museum, Los Angeles, California.)

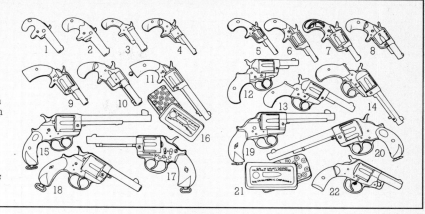

QUICK ON THE DRAW

No gunfighter worthy of the name could ever be described as slow when it came to getting his gun into action. But so preoccupied were the old-time writers with the speed and accuracy attributed to the man-killers that little attention was paid to practicalities. Rather, they were more concerned with speed and notches on their guns than realities. Consequently, the careless reference to someone being fast on the draw is rarely questioned, particularly when it is inextricably linked with the gunfighter myth. But no gunfighter of the time, if asked to explain how he got his gun into action, would have described himself as fast. Fast to the inhabitants of the old West was an expression they might have used when referring to a loose woman or a town that was lax in morals or legal restraint. 'I have seen many fast towns,' declared John Wesley Hardin, but I think Abilene beat them all.' 'Quick' was a term more commonly used, but even this emphasis on speed took second place to 'the drop' – seeking an advantage. Interviewed in 1865, Wild Bill Hickok is reported to have declared: 'Whenever you get into a row be sure and not shoot too quick. Take time. I've known many a feller slip up for shootin' in a hurry.' This emphasis upon accuracy rather than speed might appear to diminish the legendary prowess of those old-timers, but not a bit of it. When they spoke of 'taking time' it was the split second it took to make the decision to draw or take whatever evasive action might be required. In effect, the so-called fast draw was a reactional response and not speed, although an onlooker unversed in the finer points of gunplay might be excused for thinking that he was witnessing a quick draw.

Writing in the *New York Herald-Tribune* on 3 January 1930, Arthur Chapman described the extraordinary lengths to which some of the old-time gunfighters were reputed to have gone in order to stay alive. Despite its fictional overtones, it makes interesting reading:

> . . . It was not magic which enabled Bat Masterson to produce some wizard-like effects with the draw. It was hard and unrelenting practice. Just what it meant to acquire the degree of Doctor of the Draw at Dodge City in those days, was recently revealed to the writer of this article by John L. Amos, a prominent official of the Union Pacific Railroad at Salt Lake City. Mr. Amos, as a youth seeking adventure, found himself in the whirl that was Dodge City. His roommates were Masterson and 'Conk' Jones. 'Conk Jones was a wonderful gunfighter,' said Mr. Amos. 'He did not gain the prominence of many others, but I happen to know that for nerve and skill, he could not be beaten. He and Bat seemed to have taken a shine to me as a youngster. The only complaint I had against my roommates was that they were always practising gunplay. For at least an hour every day, they would practise with unloaded guns, draw and click, draw and click. Bat had a most peculiar way of carrying his revolver. It was tied on a string which was hung around his neck. He would reach inside his coat, and bring out the revolver, breaking the string in the same motion. Evidently it was a scheme he had developed himself. Masterson and Conk practised their gunplay in the room and generally, I was the target. I would hear a click behind me and would turn around to find that one of them had snapped his revolver at me. If I came in the door, perhaps both of them would go through the motion of drawing and firing at me as I entered. I liked both of them a lot, but finally I had to tell them that my nerves were going to pieces, and I would have to hand in my official resignation as their target.
>
> 'But no matter whether they aimed at me or at a bedpost, they would put in just so much time every day, perfecting themselves in the draw. And they never failed to inspect and clean their revolvers daily . . .'

The suggestion that Bat Masterson carried a pistol on a piece of string slung around his neck that 'broke' each time he drew his revolver makes no sense at all. Assuming he was armed with a .45 caliber Colt revolver, which when loaded weighed about three pounds, it would have taken more than a piece of string to hold that weight! But Chapman's yarn does serve to show how the mystique of speed played such a big part in the fast draw myth.

Curiously, little reliable evidence exists either to boost or deflate some of the stories

Below: *Bat Masterson's career covered a lot of territory. During his Dodge City days he exhibited a journalistic streak, and in later years became a sports writer for the* New York Morning Telegraph.

that have been handed down concerning speed and skill. Wild Bill Hickok is generally regarded as the epitome of the Western gunfighter both in performance and accuracy, yet no authentic targets are to hand, although this writer has been advised of several that are claimed as such. One exhibited to me some years ago was an envelope that had been tacked to a tree and the postage stamp affixed to its center. There were six holes in the paper, two of which clipped the stamp. It was claimed that Hickok fired from ten yards. Unfortunately, it had not been signed or otherwise authenticated.

In 1865 Colonel George Ward Nichols met Hickok at Springfield, Missouri, and in the February 1867 issue of *Harper's New Monthly Magazine* claimed that Wild Bill offered to demonstrate his skill with his Colt's Navy pistol, and proceeded to empty all six shoots at a signboard fifty yards away which included the letter 'O'. 'In an off-hand way, and without sighting the pistol with his eye, he discharged the six shots of his revolver. I afterward saw that all the bullets had entered the circle.' Bearing in mind that only weeks before Hickok had put a pistol ball through one Dave Tutt's heart at 'one hundred paces' such a feat does not seem unreasonable, except that Nichols weakens his case by suggesting that Hickok did not take aim. Similarly, in 1910, Bat Masterson reported a similar incident, only this time it took place at Kansas City, Missouri, and the distance was increased to 100 yards. Expert pistol shots have no difficulty in hitting targets at 100 yards with the Colt Navy pistol, but they do so with carefully aimed shots. Attention is also paid to the loading of each chamber. Nevertheless, neither the colonel nor Bat thought it necessary to explain how Wild Bill could discharge a pistol within city limits and escape a fine!

That Hickok was considered a good pistol shot is not in doubt. His contemporaries were in awe of his reaction to danger and his uncanny ability to hit targets, but even they agreed that some of the feats attributed to him were fictional. One acquaintance, W. E. Webb, who met him at Hays City in 1869, declared in his *Buffalo Land* published in 1872: 'I do not believe, for example, that he could hit a nickel across the street with a pistol-ball, any more than an Indian could do so with an arrow. These feats belong to romance. Bill is wonderfully handy with his pistols, however.' To which Luther North added: 'Wild Bill was a man of Iron Nerve and could shoot straight enough to hit a man in the right place when the man had a gun in his hand, and just between you and me, not many of the so called Bad Men could do that.'

John Wesley Hardin was considered by many of his contemporaries to be a good pistol shot, and shortly before his death fired several shots into a card at close range and signed his name. But by his own word he knew all the tricks of the trade and claimed to have fooled Wild Bill with the 'roadagents' or 'Curly Bill' spin back in 1871. Descriptions of it vary. Earlier we reported how a cowboy performed one version in an El Paso gun store – by spinning the barrel forward on the trigger finger and catching the butt and cocking the pistol as it came back to the hand. In the Hardin version

Above: *Wild Bill Hickok from a family tintype, circa 1863–4. Photographed when he was a contract scout for the Union Army, Hickok is dressed in the typical nondescript garb of the time.*

the pistol is offered butt first, but the index finger stays in the trigger guard. As the victim reaches for the butt, it is spun back into the hand, cocked and 'what are your favorite flowers?' The only problem with Hardin's story is that he says Hickok had two cocked pistols on him when he tried that trick. As Hickok reached for his pistol, he jumped back and cocked it. What is not explained is how Hickok could have two cocked pistols on Hardin and yet reach for his!

Topping the list of Texas 'bad men' with a reputation for violence and as a shot was Ben Thompson, the British born gambler-gun-fighter. His cronies always maintained that Ben was a good shot and that had he and Wild Bill met face-to-face following Hickok's shoot-out with Ben's erstwhile partner Phil Coe at Abilene, the outcome would have been very close. But Ben was in Kansas City at the time and any such speculation is academic. It does seem evident that he was a good shot, and in 1879 took part in a shooting match against William ('Buffalo Bill') Cody. Buffalo Bill at that time was touring with his Combination and, following a performance at Austin, Texas, he was introduced to Ben Thompson. We suspect that it was not a first time meeting for either of them, for it is likely that they first met in Kansas. The *Austin Daily Statesman* of 10 December 1879 reported that 'Buffalo Bill went out of town yesterday with Mr Ben Thompson and some other gentlemen, and he showed them a little crack shooting. With Mr Thompson's rifle he

struck six half dollars out of seven that were thrown up.' Ben was impressed, as indeed were the others, for Cody's reputation on the plains as a rifle shot was second to none. But when it came to pistols, Cody was outclassed. Old-time plainsmen recalled that Buffalo Bill had never been any great shakes as a pistol shot, and although in later years he improved, there was a sneaking feeling in some quarters that much of his ring work was done with smooth-bore pistols firing bird-shot. True or not, he was man enough to admit that he had met his match with Ben. Proof of his admiration for the gunfighter came to light in 1881 when, according to the *Statesman* of 15 June, 'Yesterday morning Marshal Thompson [Ben had been elected City Marshal and Chief of Police in the election held the previous December] received a very handsome present from Buffalo Bill . . . a costly target pistol manufactured by Stevens & Co. of Chicopee Falls, Massachussetts . . .'

Following Ben's murder on 11 March 1884, his wife disposed of the pistol which eventually ended up in the hands of a private collector who placed it on loan at the National Cowboy Hall of Fame, Oklahoma City. It is described as a target pistol chambered for the Colt .32 caliber center-fire cartridge, and it is fitted with a ten-inch barrel. Superbly engraved, with nickel-plating and a gold wash finish to the barrel and frame, the grips are made of pearl. The back strap bears the inscription 'BUFFALO BILL TO BEN THOMPSON'. A similar weapon was also ordered which bears the backstrap inscription 'W. F. CODY.' It was not uncommon for engraved pieces to be given as tokens of admiration.

Above: *William Frederick ('Buffalo Bill') Cody in stage costume, circa 1873. He was never a 'pistol fighter' but his interpretation of the 'Wild West' in his stage and later exhibition days was influential.*

In July 1880, when Ben's homicidal brother Billy got into trouble at Ogallala, Nebraska, and wounded a bartender who in turn wounded Billy, Ben asked Bat Masterson to get him out of trouble, and en route to Dodge City the pair stayed at Cody's ranch at North Platte.

Attitudes to gunfighting varied. Hickok was philosophical on the subject. He believed that no one could outrun a bullet, so if one was coming it was better to face it – an ironic comment considering his demise at the hands of a back-shooting coward. He also thought it better to aim for the body rather than anywhere else for the simple reason that if one shot a man 'in the guts near the navel; you may not make a fatal shot, but he will get a shock that will paralyze his brain and arm so much that the fight is all over.'

'The first man you kill,' mused Jim Moon (whose real name was Henry Wilcoxon), 'it goes pretty hard with you for a while, but after the second or third you don't mind knocking over one of these gunfighters any more than you would a sheep,' he remarked to E. D. Cowan shortly before he was killed by Charley Wilson at Denver. 'The man who pulls a gun on you when you have nothing in sight is a cur. All you need to do is walk right up to him, take it way and beat him over the head with it, so he won't try it again. Nearly all my men came for me. Of course, I went after some of them, – had to.' Cowan then described in his *Daily News* story of 23 October 1898, how Moon handled such encounters, one of them with 'a bad man from Breckenridge':

Only a few weeks previously Moon, while seated with a friend and two women at a restaurant and having a rather merry time not objected to by the proprietor, was, according to his way of thinking, insulted by a lieutenant and officer of police. He beat both of them nearly to death with the chinaware and chairs, hurried his three companions into a hack, which he ordered driven to a half-way house outside the city limits, and held his impromptu block-house a week with a double-barreled shotgun against the combined police and the sheriff's force. He surrendered only when liberty was guaranteed him.

Shortly after, a bad man from Breckenridge pulled a six-shooter on Moon in a gambling room. He captured it and hit his assailant over the head with the butt. The blow knocked the Breckenridge killer down a flight of stairs and the body was taken to the morgue; the neck was found to have been broken. Moon was acquitted.

Then came Jim Moon's last attempt to brain or shoot a man with his pistol. A woman was at the bottom of the trouble. Clay Wilson was a mild-mannered, inert sort of a young fellow. Moon got entrance to his room one night and made him dance a jig in his night shirt while the 45-caliber bullets cut splinters out of the floor around his feet . . .

The following morning Wilson put in his pocket a 'Colt's sawed off' [presumably a large caliber pistol with a shortened barrel] which was the favorite weapon of the happy bad man. He went into the Arcade to take a drink. Moon was there and ordered him out. He obeyed, but came back with the six-shooter in his hand. He fired twice before Moon grappled with him, both bullets plowing through the heart. With that strange vitality which is explicable in the deer when it bounds for hundreds of yards after having received a mortal wound, but unaccountable in man, Moon fought for the possession of the six-shooter, which Wilson discharged a third time, the bullet again passing through the body. Moon did not quit the fight until a fourth bullet broke his neck.

Nothing in the annals of border tragedy is so remarkable as the last battle of Jim Moon, waged with animal like instinct after he had been shot fatally. His own six-shooter was found in his coat pocket. Moon was large, alert, athletic, red-headed, and of course blue-eyed. Before settling in Colorado he disposed of some of the most troublesome junior bad men in Arizona.

Cowan's final comment on Moon's eyes is another tribute to the stereotype gunfighter. In more recent years George D. Hendricks devoted a whole volume (*The Bad Man of the West*) to characteristics that set them apart. Out of fifty-seven so-called badmen examined, thirty-eight of them had blue or blue-grey eyes!

In contrast to Moon's violent reaction to what he considered to be personal insults, Cowan declared that 'Bill Hickok was a finer type of the happy bad man than such as Jim Moon, because he was a genuine lover of law and order. When Wild Bill ruled in the name of good citizenship it fared ill with every pistol expert who undertook to run the town. His assassination at Deadwood was one of the most cowardly acts remembered in the mining camps,' a view shared by many of Hickok's contemporaries. In Hays City, where Wild Bill lived for several years and for a brief period enforced the law, he was known and admired as a 'law and order man'. Anyone who let it be known that they 'had it in for him' was advised to put up or shut up, for it was well known that Hickok usually hunted up those who made such threats. The Hays City *Sentinel* of 2 February 1877 added:

> The many tributes to his bravery, coolness, and generosity are not exaggerated. Bill was a quiet, peaceably disposed man – never boisterous and quarrelsome – and never starting a row. But when Bill was once convinced of an adequate cause for taking a hand in a row, there was always a funeral. This is where he differed from the generality of frontiersman. The ordinary ruffian, when involved in a row, would bluster around until, in the natural course of events, he would get shot; while Bill would perforate his opponent and then do his blustering at the funeral.

Above: *Deadwood, Dakota Territory, circa 1877. Founded in April 1876, it soon attracted a large population of would-be goldminers who flocked to the place once gold was discovered.*

Below: *Transportation in early Deadwood was limited to ox trains (as depicted) or the Cheyenne & Black Hills Stage Line coaches that plied between the Hills and Cheyenne. Shipments of gold 'dust' were well guarded.*

Below: *The murder of Wild Bill Hickok by John ('Jack') McCall on 2 August 1876 created a sensation. Then as now, tourists and others visited his grave, many of them carefully noting Charley Utter's moving epitaph.*

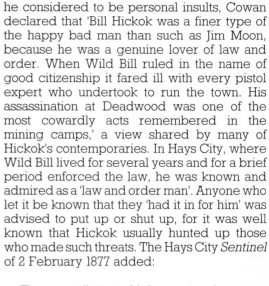

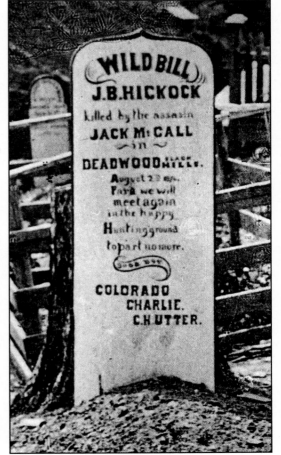

THE COLT SINGLE-ACTION ARMY

Few firearms were as easily identified with the gunfighter and the settlement of the West as the Colt single-action Army revolver. Even its nicknames convey ideas of frontier lawmen and gunmen. Known variously as the 'Peacemaker', the 'Frontier Six-Shooter', the 'Thumb buster' and the 'Hog Leg', this gun was popularly used and relied upon by men and women on both sides of the law, and by both civilians and the military after its first release in 1872.

1. Model 1862 pocket Navy revolver, .36 caliber centerfire, c. 1873.
2. Model 1851 Navy conversion from .36 caliber percussion to .38 caliber rimfire, about 1873.
3. Richards-Mason Colt conversion revolver.
4. Thuer conversion of Model 1861 Navy revolver from percussion to front loading, tapered brass cased cartridge,

caliber .36, c. 1869.
5. Experimental .44 rimfire Colt cartridge revolver, c. 1868–9.
6. Gauges used for initial manufacture of the Colt single-action Army revolver, 1872–4.
7. Serial number 1, 's' Colt single-action Army, the first manufactured in 1872, shipped to England for promotional purposes.
8. Factory cutaway single-action, .45, showing internal mechanism.

9. Experimental .45 caliber single-action with automatic cartridge extractor.
10. Typical, inexpensive, machine embossed holster and belt for single-action Army Colt.
11. Gold plated, pearl steer head grips, and with silver inlaid name on the backstrap, 'Albert W. Bonds'.
12. Box for .45 Colt cartridges, made by Remington–U.M.C.

13. Brass cased .44 Smith & Wesson cartridges.
14. Nickel plated, ivory gripped Colt single-action .45 known to collectors as the 'Sheriff's' model; was manufactured without the cartridge ejector.
15. Carved Mexican eagles on ivory grips were especially popular south of the border where the Colt single-action Army .45 became a weapon of choice.

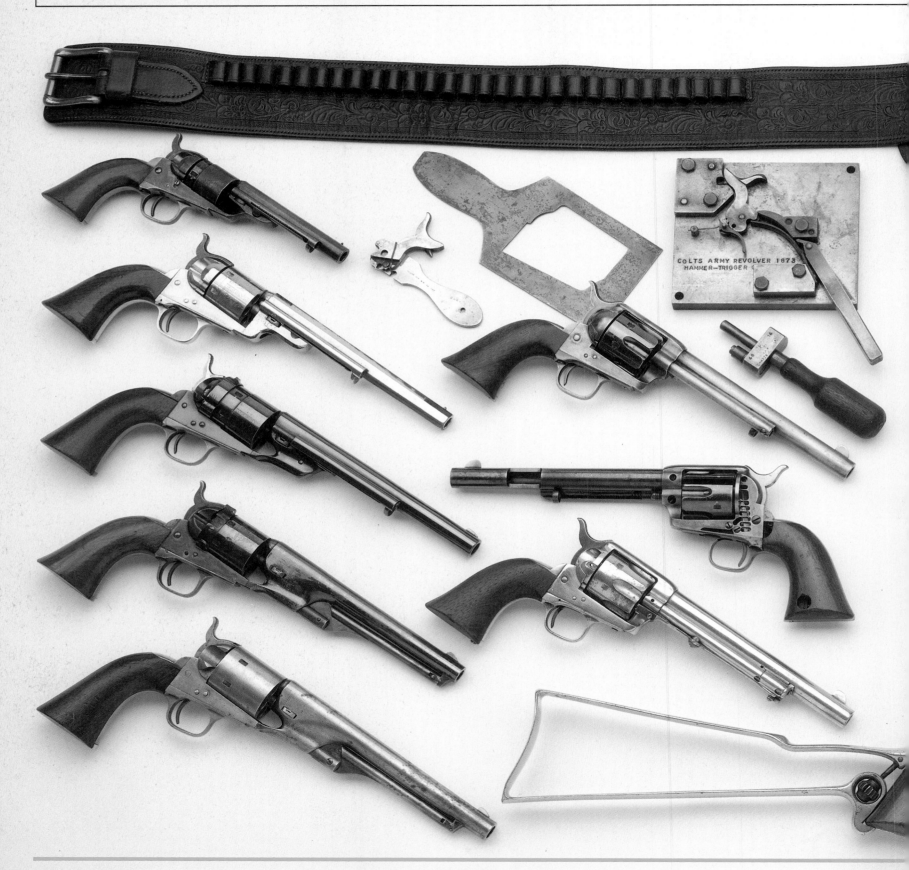

16. Although available in many barrel lengths, the 4¾ in. model such as this .45 nickel finished version was among the most popular of the single-action Colts.

17. Colt single-actions with detachable shoulder stocks and extra long barrels could be ordered from the factory. This example was the first made, 1876.

18. Wells Fargo Express ordered a number of these .45 Colts for use by security personnel in 1909.

19. The same weapon proved reliable for Adams Express Company.

20. A .45 caliber Colt, factory ivory grips decorated with carving.

21. Second in popularity to the .45, the .44-40 received wide use.

22. With longer curved grips and special target sights, the Bisley model single-action gained popularity in England and the United States.

23. With fixed sights and custom finish and grips, the Bisley also saw use in the West.

24. Standard Bisley model with fixed sights and 5½ in. barrel.

(Artifacts courtesy of Gene Autry Western Heritage Museum, Los Angeles, California.)

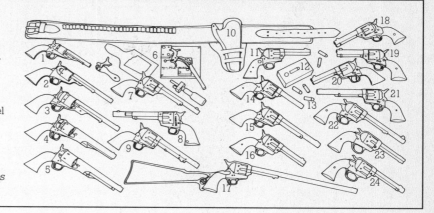

E. D. Cowan also described the demeanor and character of John Holliday, whose professional calling as a dentist earned him the title 'Doc' on the frontier. It was said of him that he was well 'drilled in the art of dentistry, but for those who doubted his ability, he would drill 'em for free'. Born in Georgia in 1851, Holliday came from a genteel background, but early in life had displayed characteristics that later led to his reputation as a killer. His already bad disposition was not helped when he contracted tuberculosis which necessitated a life in a high, dry climate. Holliday's relationship with Wyatt Earp often proved an embarrassment both to Earp who had political as well as social ambitions, and to his friends who were said to detest him. But it was Doc Holliday who stood by him when the Earp brothers fought it out with the Clantons and the McLaurys at the O.K. Corral in 1881. His later involvement with the Earps after the murder of Morgan caused him most problems. Holliday was arrested on trumped up charges in Denver in an attempt to get him extradited to Arizona. Cowan's version of what happened is informative if perhaps embroidered:

To Holliday's record is accredited the breaking up, if not the extermination, of the Pimo [sic – Pima] county, Arizona, 'rustlers', a class of murderous cattle thieves who prospered in New Mexico and Arizona until wiped out by the happy bad men [obviously a reference to the O.K. Corral fight and the local rustlers]. Holliday was tried for murder in Pima County, whose official life at the time was dominated by the rustlers' conspiracy, and in spite of this adverse influence was acquitted.

Tom Fitch, of California, who defended him, told me that the witnesses for the prosecution were the best witnesses for the defense, since by their testimony it was clearly proved that Holliday killed all his men under fire, and with the odds often against him. He was incredibly swift and accurate with the six-shooter and ambidextrous. Given two men for objects, anywhere within the semi-circle he could hit both at the first discharge . . .

After Holliday got free from the Pima County trials he made his way with all haste to Colorado. Under a trumped-up indictmen a warrant was issued for his arrest and he was taken at Denver. The plot of the rustlers was to get him across the border of New Mexico and lynch him. Bat Masterson, who was greatly attached to Holliday, made a plea for assistance in the *Tribune* editorial rooms the night of the arrest. He submitted proof of the criminal design upon Holliday's life. Late as the hour was, I called on Governor Pitkin and he agreed to order a public hearing of the requisition.

The true motive of the arrest was sufficiently proved out of the mouth of the deputy sheriff. Governor Pitkin refused to grant the requisition, reprimanded the deputy sheriff, gently lectured Holliday as to the requirements of good citizenship in Colorado and dismissed him.

Whether Bat Masterson really liked Holliday or not is uncertain. His own assessment

DENTISTRY.

J. H. Holliday, Dentist, very respectfully offers his professional services to the citizens of Dodge City and surrounding country during the summer. Office at room No. 24, Dodge House. Where satisfaction is not given money will be refunded.

Above: *Denizens of Dodge whose 'miscreant molars' gave trouble were able to be 'drilled' by Doc without suffering from lead poison. One wonders if there were any dissatisfied customers with nerve enough to complain!*

Below: *John 'Doc' Holliday appeared in a number of Western boom towns in their heyday, including Dodge City, Tucson and Tombstone. Ravaged by alcoholism and tuberculosis, he died at thirty-six.*

was that he had 'a mean disposition and an ungovernable temper, and under the influence of liquor was a most dangerous man'. But Bat, like many of Wyatt Earp's friends, tolerated Holliday simply because he was a friend of Earp's. Of the incident involving Governor Pitkin, Bat did state in *Human Life*: 'I was in Denver at the time, and managed to secure an audience with Governor Pitkin who, after listening to my statement in the matter, refused to honor the Arizona requisition for Holliday.' Bat then declared: 'I then had a complaint sworn out against Holliday charging him with having committed a highway robbery in Pueblo, Colorado, and had him taken from Denver to Pueblo, where he was put under a nominal bond and released from custody. The charge of highway robbery made against Holliday, at this time, was nothing more than a subterfuge on my part to prevent him from being taken out of the state by the Arizona authorities, after Governor Pitkin went out of office, but the Colorado authorities did not know it at the time. Holliday always managed to have his case put off whenever it would come up for trial, and, by furnishing a new bond, in every instance would be released again.'

Jack DeMattos, editor of an annotated version of Masterson's *Human Life* articles, discovered that the actual charge leveled against Doc was not highway robbery but 'bunco'. The case was continued indefinitely, which meant Holliday could not be extradited from the state.

Doc Holliday's luck finally ran out. His pulminary condition worsening, he went to Glenwood Springs, Colorado, seeking some relief, but galloping consumption set in and he died at 10 a.m. on 8 November 1887, at the Hotel Glenwood. They buried him that afternoon in the Linwood Cemetery close by. He was thirty-six years old, but his ravaged body made him look like a man in his eighties.

David Allen ('Mysterious Dave') Mather shared in demeanor and general behavior Holliday's anti-social characteristics. Born on 10 August 1851, the first of three sons born to Ulysses and Lydia Mather, he and his younger brother Josiah Wright Mather, born on 11 October 1854, both made their way West. Josiah also became a noted figure in the West but he did not achieve anything like the reputation of his brother. Josiah was to die with his 'boots off' at Grangeville, Idaho, on 18 April 1932. In their time, however, the Mather brothers were known as tough characters and Dave was a particularly hard case with not too many redeeming features.

According to his biographer Jack DeMattos, Dave Mather probably appeared out West post-1870 where, it is claimed, he had some links with a gang of outlaws in Arkansas before moving on to achieve a notoriety in places as far apart as Texas and Missouri. His first prominent mention, however, was in New Mexico, where he became mixed up in gambling and alleged crooked activities at Las Vegas. Here he met and became friends with several ex-Dodge City types, including Doc Holliday. Mather was also ambitious. He applied for and was appointed as a deputy U.S. marshal. This appointment came at a time when he, together with others, was under suspicion for alleged involvement in stagecoach hold-ups and other

Above: *David ('Mysterious Dave') Mather photographed at Dodge City in 1883 – note the 'Assistant Marshal' band on his hat. To some Dave was a 'wicked' man and a 'killer of killers'. His death remains a mystery.*

robberies, but he was never indicted for any of those crimes. Instead, he was busily serving writs upon some of those with whom he was alleged to be in cahoots!

Mather, however, is best remembered for his exploits in Dodge City where he settled in May 1883. His arrival coincided with the famous so-called 'Dodge City War' (mentioned elsewhere) between Luke Short and his partner William H. Harris and the town council over prostitution. Dave was not involved in that fracas. On 1 June 1883, Dave was appointed assistant city marshal, and celebrated the event by having the only known photograph of himself made which depicts him wearing a ribbon around his hat bearing the words 'Assistant Marshal'. He was also appointed as a deputy sheriff of Ford County. His appointment as an assistant marshal, however, was not welcomed by everyone. One man even wrote a letter of complaint to the governor about Mather's behaviour, and inferred that the police force was intimidating the citizens. If any action was taken it was not recorded and Mather remained on the force. At that time the marshal was Jack Bridges who was earning $100 per month, and his assistant $75, which was good money. On 6 July the council boosted both the marshal's and the assistant marshal's salaries to $150 and $125 respectively, which prompted the *Ford County*

Below: *Las Vegas, New Mexico. Depicted is the South East Plaza in 1881. Cattle wander or lay in the streets, in what appears to be rural peace. But in the saloons and gambling 'hells' violence was never far away.*

Above: *George Hoover erected the first saloon in Dodge in a sod hut on 17 June 1872, thereby creating the place. He later became the town's first mayor and bank president. He died in 1914.*

Above: *Thomas C. Nixon, buffalo hunter, rancher and lawman. His feud with Dave Mather finally led to bloodshed. Although fault lay on both sides there were many who thought that Tom had been the aggressor.*

Above: *Orlando A. ('Brick') Bond who hailed from New York and settled in Dodge in 1872. He is credited with the deaths of 6,183 buffalo between 1874 and 1875. He joined with Nixon in the saloon business.*

Globe of 24 July 1883, to comment: 'Dodge City pays her marshal $150 per month and the assistant marshal $125 per month. Besides this, each of them is entitled to kill a cowboy or two each season.' But both Bridges and Mather lost their jobs following the election of April 1884. The incoming mayor, George M. Hoover, himself an old-time saloon keeper and wholesale liquor dealer, replaced them with William M. ('Bill') Tilghman as the new city marshal and as his assistant he chose Thomas C. Nixon.

Dave Mather managed to retain his commission as a deputy sheriff, but he was increasingly concerned with local politics, which were in something of a turmoil when he joined the Democratic party. The Kansas statutes that had introduced prohibition into the arena met with a mixed reaction among those who argued the case for keeping Kansas wet or making her dry. Added to this, Mather and a Texan friend named David Black had become proprietors of the Opera House saloon with the intention of turning it into a dance hall. This was much against the wishes of the new mayor and council, which soon led to friction. To add insult to injury, Dave's rival and bitter enemy Tom Nixon not only had his old job but in partnership with Orlando A. ('Brick') Bond he owned the Lady Gay saloon which was operated as a saloon-cum-dance hall. On 22 May the council passed legislation to forestall any plans by Mather & Black for a dance hall by passing Ordinance No. 83 which in part claimed that it would be unlawful for anyone to maintain in Dodge City 'what is commonly known as a dance hall, or any other place where lewd women and men congregate for the purpose of dancing or otherwise'.

For reasons not disclosed, Nixon's establishment was not touched. In reprisal, Mather & Black advertised in the Dodge City *Democrat* on 7 June that they intended to sell their

beer for only 'five cents a glass' which was less than half the going rate. Nixon and his cronies soon reacted: pressure was placed upon local liquor dealers and beer wholesalers and the Opera House saloon soon dried up. On the 12th, the *Times* reported a court ruling concerning potential jurors and the demon drink, which took a great swipe at the partners:

> . . . a man who is engaged in selling liquors, or in any other unlawful business, is incompetent to act as a juror. This is a virtual disfranchisement of a large class of people in Dodge City, and if the rule was applied to the country, it would make a vast army of incompetents.
>
> Little by little, prohibition is taking hold in this city. It may appear insignificant, but the 5 cent beer business lends to prohibition . . .

It soon became increasingly obvious to Mather & Black that Nixon was a leading light in their problems, and it would only be a matter of time before there was trouble. Black was not personally involved in the dispute between Mather and Nixon. Tom Nixon, like Mather, had a shrouded past. It is known, however, that by 1870 he and his wife Cornelia and young family were living near Fort Dodge, where Tom had a local reputation as a buffalo hunter. He also owned a small ranch, but later set up in business at Dodge City repairing wagons. Madam Rumor had it that a woman was the cause of the friction between himself and Dave, and that the saloon feud was a smoke screen. Some even claimed that there was a relationship between Mather and Mrs Nixon. This was all conjecture: the real reason (if it had nothing to do with the saloon feud) was never disclosed.

Tom Nixon made the first move. On 18 July 1884, as Mather stood in the doorway of his

Above: *Tom Nixon's wife Cornelia and their son Howard Tracy, circa 1877. Innuendo asserted that one of the reasons Nixon and Mather fell out was over her favors; but no evidence of a liaison has come to light.*

Opera House saloon, Nixon took a shot at him from the bottom of the porch stairs. The bullet missed Mather who suffered only powder burns and the odd splinter.

Sheriff Pat Sughrue rushed up at the sound of the shot and promptly disarmed Nixon and took him over to the jail. Mather dismissed his wound as superficial, but protested that he had not been armed; Nixon claimed that he was and that he had only fired because he believed Dave was going for his gun. Mather said that he would not press charges, and many people expressed the opinion that the

Above: *Robert M. Wright, one of the early day businessmen of Dodge whose book did much to publicise its status as the 'Cowboy Capital' that is remembered to this day. He knew most of the famous frontier characters.*

Above: *Patrick Sughrue (and his twin brother Michael) both served as policemen during the hectic days of 'cowboy chaos' in Dodge City. Pat later became sheriff of Ford County and Mike of Clark County.*

Above: *Michael Sutton was a prominent lawyer in early day Dodge who acted for the defense in Dave Mather's trial. Once, in 1879, he assisted Sheriff Bat Masterson in the capture of horse thieves.*

matter was far from over. Nixon was bound over in the sum of $800 to appear at the next term of court charged with 'assault with intent to kill'.

Robert M. Wright, a local merchant and the author of *Dodge City The Cowboy Capital*, stated that Dave Mather was 'said to be a very wicked man, a killer of killers. And it was and is an undoubted fact that Dave had more dead men to his credit, at that time, than any other man in the West.' On 21 July 1884, yet another victim was added to his tally. Almost seventy-three hours after their first encounter, and ironically in approximately the same spot (but their positions were reversed) Dave Mather shot and killed Tom Nixon. The *Globe and Live Stock Journal* on 22 July, under the heading 'THE MURDER' declared that Mather shot Nixon at 10 p.m. the previous evening as the assistant marshal was 'on duty at the corner of Front Street and First Avenue . . . ' The paper described how Mather 'came down the stairs from his saloon and on his arrival at the foot he called to Nixon who was standing at the corner, and on Nixon turning around Mather commenced shooting at him, firing four shots, two of them striking him in the right side one on the left side and one passing through the left nipple, killing him instantly.'

Mather was immediately placed under arrest, and a preliminary hearing was arranged for 30 July at the Ford County Courthouse at Dodge City. DeMattos unearthed the original court records which contradict some of the published accounts of both the shooting and testimony. Witnesses testified that Nixon was looking in on a game of cards when he was shot, and was oblivious to his danger. When Mather called out 'Tom' which was immediately followed by four shots, Nixon was heard to say 'Oh, I'm shot' or 'I'm killed', before collapsing. It was also claimed that he had

turned to face whoever spoke just as the shots were fired. Nixon never had a chance to draw his own revolver. Following the shooting, Mather walked up the stairs to his saloon.

Witness Archie Franklin stated that 'Nixon did not fall after the first shot. He fell between the second and third shots. Mather advanced after the first shot. I could not say that he shot Nixon at all after he was down.'

Bat Masterson, who appeared on the scene moments after the shooting, testified that he was among the first to reach the body. He added:

'I was probably the first that took hold of him. He was lying on his right side and back, with his head south west, and his feet north east. His right hand was up and his left was on his left hip.

'This was about a minute after the last shot was fired. He had his revolver on. He was lying on it. It was in his scabbard [holster]. It looked as if it might have fallen partly out or been drawn partly out. I did not see any other weapons on him or in his hands.'

Sheriff Pat Sughrue testified that Mather did the shooting with a Colt's .45 caliber pistol, but he did not 'see the pistol while it was being shot'.

In court the following day, 31 July, the reporter for the Topeka *Daily Commonwealth* claimed that he was seated close to Mather. In his report, published on 3 August, he described Dave as 'calm and collected, and being unrestrained, the best observer of human nature could not have selected him as the man whose life was in jeopardy . . . ' Michael Sutton, a well-known lawyer in Dodge, acted for the defense and tried unsuccessfully to impeach one of the witnesses.

Mather's attempt to obtain bail was denied and he was placed in jail to await trial for first degree murder.

Following some wrangling and legal hassle for a change of venue, the trial was finally fixed to take place at Kinsley, Kansas, on 29 December. On 31 December the jury retired and twenty-seven minutes later rendered a not guilty verdict. The consensus of opinion on all sides seems to have been that Nixon was the aggressor and that Mather's actions were justifiable.

Mysterious Dave Mather's subsequent career was fraught with scrapes, and his final disappearance only adds to the mystery surrounding him. A body found on the tracks of the Central Texas Railroad was thought to be that of Mysterious Dave, but the dead man's identity was never disclosed. But the description tallied with Dave's. The Kingman, Kansas, *Courier* of 21 May 1886 described the body as that of a man aged about 'thirty-five or forty-five years of age, with a long black moustache. There is a hole in the side of the head, the nature of which can not be determined without a surgical examination, but it is believed to be a bullet wound. He had near him two bottles of whiskey and some cigars.' Curiously, DeMattos unearthed a document in the court records of Ford County which claims that Mather was driven out of Dodge under threat of death, but his ultimate fate remains a mystery. Yet like Billy the Kid, Jesse James and other notorious characters, stories of sightings continued to circulate long after the subject ceased to exist. Even Dave's own brother Josiah was later to confess that he had no idea what had happened to his brother, or where he went after leaving Dodge. In his heart of hearts he secretly hoped that 'Mysterious Dave' would one day become 'Prodigal Dave' but he never did.

SIPS, SLAPS AND SHOTS

Personal diputes, feuds and rows over wine, women and cards beset frontier towns and settlements, and the outcome of such disputes invariably led to violence or sudden death. Perhaps the most memorable of Dodge City's gunfights was that which took place between Levi Richardson and Frank ('Cock-eyed Frank') Loving in the Long Branch saloon on 5 April 1879. This encounter had all the ingredients of the classic Western gunfight, but there was also a touch of graveyard humor about it, for as it turned out it was almost a farce.

The fight was graphically described by the *Ford County Globe* on 8 April:

There is seldom witnessed in any civilized town or county such a sense as transpired at the Long Branch saloon, in this city, last Saturday evening, resulting in the killing of Levi Richardson, a well-known freighter, of this city, by a gambler named Frank Loving.

For several months Loving has been living with a woman toward whom Richardson seems to have cherished tender feelings, and on one or two occasions previous to this which resulted so fatally, they have quarreled and even come to blows. Richardson was a man who had lived for several years on the frontier, and though well liked in many respects, he had cultivated habits of bold and daring, which are always likely to get a man into trouble. Such a disposition as he possessed might be termed bravery by many, and indeed we believe he was the reverse of a coward. He was a hard working, industrious man, but young and strong and reckless.

Loving is a man of whom we know but very little. He is a gambler by profession; not much of a roudy [sic], but more of the cool and the desperate order, when he has a killing on hand. He is about 25 years old. Both, or either of these men, we believe, might have avoided this shooting if either had possessed a desire to do so. But both being willing to risk their lives, each with confidence in himself, they fought because they wanted to fight. As stated in the evidence below, they met, one said 'I don't believe you will fight.' The other answered 'try me and see', and immediately both drew murderous revolvers and at it they went, in a room filled with people, the leaden missives flying in all directions. Neither exhibited any sign of a desire to escape the other, and there is no telling how long the fight might have lasted had not Richardson been pierced with bullets and Loving's pistol left without a cartridge. Richardson was shot in the breast, through the side and through the right arm. It seems strange that Loving was not hit, except a slight scratch on the hand, as the two men were so close together that their pistols almost touched each other. Eleven shots were fired, six by Loving and five by Richardson. Richardson only lived a few moments after the shooting. Loving was placed in jail to await the verdict of the coroner's jury, which was 'self defense', and he was released. Richardson has no

Above: *The interior of the Long Branch saloon at Dodge City. In place of TV's 'Miss Kitty' one finds an all-male domain. The angle of the photograph clearly shows how much room was taken up by the bar.*

Below: *A famous street scene that was the basis for the present-day 'Front Street' recreation at Dodge City. Clearly visible is another street view of the Long Branch and Beatty & Kelley's saloon facing the tracks.*

relatives in this vicinity. He was from Wisconsin. About twenty-eight years old.

Together will all the better class of our community we greatly regret this terrible affair. We do not believe it is a proper way to settle difficulties, and we are positive it is not according to any law, human or divine. But if men must continue to persist in settling their disputes with fire arms we would be in favor of the dueling system, which would not necessarily endanger the lives of those who might be passing up or down the street attending to their own business.

We do not know that there is cause to censure the police, unless it be to urge upon them the necessity of strictly enforcing the ordinance preventing the carrying of concealed weapons. Neither of these men had a right to carry such weapons. Gamblers, as a class, are desperate men. They consider it necessary in their business that they keep up their fighting reputations, and never take a bluff. On no account should they be allowed to carry deadly weapons . . .

In establishing the lurid details of the fight, the *Globe* cited several witnesses. Adam Jack-son, the bartender in the Long Branch, claimed that Richardson was on his way out of the saloon when Loving came in:

> Richardson turned and followed him back into the house. Loving sat down on the hazard table. Richardson came and sat near him on the same table. Then Loving immediately got up, making some remark to Richardson, could not understand what it was. Richardson was sitting on the table at the time, and Loving standing up. Loving says to Richardson: 'If you have anything to say about me why don't you come and say it to my face like a gentleman, and not to my back, you dam[n] son of a bitch.' Richardson then stood up and said: 'You wouldn't fight anything you dam[n] —' could not hear the rest. Loving said 'you try me and see'. Richardson pulled his pistol first, and Loving also drew a pistol. Three or four shots were fired when Richardson fell by the billiard table. Richardson did not fire after he fell. He fell on his hands and knees. No shots were fired after Richardson fell. No persons were shooting except the two mentioned. Loving's pistol snapped twice and I think Richardson shot twice before Loving's pistol was discharged.

City marshal Charles E. Bassett testified that when the shooting started he was at Beatty & Kelley's saloon. He ran to the Long Branch and was on time to witness the remarkable sight of both men running around the billiard table, then the stove, shooting at each other.

> I got as far as the stove when the shooting had about ended. I caught Loving's pistol. Think there was two shots fired after I got into the room, and positive there was one. Loving fired that shot, to the best of my knowledge. Did not see Richardson fire any shot, and did not see him have a pistol. I examined the pistol which was shown me as the one Richardson had. It contained five empty shells. Richardson fell while I was there. Whether he was shot before or after I came in am unable to say. I think the shots fired after I came in were fired by Loving at Richardson. Richardson fell immediately after the shot I heard. Did not see any other person shoot at Richardson. Did not see Duffey take Richardson's pistol. Do not know whether Loving knew that Richardson's pistol had been taken away from him. There was considerable smoke in the room. Loving's pistol was a Remington, No. 44 and was empty after the shooting.

'Duffey' was William Duffey who testified that Loving fell at one point and he imagined that he had been shot. He then grabbed Richardson's pistol and recalled that there 'might have been a shot fired by one or the other while we were scuffling'. He added that he was not sure if Richardson had been shot or not, 'but think he had, as he was weak and I handled him easily'. He also stated that he thought that Loving was unaware that he had disarmed Richardson.

Bassett's reference to Loving's pistol as a 'Remington, No. 44' is confusing. It seems that the marshal was referring to is caliber – .44 Remington – rather than the weapon's serial number. Possibly it was the New Model Army revolver of 1875 that was chambered for the .44 Remington cartridge, or perhaps it was one of the thousands of original 1863 New Model Army percussion revolvers that the company began converting to center-fire ammunition during the early 1870s. Of greater significance, of course, is the extra-ordinary fact that two men, bent upon killing each other, could run around a billiard table and a stove in a crowded saloon, firing wildly. And that those shots that missed either antagonist also missed anyone else! But both men dispelled the vision of the cool, calm gunfighter of legend. Indeed, they let emotion rather than their heads rule the day. It was an outcome that surprised men versed not only in the art of gunplay, but familiar with both combatants. The coroner's jury's verdict was unanimous: 'The said Levi Richardson came to his death by a bullet wound from a pistol fired by Frank Loving in self defense.' Loving's own career following that fight was short-lived. He was killed at Trinidad, Colo-rado, in 1882 by John ('Jack') Allen, who him-self had been forced out of Dodge in 1876 fol-lowing a row with some Texans.

Texas witnessed a lot of violence, and she also exported a number of noted gun-toters.

On home ground, however, she still harbored a number of hard cases. El Paso, scene of several shoot-outs, paid host to several that are testimony to the reactions of men bent upon jealous revenge. On 14 April 1885, the city found itself virtually without law when the city marshal and the county sheriff, accompanied by deputies, were attending a murder trial in Presidio County. The marshal had left Charles M. ('Buck') Linn in charge. Linn, a former Texas Ranger, was at that time in charge of the city jail. Buck was regarded as a man to be depended upon just so long as he remained sober; but when drunk he was described as 'crazy.' Unfortunately, that was the night he chose to hit the bottle, and when he heard that Sam Gillespie, a friend of a man he is reported to have pistol whipped, was demanding that Buck be locked up and tried by a grand jury, he was furious. He sent word to Gillespie that he would shoot him on sight. Sam prudently armed himself and hid in a convenient doorway to wait, but Linn saw him and hesitated, then turned and hurried into the Gem saloon where he bumped into an old crony named William P. Raynor, described by some as 'the best-dressed bad man in Texas'. Raynor was an interesting character. By profession a gambler, he had also been employed as a Collector of Customs at Clinton, Texas, and later had served for a brief period on the El Paso police force, so he was well versed, as was Linn, in the finer points of gunplay.

Raynor, generally popular with most people, had a reputation for interfering in other people's affairs, and before long the pair were showing the effects of several hours of drinking in various saloons. George Look, an early day resident of El Paso who in later years compiled a personal memoir, recalled that the pair had a row in the Gem saloon with Bob Cahill, a young faro dealer. After Linn and Raynor parted, Look warned that there might be trouble, particularly when it became clear that both men had been having their drinks 'charged up on ice' when their money ran out. The peace of what appeared to be a quiet enough evening was then abruptly shattered as Raynor suddenly appeared at the entrance of a theater which adjoined the main bar room of the Gem saloon. The entertainment of soldiers relaxing on furlough was sharply curtailed by Raynor bawling out: 'Where is that son of a bitch who came to town tonight?' Most of the troopers hit the floor immediately; others escaped via the exit. At that moment Raynor noted that Look and the saloon's proprietor were themselves seated in the audience. Confused and embarrassed, he holstered his pistol, removed his hat, and bowed his way out. 'Excuse me, gentlemen – excuse me,' he apologized and was gone. Whoever it was that Raynor was looking for kept silent and hidden.

According to his biographer, Wyatt Earp was present on that occasion visiting his friend Lou Rickabaugh. This account claims that Raynor had tried to provoke Wyatt into a fight, which he declined. Raynor then started to insult a man standing at the bar sporting a white hat. Raynor's taunts ceased when the man known as Robert ('Cowboy Bob') Ren-

nick assured him that he was unarmed. Disgusted, Raynor left the bar, leaving Rennick fuming. His reputation had been insulted and he determined to get even. He walked across to the faro dealer and asked to borrow a pistol, stating that he would not be imposed on. The dealer shook his head: 'Have no trouble – go on out.' Ignoring him, Rennick reached into the drawer and grabbed the dealer's pistol.

It was just as well for him that he did, for the door burst open and Raynor rushed in, firing wildly. Rennick, with remarkable coolness, dropped to one knee, cocked the pistol, and holding it firmly in both hands, opened fire, cocked and fired again, hitting Raynor first in the shoulder and then in his stomach. Raynor, dazed and numbed by the shock of the heavy lead slugs, continued to shoot, ruining a billiard table with his final shots, before turning away and staggering into the street where he clambered on to a passing street car and collapsed across a seat. Passengers heard him mumble that his mother should be informed that he had 'died game'.

Rennick apeared in the doorway of the Gem saloon but he took no further action. What is more, he followed George Look's advice and left town, slipping over the border to Ciudad Juarez. Furious at the demise of his partner, Linn searched every saloon for the hapless Cahill, convinced that the faro dealer with whom he and Raynor had rowed earlier in the evening was responsible. Stuart Lake has credited Wyatt Earp with the advice to the worried Cahill, who was no gunfighter, to get himself

'heeled', to have his gun cocked and not to shoot until he was ready. He advised him, too, to aim low, for the belly. When Linn eventually burst through the door of Cahill's saloon, gun in his hand, the denouement was swift. Responding to Linn's opening fire deliberately and with great coolness Cahill aimed his pistol and fired twice. One ball struck Linn in the heart and he was dead before he hit the floor, ironically almost exactly where Raynor had earlier been shot. It was now Cahill's turn to flee across the border where he joined Rennick.

Raynor lived for several days. Some reports claimed that Rennick had expressed the wish that someone should have killed him years ago, but hastily added that 'if Bill gets well, what I said don't go'. Soon after Raynor's death Rennick and Cahill returned to El Paso where they were acquitted on a plea of 'self-defense'.

El Paso also witnessed the exploits of one of Texas's most publicised peace officers, and a man who but for the demon drink might well have joined the ranks of the immortals. Dallas Stoudenmire was not a native Texan, but a Southerner nonetheless, having been born at Aberfoil, Alabama, on 11 December 1845. He came from a large family and is reported to have joined the Confederate army in 1862, surviving the war despite several severe wounds. Having tried a stint as a farmer near Columbus, Texas, he finally took the plunge and enlisted in Company A of the Frontier Battalion of the Texas Rangers. His service papers describe him as being six feet two inches tall, with hazel eyes, auburn

hair, and others recalled that he had a broad, pale face, and a 'granite jaw'. As a Ranger he proved very effective, but there were those who were concerned about his attitude. Utterly fearless, Stoudenmire, if provoked or convinced that he was right, could kill without compunction – characteristics judged by some to be necessary when upholding the law in a lawless society, but by others to suggest a mad dog on a leash.

When Stoudenmire arrived there in 1881, El Paso was a curious mixture of old and new. Its proximity to Mexico (Paso del Norte, later to be renamed Ciudad Juarez, was separated from El Paso by the Rio Grande River), and the anti-Mexican attitude of many of its predominently white population, boosted by the fact that there were was little law enforcement, created problems on both sides of the river.

Stoudenmire at that time was marshal of Socorro, New Mexico, where his reputation with a gun was already known. Since leaving the Rangers he had been involved in several shoot-outs, some on a personal basis, and the others in an official capacity. His brother-in-law, Doc Cummings, was the proprietor of the Globe Restaurant in El Paso and is believed to have been responsible for persuading Dallas to come to the place. Just prior to his arrival there had been a dispute with Mexicans over the shooting of a Mexican peddler by Americans, some of whom had escaped back across the border. Others had been captured and jailed. Aided by some friendly prostitutes, the men had been helped to escape, but had been killed

Left: *The Overland Building, corner of El Paso and Overland Street. The Texas Rangers headquartered here when in town, and it was to where George Campbell was carried. He died there the next morning.*

Above: *Dallas Stoudenmire photographed when Marshal of El Paso (badge prominently displayed). He cuts a fine figure. No pistols show for he carried them in specially made hip pockets. He also carried a 'belly gun'.*

Below: *The Mexican jail at Paso del Norte in 1880. From here a number of Texans escaped after being jailed over the shooting of a peddler. They tried to cross the Rio Grande, but were gunned down,*

SPENCER RIFLES AND CARBINES

According to the report by Brigadier James W. Ripley, Chief of Ordnance to the Secretary of War in 1864, the Spencer rifles and carbines were the 'cheapest' and most 'durable, and most efficient' of the many arms at the time in use by the Union forces. Its reputation among cavalry regiments was reknowned. This seven-shot weapon, fitted with a Blakeslee quick-loader, was designed so that the ammunition was contained in a tube set into the stock. It took a matter of seconds to remove a tube and replace it. More than 90,000 carbines were purchased during the Civil War and, following the conflict, the Spencer enjoyed a great frontier reputation. In 1865, the company introduced a .50 caliber version, complete with a magazine cut-off that enabled it to be used as a single-shot weapon if required. Issued to various cavalry regiments, including the Seventh, the Spencer was considered to be the finest weapon of its type then available.

What the Spencer lacked in magazine capacity compared with the Winchester, it made up for by being easier to carry and faster to load. In 1874 the Spencer was superseded by the Springfield Model 1873, a single-shot carbine in .45-70 caliber capable of firing twelve or thirteen rounds a minute. Poor ammunition and lack of proper means of removing jammed cases led to the disaster at the Little Bighorn. Had the Spencer been used, it may well have saved lives.

1. Spencer caliber .36 light sporting rifle (s.n. 15).
2. Spencer caliber .44 light carbine (s.n. 5).
3. Spencer U.S. Navy contract caliber .36-56 military rifle (s.n. 121).
4. Four rounds of Spencer caliber .56-52 rimfire ammunition.
5. Spencer U.S. Army caliber .56-56 military carbine (s.n. 30670), carried at the battle of the Little Bighorn by a Cheyenne warrior.
6. Spencer U.S. Army Model 1865 caliber .56-50 military carbine (s.n. 5909).
7. Spencer caliber .56-56 rimfire cartridges.
8. Spencer caliber .56-46 sporting rifle (s.n. 17444).
9. Seven round tubular magazine for Spencer rifles and carbines.
10. Spencer caliber .38 prototype sporting rifle (no s.n.).
11. Spencer caliber .56-50 carbine (s.n. oblit-erated), rebarreled to a sporting rifle.
12. Spencer caliber .56-46 sporting rifle (no s.n.).
13. Spencer caliber .56-56 carbine (s.n. 35862), rebarreled to caliber .56-50 by John Gemmer of St Louis under S. Hawken's stamp.
14. Pair of typical Western saddle bags which might carry loose ammunition.

(Artifacts courtesy of Buffalo Bill Historical Center, Cody, Wyoming.)

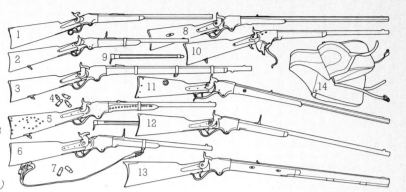

by a Mexican armed with a rifle as they struggled through the water to escape. This led to a revenge attack by some of the citizens, but the locals were more concerned with establishing law and order within city limits.

Among the early peace officers appointed by the city council was George W. Campbell, a native of Greenup County, Kentucky, who was born on 23 December 1850, and went West in the middle 1870s, eventually arriving in Texas where he served for a time as a deputy sheriff. Later, on the recommendation of the Texas Rangers, he was appointed marshal of El Paso on 1 December 1880. But George, like his predecessors and his successors, had problems with the local mayor, Solomon Schutz, who seems to have run things pretty much his own way. When Mexicans were arrested, he sought to drop the charges. In his biography of Campbell, *El Paso Lawman*, Fred R. Egloff suggests that this was because Schutz did not wish to upset his Mexican customers both sides of the border. There is some suggestion that to supplement his income, Campbell 'shook down' the local gamblers and brothel keepers. Word was that the Rangers intervened and Campbell resigned, but in effect the Rangers had interceded to assist Campbell. He actually left office when he and the mayor fell out over the non-payment of back pay and expenses. His departure from office led to a wave of lawlessness that involved the Rangers.

Dallas Stoudenmire became marshal of El Paso on 11 April 1881, following the enforced resignation of his predecessor Bill Johnson, whom many considered to be an alcoholic. Within days of Stoudenmire's appointment, there was a major upset between the Mexicans and Americans. A number of Mexican cattle had been driven across the border and were found on John Hale's ranch. It was alleged that he and the Manning brothers, Frank and Jim, were involved with him. The major, anxious to keep in with his Mexican customers, gave them the right to carry arms on Texas soil, which caused an uproar. On the way to the Hale ranch some of the Mexicans were ambushed and murdered. Once news of this reached Mexico, more armed men came over and Gus Krempkau, a Spanish-speaking constable at El Paso, was called in to act as an interpreter. An inquest was opened and adjourned and the Mexicans recrossed the border bearing their dead. But behind them they left a simmering resentment both over the deaths and the decision to allow so many armed Mexicans into the area.

Mr Egloff learned much of Campbell's part in El Paso's early history from his family and surviving correspondence. He also discovered that Campbell's hometown newspaper carried an account of what happened to George Campbell following the inquest and it gives us another insight into the activities of Dallas Stoudenmire. George's brother Abe visited El Paso to learn more of his brothers death, and in May 1881 the *Ashland Independent* carried a letter from him which gave a resume of the cause and the outcome. His report disclosed a campaign to blacken characters or distort the facts. Tradition as-

Above: *George W. Campbell photographed at Ironton, Ohio, in 1877 aged 27. The plate was made during a trip to his home. Largely ignored by historians, George was highly regarded by his contemporaries.*

serts that following the inquest Campbell was drunk and yelling that Stoudenmire should have arrested the Mexicans. When Krempkau appeared on the street, Campbell abused him, but Gus ignored the tirade. At that moment John Hale, the worse for liquor, leapt to his feet, drew his pistol and ran at Krempkau, ordered Campbell out of the way and shot Krempkau through the lungs. Realizing his action, he jumped behind a pillar. At that moment, Stoudenmire arrived, took in the situation and opened fire, killing an innocent Mexican bystander. But his next shot hit Hale right between the eyes. Campbell, meanwhile was yelling that he was not involved. The dying Krempkau pulled his pistol, cocked it and put a ball through Campbell's wrist, forcing him to change his pistol to his left hand; Gus's next shot hit him in the foot. Stoudenmire then joined in and brought Campbell down, who in his dying moment accused the marshal of murdering him. The Rangers, however, who had stood by during the shooting, later stated that they believed that Stoudenmire had had the situa-

tion under control. The *Independent* article, however, gives us reason for doubt.

When reviewing the events that led to the shooting, Abe admitted that there was evidence of a dispute between Campbell and Krempkau, but that Campbell had been trying to avoid gunplay, especially when Hale interceded and opened fire. It was Krempkau or Hale who hit Campbell in the foot, and Stoudenmire who hit him in the arm, after he had shot the innocent Mexican and then blown Hale's brains out. As Campbell tried to grasp his pistol with his left hand Stoudenmire shot him again. 'This was about six o'clock, P.M. and he died about five o'clock the next morning. He was perfectly rational up to the second before he died. He made his dying declaration in the presence of the State's Attorney, in which he stated the facts as I have given them above. Said that he did not want to have any difficulty, and that he understood Knowcamp [Krempkau] to accept the explanation.'

Follow-up reports in the Western press further confused the issue, and there are a number of unanswered questions. Egloff raises the point that Dallas was not charged with murder which may have been because the mayor and council were anxious to get rid of Campbell, so they backed their own man, Stoudenmire.

Above: *This photograph of George Campbell and Jim Manning was made in 1881. George had no quarrel with the Mannings. Rather, he kept in with them as he did others among the sporting set. His ivory stocked Colt .45 is worn butt forward as was still common at the time. The pistol still exists and is now owned by a member of his family. Its serial number is 22459 which means it was manufactured in 1875.*

Dallas himself continued in office, where his presence and reputation kept the lid on. His armament was a pair of .44 Smith & Wesson .44 caliber No. 3 'American' pistols, silver-plated and ivory stocked, which he carried in specially made leather-lined hip pockets. He also carried a 'belly gun', a .44 Richards-Mason conversion of the Colt 1860 Army revolver, the barrel cut down to about two inches.

Late in the evening of 17 April, Bill Johnson tried to ambush Stoudenmire as he and Cummings took an evening stroll, but was himself shot dead by both men. Eight bullets were found in his body. Others are reported to have joined in but missed. For his part, Stoudenmire blamed the Manning family but could not prove it. His handling of the situation in El Paso met with general approval, but the strain began to tell and he took to drink. Soon after, he was reported to be planning marriage and during his absence on honeymoon James B. Gillett, a deputy marshal, took over (the same Gillett who later made a name for himself as a Texas Ranger). Cummings made the mistake of falling out with the Mannings and was shot dead in a saloon fight.

On his return, Dallas declared open war on the Mannings. The city council interceded and persuaded both sides to make peace but the strain took its toll, and Dallas again took to drink. He ultimately resigned, his place being taken by Gillett. On 18 September 1882, Dallas decided the time had come to have a showdown with the Mannings, claiming that they had put the word about that he wanted a fight. He found two of the brothers in the Coliseum, Jim standing beside the bar and Felix (known as 'Doc') playing billiards. Brother Frank was summoned. 'Doc' and Dallas got into a slanging match, and Walt Jones, who had accompanied Dallas to make sure there were no problems, tried to intervene and Dallas pushed him aside, a fatal mistake. 'Doc' pulled his .44 double-action and fired, the ball smashing into Stoudenmire's pocket book. Again Manning fired and this time he hit Dallas in the left breast. Now severely wounded, Dallas managed to draw one of his own pistols and shot Manning in the right arm above the elbow, causing him to drop his pistol. Pluckily Manning threw himself against Dallas before he could fire a second time, and locked together the pair staggered about in a *danse macabre* until they fell into the street. At that point, Jim arrived armed with a .45. His first shot thudded harmlessly into barber's pole, but he took careful aim for the second one and blew Stoudenmire's brains out. Doc Manning, free from Stoudenmire's embrace, grabbed one of his pistols and started to beat the now lifeless body around the head, before he was finally pulled off.

The inquest found that Jim acted in self-defense to protect his 'unarmed' brother and no further action was taken. Old-timers, however, were adamant in their view: a bullet may have been the instrument, but it was alcohol that destroyed Dallas Stoudenmire. He was considered to be a man who, in his better moments, had deserved his good reputation.

'WALK 'N DRAW'

Tradition asserts that gunfighters approached gunfights in the manner of duelists – face-to-face and firing on a given signal, or on the command of one of them. This over-simplification has remained a constant feature of film and fiction for more than a century. Few Hollywood-style gunfights took place, and those that did were not quite as the storytellers might wish. Perhaps the one gunfight that best illustrates the face-to-face, 'walk 'n draw' encounter took place at Springfield, Missouri, on Friday 21 July 1865, between Wild Bill Hickok and Davis K. Tutt. The pair were reported to have been friends for some time, but had fallen out the day before over a game of cards. Both men believed that they were in the right and were prepared to back their opinions with pistols if necessary.

Although James Butler Hickok was generally known in southwest Missouri and parts of Arkansas as 'Wild Bill', he had yet to establish the reputation he eventually achieved on the plains. He won the name of 'Wild Bill' as a result of his activities during the Civil War as a Union Army scout, detective and spy. He was admired by most of the officers he had worked for, and had a number of friends within the city. Tutt, on the other hand, was not well known and even today is obscure. In his youth, Dave became embroiled in the Tutt–Everett feud that clouded the horizon for some years, and led to his own father's death. When the Civil War broke out the family were living at Yellville, Arkansas. Here Dave enlisted in the First Regiment, McBride's Brigade, Arkansas (Confederate) Infantry, early in 1862. Military records indicate that he served only one year with the regiment before being detached to the quartermaster's department as a brigade wagonmaster in 1863. Confederate military records (such as exist) contain no further information. The question then is: when did he meet Hickok and where? It was understood that the pair had been acquainted for some years, which suggests either that Dave changed sides or got to know Hickok when the latter was himself working behind enemy lines. Hickok also spent some time at Yellville, which might explain the connection. Early in 1865, Dave had brought his mother, a sister and a half-brother to Springfield, which would suggest late pro-Union sympathies on their part.

The fateful card game that led to the pair falling out took place in the old Lyon House or Southern Hotel. Tutt is reported to have lost a lot of money to Wild Bill and he reminded Hickok of a forty dollar debt he owed him for a horse trade. Hickok paid up, but when Tutt said he still owed him thirty-five dollars from a previous game, Wild Bill claimed it was only twenty-five. Dave then reached across the table and picked up Hickok's prized Waltham watch, said to have been a present from his mother. In later years, the Tutt family was to claim that the watch was in fact Dave's, and it was Hickok who picked it up! This conflicts with the evidence given at the trial and penned by Colonel Albert Barnitz, post commander at Springfield, on the day of the shooting. Tutt made it known that he would wear the watch next day on Public Square, despite Wild Bill's suggestion that this was an unhealthy decision.

Accounts of what happened on 21 July are as numerous as the allegations that led to the shoot-out, but the simple facts are that at about 6 p.m., as Hickok walked on to the square from the direction of the Lyon House, Tutt appeared beside the court house. Both men pulled their pistols and, while still on the move, opened fire. Colonel George Ward Nichols, who first publicised the fight nationwide in an article on 'Wild Bill' published in *Harper's New Monthly Magazine* for February 1867, gave the distance between them as both 'fifty paces' and 'fifty yards', a distance that dispels much of the mystique of a face-to-face conflict. Nevertheless, within hours of the shoot-out, Colonel Barnitz, who witnessed the fight from the balcony of the Lyon House where he had his headquarters, wrote in his journal that both men 'fired simultaneously, as it appeared to me, at a distance of about 100 paces. "Tut" [*sic*] was shot directly through the chest . . . ' Colonel Barnitz also confirmed that the fight was over cards and that Tutt had provoked Hickok.

It says much for Hickok's marksmanship that he could hit a moving target (and one that was firing back) at such a distance with an awesome accuracy. The pistol he used has been a controversy in itself. Some writers have claimed that he shot Tutt with a .44 Colt Dragoon and actually rested it on a hitching-post to steady his aim. Others alleged that the pistol was a .32 caliber Smith & Wesson No. 2 Army revolver. The actual weapon was a .36 caliber Colt's Navy pistol: Wild Bill carried two of them, worn butts forward in holsters attached to a military belt. Colonel Nichols also noted that his waist was 'girthed by a belt which held two of Colt's Navy revolvers'. The recent discovery of a photograph made at the time clearly shows Wild Bill with his Navy pistols, worn as described.

Below: *The old Greene County courthouse at Springfield, Mo., circa 1865. From this point Dave Tutt stepped out to meet Wild Bill for the last time. A chance shot (?) or deadly accuracy at 100 paces ended his career.*

Right: *The original print of this photograph of Wild Bill is a* cartes-de-visite *by Wilbur Blakeslee of Mendota, Ill., where Hickok appeared in 1869, en route from the plains to his mother's home at nearby Troy Grove.*

Some have dismissed Hickok's heart shot at such a distance as luck and they may be right, but they do an injustice to the pistol. Despite the reams of nonsense written about both marksmanship and the miraculous accuracy of the old-time gunfighters, the real answer lay in their pistols. The Navy was sighted in for about sixty yards, but in the hands of an expert it is accurate up to about two hundred yards, that is to say with carefully *aimed* shots. The ball itself has been known to go as far as 600 yards, but at that distance would be totally ineffective. The only drawback to the Navy (and weapons of like caliber) was its comparatively small size (equivalent to the modern .38) and limited stopping power. This problem was encountered in India during the Mutiny of 1857 when maddened Sepoys sometimes took all six bullets from a Navy before expiring, by which time they had occasionally cut down the pistoleer. To rectify this problem, Colt's London Agency shipped out a large number of Dragoons, and these, in company with the big .442 Adams pistols (and a limited number of the company's .50 caliber 'Dragoon' pistols), proved to be very effective. Even out West, it was claimed that when used in combat with Indians the Colt Dragoon was the preferred weapon. Nevertheless, the West produced a few situations where the smaller calibered pistols failed to work. As a result, close encounters of the revolver kind were often fatal.

Following the Tutt fight, Barnitz had Hickok arrested and handed over to the civilian authorities, and he was promptly charged with murder, later reduced to manslaughter. On 5 August Hickok went on trial. The judge went to great lengths to explain the law in respect of self-defense, and how it was not a plea if the defendant had intimated that he was prepared to fight rather than avoid any conflict. He also dismissed testimony which repeated hearsay claims that Tutt had threatened Hickok. The jury, however, decided that Hickok did act in self-defense and acquitted him.

Reaction among the citizens was mixed. Barnitz advised his wife that opinion was equally divided between Hickok and Tutt, but the press was adamant that street shoot-outs had to be discouraged. On 10 August the *Missouri Weekly Patriot* complained that the jury only took ten minutes to reach a verdict, but that the 'general dissatisfaction felt by the citizens of this place with the verdict in no way attaches to our able and efficient Circuit attorney, nor to the Court . . . Those who censure the jury for what they regarded as a disregard of their obligations to the public interest, and a proper respect for their oaths, should remember that they are partly to blame themselves.'

The editor then went on to suggest that the citizens of the town were 'shocked and terrified' at the thought that a man could arm himself and lie in wait for his victim, with the connivance of cronies anxious to see bloodshed, yet failed to 'express the horror and disgust they felt, not from indifference, but from fear and timidity.' This comment must have come as a surprise not only to Hickok (who like many others had walked around the place for several years armed with one or two revolvers and other weapons) but also to those citizens who had endured four years of war without feeling terrorised by the sight of armed men.

BURGESS, WHITNEY VARIENTS

Andrew Burgess was a prolific inventor who, in 1873 and 1875, patented a lever action for rifles that also included features patented by G.W. Morse in 1856. He contracted with Eli Whitney, Jr. (whose company had made Sam Colt's Walker pistols back in 1847) to produce a magazine lever-rifle that competed with the Winchester. The venture was not a success and in the mid-1880s Colt also manufactured an improved Burgess lever-

action rifle. Tradition has it that Winchester threatened to produce revolvers if Colt continued to manufacture the Burgess. Production stopped! Whitney, however, did produce other lever-action weapons, notably the Whitney-Kennedy series (one such was owned by Billy the Kid).

The Whitney range of lever-action rifles was designed for frontier or sporting rather than military use, and an estimated 20,000 such rifles were made. Like the Winchester arms, the carbine version had a 20-inch barrel, and the rifle a 24-inch

barrel. The company also produced several bolt-action models designed for military use, but none was purchased by the Ordnance Department. However, it is reported that a number of these latter arms also found favor in Central and South America. In 1886, the company introduced another lever-action rifle, based on William A. Scharf's patent which looked uncannily like the Winchester Model 1873. But it was too late to save their dwindling finances; in 1888 Whitney sold out to Winchester.

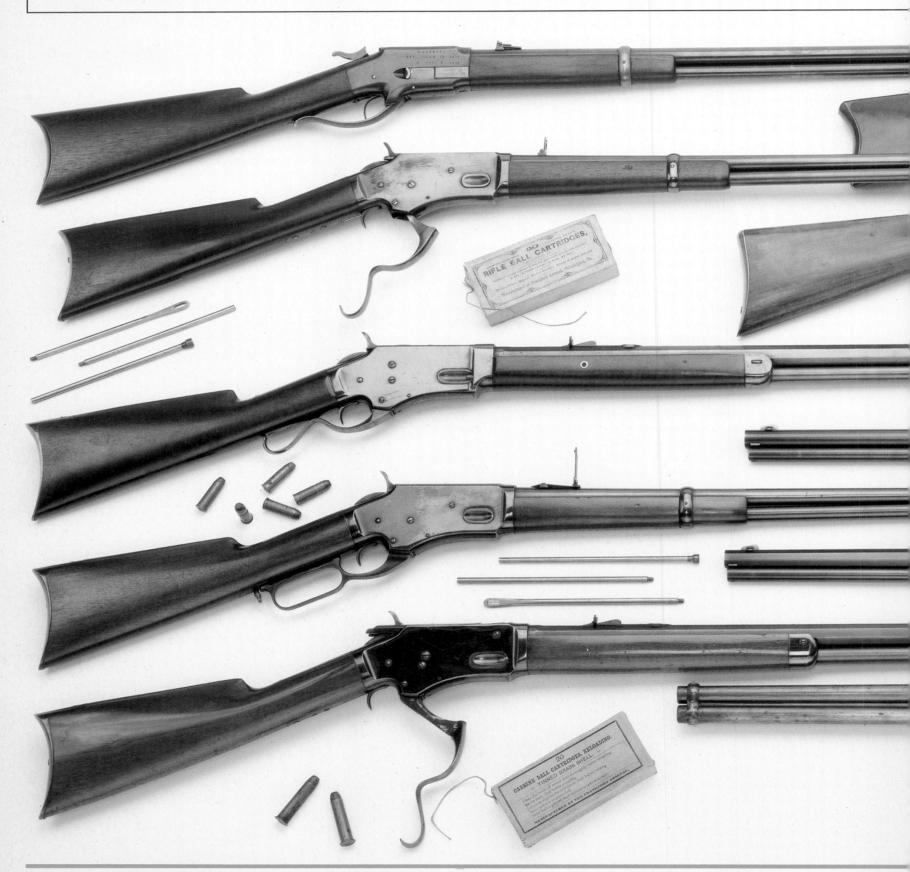

1. Whitney-Burgess carbine in .40 caliber.
2. Whitney-Kennedy lever-action carbine showing the 'S' lever on early models.
3. Three-part cleaning rod for the above carbine.
4. A box of .45 caliber 'Rifle Cartridges'.
5. A Whitney-Burgess-Morse lever-action rifle in .44 caliber.
6. Its ammunition. Cartridges were called 'shells' out West.
7. Whitney-Kennedy carbine fitted with a full loop lever.
8. Cleaning rod for the above weapon.
9. Whitney-Kennedy rifle in .40-60 caliber.
10. .40-60 cartridges for the above rifle.
11. Whitney-Scharf lever-action hunting rifle. It was sold in .32-20, .38-40 and .44-40 cals.
12. Hunting rifle cartridges.
13. Another version of the sporting rifle.
14. Government 'loads'.
15. Typical Stetson type broad-brimmed hat.
16. Colt-Burgess lever-action rifle.
17. Cleaning rod for the Colt-Burgess rifle.
18. Colt Lightning slide-operated rifle. Colt produced a number of variants of this rifle.
19. Remington-Keene magazine bolt-action rifle in .45-79 caliber.

(Artifacts courtesy of Buffalo Bill Historical Center, Cody, Wyoming.)

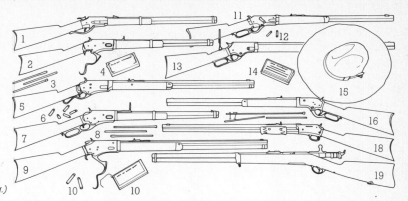

Above: *Ellsworth in 1879 was beginning to lose its 'shacks and tents' image and assume respectability denied it during the hectic 1860s and its cowtown period. Still dominant are the railroad tracks dividing the place.*

Within months of the shooting, whatever animosity there might have been disappeared. Hickok became the focus of much attention, and his write up in *Harper's* not only gave him nationwide fame but established the tradition of the Western gunman's role as a latter-day duelist.

Understandably, gunfights were never welcomed in populated areas, and while it was also true that such drastic action was an expedient means of ridding the place of unwanted or dangerous individuals, its effect could be demoralizing and certainly dangerous to others if the shooting got out of hand. In an environment where most people either went armed or had access to pistols or other weapons, there was always the danger of community shoot-outs. This problem was addressed very early by both cattle towns and other boom towns. Ordinances against the use and carrying of firearms within city limits were passed but frequently ignored. In 1868, a year after it was founded, Ellsworth, already worried by the violence in its midst that threatened to engulf the place (a fact that was almost gleefully publicised in the newspapers of rival townships), feared the worst. But it was 1870 before it got around to tackling the problem in earnest. On 1 April 'Ordinance No. 1' included a section devoted to firearms, with particular attention to places where their use was strictly prohibited. The ordinance was very specific in its definition of just where the inhabitants of Ellsworth could or could not 'burst a cap and burn powder'. Other towns tried similar legislation with varying results. Only when the cowtown era ended did they claim any real success, by which time the age of the six-shooter was also a thing of the past. Meanwhile, fines took care of most of those who would rather pay up than disarm. It was an ongoing problem, however, and one that was not helped by individuals who, perhaps dismissed from the police force for some reason or other, willfully disobeyed the roles and continued to carry arms.

John ('Happy Jack') Morco, whose activities during the disturbances at Ellsworth which led to the death of Chauncey Whitney at the hands of Billy Thompson have already been noted, was generally regarded as an obnoxious individual, and was the particular 'hate' of the Texans. His demeanor was such that most of the people he encountered shunned him, which is perhaps why some wag named him 'Happy Jack'. One wonders why such a character should have been employed by the police force in the first place, but few cowtowns were that fussy when they feared 'cowboy chaos' and leapt at someone who might be tough enough to stand up to them. Following his dismissal from the police force, Morco went to Salina, but returned to the city where he paraded about attached to a pair of 'ivory-handled' six-shooters. His presence was unwelcome and he was advised to disarm or leave town. Morco chose to stay, which was a mistake on his part.

Following some quite disastrous appointments to the police force following the Thompson brothers episode, J. Charles Brown, a former farm boy from Illinois who had proved himself an able assistant marshal, was elected city marshal of Ellsworth. He was very familiar with Morco's personality and had been personally involved in a dispute over the two pistols that he carried. It was claimed that when Jack left Ellsworth following his dismissal from the police force on 27 August, he took with him a pair of pistols valued at $100 which belonged to John Good. A telegram was despatched to Salina, and when the train on which Morco was traveling stopped at the depot the police boarded it and arrested him. Good and Brown followed and gave some testimony before returning to Ellsworth. Morco had pleaded that the pistols were his, and without them his life would be worthless, for he had made many enemies among the Texans. Before returning to Ellsworth, Brown advised Jack to keep on the move and away from Ellsworth but for reasons best known to himself Morco followed on the next train.

When word reached police headquarters that Morco was back and armed, and boasting that he would 'make away' with anyone who upset him, Marshal Brown realized that he had trouble on his hands. On the evening of 4 September, Brown confronted Morco and ordered him to disarm. Morco refused. Some reports have him offering resistance to arrest, others that he tried to draw his pistols on the marshal, but the outcome was that Brown shot him through the heart. Morco's death was viewed with a sense of relief by most people. His wife, from whom he had been separated for some years, happened to be in town with a theatrical troupe when he died, and she stated that he had a habit of boosting his own image. Of the 'twelve' men he claimed to have killed, his wife said she only knew of four, and they were men who had come to her assistance when he was beating her up in a drunken rage.

Any feelings of remorse Marshal Brown might have had following the shooting of Happy Jack was swiftly dispelled by the editor of the Ellsworth *Reporter* who remarked on 11 September 1873:

Happy Jack is gone, and considering his manner of going, we can think of him only as 'Poor Jack!'

The Coroner's inquest over the body of 'Happy Jack' decided that 'John Morco came to his death from the effects of two bullet wounds, discharged from a six-shooter in the hands of Chas. Brown, a police officer of the city of Ellsworth, in self defense, while in discharge of his duty, and was justified in the act'.

*

Below: *Ed Schieffelin, whose discovery of silver led to the establishment of Tombstone, dressed in a woolen shirt, neckerchief, sombrero, kneeboots, and armed with a Sharps, looks the part of a typical prospector.*

Below: *Richard Gird at left; Al Shieffelin, center, and Ed at the right, photographed some time after Ed discovered the silver outcropping that led to a silver strike and eventually the settlement of Tombstone.*

Above: *This photograph of Tombstone was made by C. S. Fly, circa 1885. But for the O.K. Corral fight in 1881, Tombstone might have been abandoned years ago. It is now a tourist attraction, said to be 'too tough to die'.*

Gunfights between 'consenting adults' or outlaws and lawmen were considered the norm, but when politics came into it, it also involved factions. Such a situation existed in Tombstone, Arizona, when the Earps, Clantons and McLaurys swapped lead outside the O.K. Corral, to settle a dispute that was to become the most famous gunfight of them all.

In 1877, Edward L. Schieffelin discovered a rich silver outcropping in the San Pedro Valley, some seventy miles southeast of Tucson, Arizona Territory. Legend asserts that when

Ed and his brother Al, and a close friend named Richard Gird, started prospecting some prophesied that all they would find would be tombstones. True or not, that was the name given to the Tombstone Mining District and ultimately to the town that sprang up. It attracted all kinds of people; would-be miners, gamblers, prostitutes, speculators and a breed of men who get little attention in the history books but whose activities often led to conflict. These were the land or townsite speculators. In more recent years the differences between

individuals and the eternal battles between 'cowboy rustlers' and the ranchers has also focused attention upon those who engaged in land grabs. Tombstone seems to have had its fill of them.

By 1881, Tombstone had a population of about 10,000 people. Following disputes with the land grabbers the populace had been granted incorporation and the town was the seat of the newly created Cochise County. It also boasted two newspapers, the *Tombstone Epitaph* and the *Nuggett*. Despite these apparent signs of civilization, the lawlessness in and around the place was known nationwide and, following the gunfight at the O.K. Corral, President Chester Arthur in 1882 threatened the place with martial law. But this was in the future when Wyatt Earp, his brother Virgil and younger brother James arrived there on 1 December 1879. Virgil, who had achieved some fame on his own account as a policeman, had been appointed as a deputy U.S. marshal for the Tombstone area in November by the U.S. marshal for Arizona Territory, Crawley P. Dake. If Virgil was the real leader of the Earp clan, it was Wyatt who dominated it.

Wyatt Earp's cattle town experiences were such that he was well known in Kansas, but not elsewhere, and some indication of his current reputation can be gleaned from comments in the Kansas press following his resignation from the Dodge City police force in September 1879. He went first to Las Vegas and from there to Tombstone. The *Ford County Globe* of 30 March 1880, reported that Wyatt had recently sold a mine in Tombstone for 'thirty thousand dollars. The mine is called the "Cooper Lode" and is not worked at present owing to the quality of foul air that has accumulated in the shaft . . .' Earp was then joined by other ex-Dodgeites. He soon established himself in the community. He found employment with Wells Fargo & Company as a shotgun messenger and was later appointed a deputy sheriff of Pima County. Soon, the Earp clan was joined by Doc Holliday and assorted wives and mistresses, and later by Morgan Earp, considered by many to be the 'hot-head' of the family.

In Tombstone, Wyatt also had an 'interest' in the Oriental saloon and a faro table at its rival the Eagle Brewery. The Earps soon made their presence felt, and they were also aware of the undercurrent of political pull that existed in the place, although there is no evidence of their involvement in anything but local politics where Wyatt had put himself up as a candidate for sheriff. Unfortunately the Democrat John Behan won, which did not sit well with the Republican Wyatt, a state of affairs that had repercussions later.

On a broader front, however, there was the matter of local attitudes both to people and the law. The local ranchers resented the influx of people lured to the area by gold and silver, and for their part the denizens of the gambling halls and saloons detested the ranchers and their belief that they owned Arizona. This led to a deep distrust and the threat of violence. The Earp faction was right in the middle, for besides Wyatt's role as a deputy sheriff (he served for a brief period) Virgil was city marshal. This led to open conflict with the notorious Clantons and McLaurys whose combined rancher–rustler activities were the talk of the territory. Yet they continued to obtain government contracts to feed the reservation Apaches (some alleged that the cattle for this purpose had been stolen from Mexicans).

Old Man Clanton, head of the 'clan', was a formidable character and had fathered three sons: Joseph Isiah ('Ike'); Phineas, and the youngest, Billy. The McLaurys consisted of Robert, Thomas and William Roland ('Frank'). Allied with both families was William C. Claiborne.

The Earps had little contact with the 'rustlers' until Wyatt lost a prized horse. He learned that Billy Clanton had it, but when challenged he admitted it was a mistake. However, when six mules disappeared from an Army post and Virgil was called in his capacity as a deputy U.S. marshal to track them down, things hotted up. Accompanied by Wyatt and a squad of soldiers, the posse discovered the animals at the McLaury ranch where they were about to obliterate the U.S. brands! Faced with the threat of prosecution, a trial and a possible trip to the state penitentiary, the McLaurys agreed to return the mules and pay restitution to the army. Unfortunately, soon after the posse left 'rustlers' turned up and drove the mules off. This sort of behavior, the robbing of stagecoaches and the appearance of Clantons and McLaurys as posse members did not lead to good relations. Matters were not improved either when it was rumored that Doc Holliday had also been engaged in stagecoach robbery, but this was not proved. To further complicate matters, Virgil upset county sheriff Behan when, in his capacity as a deputy U.S. marshal, he arrested two of his deputies, Frank Stillwell and Pete Spence, charging them with robbing stagecoaches.

Above: *Morgan Earp, younger brother of Wyatt, was normally a 'pleasant outgoing' man, but under stress was inclined to be hotheaded. He survived the 'Gunfight at the O.K. Corral' only to be gunned down in 1882.*

Above: *Virgil Earp, considered by many to be the leader of the Earp brothers at Tombstone. He was later ambushed and badly wounded. He later became city marshal of Colton, Cal., and died in 1905.*

Above: *Wyatt Earp, whose real and imaginary adventures have thrilled several generations of fans. But thanks to Stuart Lake's fictional biography, Wyatt remains a controversial figure. The real man was a* tough, decisive and shrewd individual, but considered by some to be a 'cold fish' devoid of any warmth. His career as a gunfighter was short. He later engaged in the saloon business; he died in 1929.

Morgan Earp was confronted on the street one day by Frank McLaury who suggested that they shoot it out, but he declined. Then on 25 October Ike Clanton fell foul of Holliday at a lunch counter in a saloon. Ike tried to back off, but Doc was 'on the prod'. 'Hey, you damn son of a bitch cowboy,' he called out, 'go get a gun and get to work.' He added a few other choice insults and claimed that Ike had been making threats against himself and his friends, which Ike denied. Ike, apparently, had also been accused of playing one side against the other, and it was rumored that Wyatt, when he had learned that Old Man Clanton had died and Ike was now head of the family, had tried to bribe Ike into divulging the names of the stage robbers. Wyatt, it was claimed, thought this information would help him in his bid for sheriff at the next election, and any reward monies would go to Ike. When this alleged arrangement became public, Ike claimed he had been set up, so there was no love lost on either side. Consequently, Ike was very unhappy when he was challenged by Holliday. Then Morgan appeared, and Ike all but ran out of the saloon, begging both men not to shoot him in the back. 'Go and get heeled,' Doc yelled after him.

On the morning of October 26, Ike appeared on the streets looking the worse for wear following a night of cards and boozing. Still in an alcoholic haze, he began mouthing threats against the Earps, and when he got his hands on a six-shooter and a rifle, someone thoughtfully suggested Wyatt should know. Wyatt promptly sought out Virgil and together they hunted up Ike. They found him in an alley, grabbed his rifle and as he went for his six-shooter, Virgil pulled it from his hand and struck him over the head with it. Ike collapsed to his knees, shaking his head. Virgil then placed him under arrest 'for carrying arms within city limits', and the brothers dragged him before the court. Here he was fined $25 for the offense. The Earps offered to pay his fine if he would fight but he declined, saying that he did not need encouragement; he would find them anywhere at any time and all he needed was 'four feet of ground'.

Outside the court house Wyatt entered into a slanging match with Tom McLaury which ended when Wyatt smacked Tom on the side of his head with the barrel of his pistol. Leaving the dazed and bleeding McLaury in the street, the Earps walked away. War had now been declared; everyone knew it was only a matter of time before shouts would lead to shots.

Advised that the combined Clanton and McLaury gang had stationed themselves

Below: *This view of Allen Street, Tombstone, is how it looked when Sheriff Behan was relaxing in a barber's chair when news of the pending shoot-out between the Earps and the Clantons sent him running.*

down at the O.K. Corral, the Earps knew that the showdown had come. Hearing of the situation, Doc Holliday hastily joined them, arming himself with his favorite shotgun, made by W. W. Greener of Birmingham, England. (Recently, however, it has been claimed that Doc carried a cutdown Meteor 10 gauge which he called his 'street howitzer'.) In his capacity as city marshal, Virgil was duty bound to avoid bloodshed if possible, but it is doubtful if that thought really crossed his mind.

Sheriff John Behan heard of the pending fracas as he sat in a barber's chair on Allen Street and hurried over to Hafford's saloon where the Earps were preparing themselves, urging Virgil to disarm rather than shoot it out. Virgil gave him no such assurance and Behan declared that he would disarm them himself. On the corner of Fremont Street he met Frank McLaury who assured the sheriff that he did not want a fight, but neither would he disarm. The pair then set off toward Fly's Photographic Gallery which was adjacent to the corral. There, Behan was assured by both Ike Clanton and Tom McLaury that neither was armed. In desperation Behan urged the others to give up their arms. 'Only if you disarm the Earps,' Frank McLaury said. Billy Clanton said he was anxious to go home, and Billy Claiborne declared that he had been trying to get them to leave town. Behan had almost talked them into accompanying him to his office when the

WYATT EARP

Endless debates have been conducted about what kind of guns were used by Wyatt Earp and his associates. Unfortunately, there is often an absence of clear evidence and specific weapons promoted as Earp guns often lack clear proof of their pedigrees. Some factors are certain. The preferred handgun was Colt, either in percussion or (post-1873) the single-action Army or Peacemaker. Reliable and well enough made to

withstand rough usage, it has been claimed that some lawmen (Earp included) 'buffaloed' would-be troublemakers by hitting them over the head or alongside the ear with the barrel.

Stuart Lake's biography of Earp established the story that Wyatt carried a Colt with an extra long barrel – 'the Buntline special'. Lake claimed that in 1876 Ned Buntline went to Dodge City and presented Earp, Bat Masterson, Neal Brown, Charles Bassett and Bill Tilghman with 'Specials' complete with

detachable carbine stocks.

The Colt company did and still does make Peacemakers with long barrels but there is no conclusive evidence to suggest that Buntline (or anyone else outside of Kansas) had heard of Wyatt Earp in 1876. Research by W.B. Shillingberg (*Wyatt Earp & the 'Buntline Special' Myth*) established that in 1929 Mr Lake was shown such a pistol and was so taken with it that he decided to equip his 'special hero' Wyatt Earp with a 'special pistol'.

1. Colt single-action .45 used by Doc Holliday. He told his nephew he carried this throughout his Western adventures.
2. Colt single-action .45 used by Wells Fargo detective Fred Dodge who claimed that Wyatt Earp borrowed the gun at the time Curly Bill Brocius was killed.
3. Colt single-action .44-40 used by John Clum while editor of the *Tombstone Epitaph* and during the capture of Geronimo.
4. Holster for Clum's Colt, purchased by him at Spangenburg gunsmith shop in Tombstone.
5. Web cartridge belt used by John Clum.
6. Diagram of Tombstone gunfight drawn by Wyatt Earp in later years.
7. Double-barrel shotgun reportedly used by Wyatt Earp to kill Frank Stilwell, one of the killers of Morgan Earp.
8. Factory holster for a long barrel Colt single-action.
9. Colt single-action .45 with extra long 16 in. barrel and adjustable rear sight.
10. Detachable shoulder stock for the long barrel Colt, used to convert the handgun into a handy carbine.

(Artifacts courtesy of Gene Autry Western Heritage Museum, Los Angeles, California.)

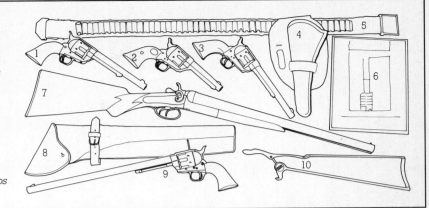

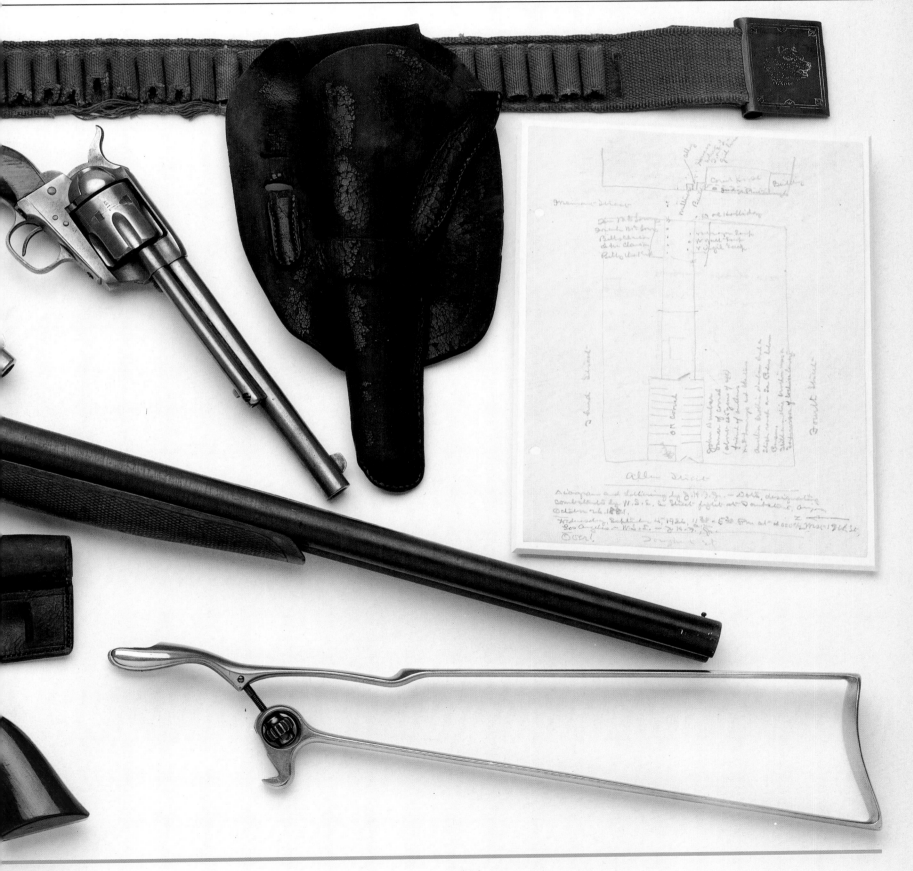

Above: *John P. Clum, Indian agent, with some of his Apache scouts at the San Carlos reservation. When editor of the* Tombstone Epitaph *he supported the Earps, and remained a life-long friend of Wyatt Earp.*

Above: *John Behan and his wife. Behan disliked the Earps who believed he was hindering rather than helping when he tried to stop them from arresting the Clanton–McLaury faction at the corral.*

Earps and Holliday appeared at the end of the street, walking in line abreast. 'Stay here,' he said, and hurried to meet them.

'For God's sake, don't go down there,' he begged. Virgil stared hard at him, then pushed him aside. 'I'm going to disarm them,' he said and the four men moved forward. Behan yelled at them to go back but he was ignored. Virgil, well aware that the situation could erupt into violence, had appointed his brothers and Holliday as deputy city marshals. Some historians think that Virgil genuinely wanted to disarm the men at the corral, but others believe that Wyatt was determined that there would be a showdown.

In dress and manner, the four Earps exemplified the typical gunfighter: wide-brimmed, low-crowned black hats and long 'Prince Albert' frock coats. Wyatt was armed not with a Colt .45 (or the mythical 'Buntline Special') but a .44 Smith & Wesson New Model No. 3 American which had been presented to him by John P. Clum, editor of the *Epitaph*. In place of a conventional belt and holster he had instructed his tailor to line one of the pockets of his coat with canvas and to wax-rub it so that the pistol would not snag and could be removed in a hurry. The others carried conventional .45 Colt 'Peacemakers'.

As the Earps approached, the Clantons and McLaurys grouped themselves on Fremont Street, almost directly in front of Fly's home and gallery, and on open ground outside rather than inside the O.K. Corral as some have claimed. When the two factions were about eight feet apart silence fell, broken only

when Billy Claiborne suddenly fled to Fly's home where he was joined by Behan.

John Behan was later to testify that Wyatt Earp started the fight by calling out: 'You sons of bitches, you have been looking for a fight, and now you can have it.' Wyatt, however, maintained that Virgil first ordered them to give up their guns, and when Billy Clanton and Frank McLaury went for their pistols, Virgil yelled: 'Hold, I don't mean that; I have come to disarm you.' Billy Clanton then shouted: 'Don't shoot me, I don't want to fight.' Tom McLaury promptly opened his coat to show that he was not armed, and shouted out to that effect.

Wyatt Earp was to claim that Behan had told them that he had disarmed the men, but the sight of pistols in the hands of Frank McLaury and Billy Clanton convinced him that they were all armed, so he opened fire. Ignoring Billy, he shot Frank whom he regarded as the deadliest of the gang. Two shots were fired almost in unison: Wyatt shot at Frank and Billy Clanton shot at Wyatt. 'I don't know which shot was fired first. We fired almost together. The fight then became general,' Wyatt later stated in evidence. Virgil then ordered them back to the street where Holliday had stationed himself. Ike Clanton took the opportunity to rush up to Wyatt and grab his left arm. Realizing that he was unarmed, Earp told him to fight or

run. Ike ran, narrowly escaping a blast from Holliday's shotgun.

Wyatt's first shot had hit Frank McLaury in the stomach, but he managed to get one shot off before staggering off toward the street. Tom McLaury then dragged his brother's Winchester from its saddle scabbard and took cover behind the terrified horse. Morgan, meanwhile, had managed to put a pistol ball into Billy Clanton's right wrist and another in his chest. The boy staggered back against Fly's Gallery, and tried desperately to use his pistol with the other hand. At that moment, Frank's horse bolted, exposing Tom McLaury to Holliday who fired his second barrel into him, almost knocking him off his feet. As his waistcoat became bloodied, Tom screamed in great agony, staggered into Fremont Street and died.

Virgil, surprisingly, had not yet fired a shot, but he received a ball in the calf of his leg which knocked him to the ground. Billy Clanton was still a threat. Frank McLaury somehow raised himself up and fired at Doc Holliday, who had tossed aside his shotgun and pulled his nickel-plated six-shooter. Both men fired together. Doc missed, but Frank's shot nicked Doc's hip, removing a piece of skin and a part of his pistol holster. Morgan, too, had problems. Billy Clanton, with his last shot, managed

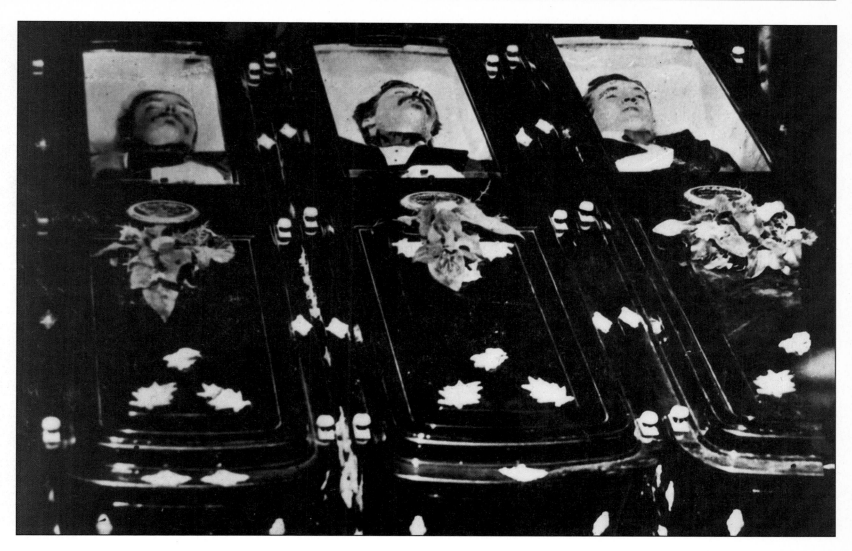

Above: *The McLaurys and Billy Clanton laid out in ornate glass-topped coffins. Some contemporary reports described them as having been 'murdered on the streets of Tombstone', which annoyed the Earps.*

Below: *Tombstone's own version of 'Boot Hill' (the first one was at Hays City, but the most famous one was at Dodge City). In more recent years some spurious epitaphs have appeared to add 'color'.*

to put a ball in his shoulder, and was promptly shot by Wyatt. A sudden silence descended over the scene. Dust and white-grey smoke from the black powder ammunition drifted slowly in the breeze. From his house came Camillus Fly, brandishing a Henry rifle. When no one made any moves, he lowered the gun and knelt beside the still breathing Billy Clanton. Gently he removed the six-shooter from the boy's hand. Billy's last mumbled words were: 'Give me some more cartridges.'

The 'Gunfight at the O.K. Corral' lasted about thirty seconds, and an estimated seventeen shots were fired. At the end,' of the eight men who had been involved three were dead, three were badly wounded and only two of them escaped without a scratch – Wyatt Earp, and Ike Clanton who turned coward and ran. It had a number of repercussions. A preliminary examination before a magistrate proved to be unsatisfactory insofar as the populace were concerned. A warrant for the arrest of the Earps was sworn out by Sheriff Behan and Ike Clanton and a hearing was had before Justice of the Peace Wells Spicer. After listening to all the evidence (which took thirty days), Spicer criticized Virgil's actions in deputizing his brothers and Holliday, even though he did admit that the 'social climate' gave him little choice. But he decided that there was insuffi-·

cient evidence to charge the Earps and Holliday with murder and ordered their release.

Across the state, however, opinion then as now was mixed. Virgil was described by the Acting Attorney General, Samuel F. Phillips, as being 'more disposed to quarrel than to cooperate with local authority'. Dake, however, resisted official attempts to get Virgil fired, and pointed out that although the Earps had not been acting in a Federal capacity, they had nevertheless rid the territory of three out of five members of the 'cowboy [rustler] element'. The press also contained plaudits and a lot of condemnation of the Earps. But closer to home other forces were at work.

Attempts were made upon the lives of the Earps following the shootings by parties not entirely connected with the Clanton–McLaury faction. Morgan was murdered in a saloon and Virgil was maimed by a shotgun blast. The blame for Morgan's murder was laid at the door of Pete Spence and Frank Stilwell, both of whom may have been in the employ of the land grabbers or townsite fraudsters whose activities remained hidden for years. But regardless of the cause, Wyatt shot Stilwell at Tucson and later killed a man associated with Spence at a camp in the Dragoon mountains.

Tombstone's relief when the Earps quit Arizona was reflected nationwide. The controversy surrounding that O.K. Corral fight has never subsided. But if nothing else, it graphically illustrates the dangers to any community when law and order either does not exist or is manipulated for other purposes. Most people prefer the gavel to the gun.

WITH THEIR BOOTS ON

In the period that witnessed the westward movement, the mining ventures, the railroads, the Indian wars and the immortalizing of the cowboy, the ubiquitous 'man-killer' or 'gunfighter' achieved a notoriety of his own. But few of those who became famous lived to a ripe old age. Some, like Edward Masterson, Tom Nixon and Tom Smith died in the line of duty, while others, such as Hickok, Stoudenmire, and the likes of Jesse James and Billy the Kid, were murdered either because of their reputations or for financial or personal gain. Of those that survived, perhaps Wyatt Earp was one of the few who, in old age, was lifted from obscurity to become 'heroic', not for what he actually did but for what he symbolized.

As early as 8 March 1879, the Dodge City *Globe* had forecast both the end of the cattle trade and a determined effort to 'civilize' the West:

> There is a class, still a large one . . . which looks with horror upon the approach of manners, customs and ideas tending to drive out the 'frontier' character[is]tics of Dodge. They look with profound contempt upon a town whose police officers are not walking arsenals. They look back with regret to the time when 'a drink was a quarter and a cigar two bits'. They are not such bad fellows after all; but they do not long for a quiet life. They are not so many as they were. Some have lately felt the cordon of grangers pressing upon them and they have flitted; some to [Las] Vegas, some to Silver Cliff, and some to Leadville.

The message was plain: change was inevitable. And by the middle 1880s police forces were being issued with uniforms. In effect, the West had adopted an Eastern appearance. The change was subtle but significant. And as its 'wildness' retreated, so did the frontier image. Gone was the familiar broad-brimmed hat, white shirt and open waistcoat, and one or a pair of pistols openly displayed. Indeed, were such a character to be seen by the turn of the century, many people would have been alarmed. Only later, when those who lived through the era grew old and reminiscent about the old days, was there any regret for their passing. Today, of course, the man with the large hat and prominently displayed pistols is the image most people cherish of what to them was indeed the Age of the Gunfighter.

Above: *There were other Boot Hills, this one at Virginia City, Montana Territory. It appears sparsely populated, but it was a constant reminder to gunfighters of their own and others' mortality.*

Right: *N.C. Wyeth's heroic vision of the West, 'The Last Stand', painted for C.P. Connolly's* The Story of Montana. *If the mode of dress is more appropriate to the early 1900s than to the 1880s, the elegiac tone of* the painting is quite unmistakable. Evident too is the dramatic action taking place around the lone figure who stands amid towering mountains, smoke drifting from the barrel of his rifle.

BIBLIOGRAPHY

(Not included in the bibliography are the numerous newspapers cited in the text)

Boessenecker, John. *Badge and Buckshot: Lawlessness in Old California*. Norman, Oklahoma, 1988.

Brown, J. Ross. *Adventures in Apache Country: A Tour Through Arizona and Sonora, with Notes on the Silver Regions of Nevada*. New York, 1869.

Burton, Art. *Black, Red, and Deadly: Black and Indian Gunfighters of the Indian Territories*. Austin, Texas, 1991.

Dalton, Emmett. *Beyond the Law*. N.P., 1918.

DeArment, Robert K. *Knights of the Green Cloth*. Norman, Oklahoma, 1982.

DeMattos, Jack. *Mysterious Gunfighter: The Story of Dave Mather*. College Station, Texas, 1992.

Dimsdale, Thomas. *The Vigilantes of Montana*. Norman, Oklahoma, 1953.

Dugan, Mark. *Tales Never Told Around The Campfire: True Stories of Frontier America*. Athens, Ohio, 1992.

Durham, Philip C., and Everett L. Jones. *The Negro Cowboys*. Lincoln, Nebraska, 1983.

Dykstra, Robert R. *The Cattle Towns*. New York, 1968.

Egloff, Fred R. *El Paso Lawman G. W. Campbell*. College Station, Texas, 1982.

Edwards, John B. *Early Days in Abilene*. Abilene, 1940.

Fellman, Michael. *Inside War: The Guerrilla Conflict in Missouri During the American Civil War*. New York, 1989.

Forrest, Earle R. *Arizona's Dark and Bloody Ground*. London, 1953.

Freeman, G. D. (edited and annotated by Richard Lane). *Midnight and Noonday: Or the Incidental History of Southern Kansas and the Indian Territory, 1871–1890*. Norman, Oklahoma, 1984.

Gard, Wayne. *Frontier Justice*. Norman, Oklahoma, 1949.

Goldstein, Norman. *Marshal: The Story of the U.S. Marshals Service*. New York, 1991.

Hardin, John Wesley. *The Life of John Wesley Hardin*. Seguin, Texas, 1896.

Hendricks, George D. *The Bad Man of the West*. San Antonio, Texas, 1950.

Jordan, Philip D. *Frontier Law and Order*. Lincoln, Nebraska, 1970.

Knight, Oliver. *Fort Worth: Outpost on the Trinity*. Norman, Oklahoma, 1953.

Krakel, Dean F. *The Saga of Tom Horn*. Laramie, Wyoming, 1954.

Lake, Stuart N. *Wyatt Earp: Frontier Marshal*. Boston, Mass., 1931.

Lamar, Howard R. (ed.). *The Reader's Encyclopedia of the American West*. New York, 1977.

McCoy, Joseph G. *Historic Sketches of the Cattle Trade of the West and Southwest*. (ed. Ralph P. Bieber). Glendale, California, 1940.

McGivern, Edward. *Fast and Fancy Revolver Shooting*. Chicago, Ill., 1975.

McGrath. Roger. *Gunfighters, Highwaymen & Vigilantes: Violence on the Frontier*. Berkeley, California, 1984.

Masterson, William B. *Famous Gun Fighters of the Western Frontier*. Annotated and illustrated by Jack DeMattos. Monroe, Washington, 1982.

Miller, Nyle H., and Joseph W. Snell. *Why the West Was Wild*. Topeka, Kansas, 1963 (republished in an abridged form as *Great Gunfighters of the Kansas Cowtowns, 1867–1886*. Lincoln, Nebraska, 1966).

Pitts, Dr J. R. S. *Life and Confession of the Noted Outlaw James Copeland*. Jackson, Mississippi, 1980.

Rasch, Philip J. 'These Were the Regulators,' in *'Ho, for the Great West!'* (The Silver Jubilee Publication of the English Westerners' Society). London, 1980.

Rosa, Joseph G. *They Called Him Wild Bill: The Life and Adventures of James Butler Hickok*. Norman, Oklahoma, 1964, 1974.

Rosa, Joseph G. *The Gunfighter: Man or Myth?* Norman, Oklahoma, 1969.

Rosa, Joseph G. *Guns of the American West*. London, 1985.

Rosa, Joseph G., and Robin May. *Gunsmoke: A Study of Violence in The Wild West*. London, 1977.

Rosa, Joseph G., and Waldo E. Koop. *Rowdy Joe Lowe: Gambler with a Gun*. Norman, Oklahoma, 1989.

Secrest, William B. *Dangerous Men: Gunfighters, Lawmen and Outlaws of Old California*. Fresno, Cal., 1976.

Settle, William A., Jr. *Jesse James Was His Name*. Columbia, Mo., 1966.

Snell, Joseph W. *Painted Ladies of the Cowtown Frontier*. Kansas City, Missouri, 1965.

Sonnichsen, C. L. *I'll Die Before I Run*. New York, 1951.

Streeter, Floyd B. *Prairie Trails & Cow Towns*. New York, 1963.

Turner, Frederick Jackson. *The.Frontier in American History*. New York, 1921.

Webb, Walter Prescott, *The Texas Rangers: A Century of Frontier Defense*. Austin, Texas, 1965.

Webb, Walter Prescott, *The Great Plains*. Boston, Mass., 1931.

Wright, Robert M. *Dodge City The Cowboy Capital*. Wichita, Kansas, 1913.

PERIODICALS

Cunningham, Gary L. 'Gambling in the Kansas Cattle Towns: A Prominent and Somewhat Honorable Profession.' *Kansas History: A Journal of the Central Plains*, Vol. 5 (Spring, 1982), No. 1.

Kane, Robert A. 'The D.A. vs. S.A. Controversy.' *Outdoor Life*, Vol. XVII, No. 6 (June, 1906).

Nichols, Col. George Ward. 'Wild Bill.' *Harper's New Monthly Magazine*, Vol. XXXIV, No. CCI (Feb., 1867).

Woody, Clara T., and Milton L. Schwartz. 'War in Pleasant Valley.' *The Journal of Arizona History*, Vol. 18 (Spring, 1977), No. 1.

MANUSCRIPTS

Author's correspondence and Western files by subject.

Records of the city councils of Abilene, Dodge City, Ellsworth, Newton, and Wichita (Microfilm copies, Kansas State Historical Society, Topeka, Kansas).

Right: *Emmett Dalton, survivor of Coffeyville, in Hollywood role.*

Below: *Pair of Colt Model 1851 revolvers, handles engraved by Gustave Young.*

INDEX

Page numbers in **bold** indicate illustrations or mentions in captions.

Below: *Playing cards; rattlesnake skin necktie; bone-handled knife.*

Dake, Crawley P. 179, 185
Dale, Ed **8**
Daley Claim **18**
Dalton, Adeline 46
Dalton, Bill 47
Dalton, Bob 14, **15**, 15, 27, 46–50, **47**, **50**
Dalton, Emmett 14, **15**, 27, 46–50, **47**
Dalton, Frank 46
Dalton, Grat 14, **15**, 27, 46–50, **50**
Dalton, Lewis 46
Dalton, Littleton 47
Daly, John 27
Daniels, Ben **137**
Daniels, James **14**
Daugherty, Roy 'Arkansas Tom' **47**
Davis, Alexander **133**
Davis, John G. 60
Deadwood 113, **159**
Deger, Lawrence E. **120**
Delano 110, 127
Denver **100**, 113, 158, 162
Dixon, William **107**
Dodge City **11**, **56**, 56–7, 60, 64, **100**, **103**, 103, 107, 110, 113, 120–1, 128, **128**, **129**, **137**, 142, **149**, **162**, 162, 163, **164**, 164–7, **166**
Dodge City Peace Commission **6**, **121**, 121
Dolan, James J. 77, **78**, 78, 82, **83**
Doolin, William M. **15**, **47**, 47
Doy, John 33

E

Earp, James 128, 179
Earp, Morgan 11, **134**, 162, **180**, 180, 181, 184–5
Earp, Virgil 11, **134**, 179, **180**, 180, 181, 184, 185
Earp, Wyatt 11, **107**, **120**, 120, **121**, 121, 128, **134**, 134, 147, 152, 162, 163, 168–9, 179–80, **180**, 181, **184**, 184–5, 186
Edwards, John B. 57, 106, 137, 142
El Paso **53**, 53, 148, 157, 168–73
Elder, James **106**
Elliott, Charles Loring 'Portrait of Colonel Samuel Colt' **22**
Ellsworth **101**, 102, **103**, 107, 110, **111**, 111–12, 125, **126**, 135, 142–7, **175**, 175

F

Farnsworth, W. K. **23**
Fetherstun, John 31
feuds 76, 84–7, 92–3
firearms, control 110, 175
Fisher, John 'King' **147**
Fly, C. S. **179**, 185
Ford, Robert 44–5
Forrest, Earle R. 50, 84–5
Forsyth, Rev. Alexander John 19
Forsythe, V. C. untitled painting **13**
Fort Dodge **56**, 57
Fort Harker **111**
Fort Smith 46, **136**
Fort Stanton **78**, 82
Fort Sumner **96**, 96
Fort Worth 60–64
Free State Army **32**, 32

G

Gadsden Purchase 76
gambling 111, 113, 116–27, 128, **163**, 163, 166, 167
Gardner, Alexander **111**
Garrett, Pat **77**, **79**, 79, **82**, 82, 83, 148
Gird, Richard **179**, 179
Gold Room, Newton 112
gold rush 10, 18, 27, 30
Goldsby, Crawford 'Cherokee Bill' **136**

Gollings, William
'Fight at the Roundup Saloon' **116**
Gonzales 53
Goodnight, Charles **96**, 96–7
Goodnight–Loving Trail 96–7, **100**
Graham, Anne Melton **85**
Graham, Billy 87
Graham, Thomas **76**, 84, **85**, 86, 87
Graham, Will Hicks 27
Graham, Tewksbury feud 84–7
guerrillas **15**, **33**, **36**, 36–7, **37**
gunfighters, speed on the draw 156–8

H

Hand, Dora **146**, 146
Hardin, John Wesley **15**, **52**, 52–3, 68, **92**, 92–3, 102, 148, 157
Harpers Ferry 33
Harris, William H. 120, **121**, 163
Hartman, Louis C. **137**
Harvey, Colonel James A. 33, 45
Hashknife Outfit 86
Hays, Colonel Jack 22, 23
Hays City **101**, 121, 133, 142, 157, 159
Helm, Jack 92–3
Hendricks, George D. 158
Henry, B. Tyler 106
Henry, E. E. **97**
Henry, Stuart 126, 140, 141
Henry, Theodore C. 140
Henry rifles 106–7
Herrera, Manuela **82**
Hickok, Wild Bill **11**, 11, 13, 56, **107**, 110, **111**, 121, **124**, 124, **125**, 128, 134, **135**, 136, 137, 140, **141**, 141–2, 148, 156, **157**, 157, **159**, 159, **174**, 174–8, 186
Hockensmith, Clark **37**
Hogue, Ed 146–7
'Hole in the Wall' 69–73
cabin **70–71**
homesteaders 88–9
Hoover, George M. 112
Hopkinson, G. S. 'Oliver F. Winchester' **107**
Horn, Tom **14**, 64–8, **65**, **68**

I

Indian Territory 32, 46, 136–7
Indians 32, 76, 132
deputy marshals **136**, 136–7
Ives, George 30

J

Jacobs, William **85**, 87
James, Frank 40, 41, 44, **45**, 45, 73
James, Jesse 14, **15**, **36**, **40**, 40–45, **44**, 73, 186
James Robert 40
James, Zerelda 40
Jarrett, Captain John **36**
Jayhawkers **33**, 33
Jennison, Colonel C. R. **37**, 37
Johnson County cattle war 88–9
Jones, 'Conk' 121, 156
judges **133**, **135**, **136**, 136
Junction City 121

K

Kansas 10, 14, 36–7, 56, 101, 120, 164
Kansas City 96, 102, 128, 141, 142, 157
Kansas–Missouri border wars 32–9

Kansas Pacific Railway **97**, 97, 127
Kelley, James **146**, 146
Kelly, Ed 45
Kelly, James 143
Kenedy, James 143, 146
Kenedy, Miflin 143
Ketchum, Thomas 'Black Jack' **73**
Kilpatrick, Benjamin 'the Tall Texan' 72
Kimmel, Glendolene 68
Kloeher, John J. 50
Krempkau, Gus 172

L

Lane, James H. **15**, **32**, 32, 33
Las Vegas **82**, **163**, 163
law and order 130–35
marshals 136–7
peacemakers 140–47
Lawrence 32, **37**, 37, **44**
Lay, William Ellsworth 'Elzy' **73**
LeFors, Joe **65**, 65, 68
legal system 133–4
Liddell, Richard **44**, 45
Lincoln County 51
range wars 76–83
Lincoln **60**, 82
Linn, Charles M. 'Buck' 168–9
Little, Theophilus 106, 137
Logan, Harvey 'Kid Curry' 69, **72**, 72
Long Branch saloon **121**, **166**, 166–7
Longabaugh, Harry 'The Sundance Kid' 14, 69, 72–3
Longley, William 68–9, **69**
Loving, Frank 'Cock-eyed Frank' 166–7
Loving, Oliver 96
Lowe, Joseph 'Rowdy Joe' 121, 124–5, **125**
Lowe, Kate 'Rowdy Kate' **125** 125
lynching 26–7, 89

M

McCall, Jack **159**
McCarty, Bridget 79
McCarty, Catherine 79
McCarty, Henry see Billy the Kid
McCarty, Joseph 79
McCarty, Patrick 79
McCoy, Joseph G. 97, 102, **103**, 127, 128, 137, 141
McCoy's Extension, Abilene Trail 97, **100**
McDonald, James H. 140, 141
McGinnis, William see Lay, W. E.
Mclain, M. F. **121**
McLaury, Frank 180, 181
McLaury, Robert 180, 181
McLaury, Thomas 180, 181, 184
McSween, Alexander 77–8, 82–3, **83**
Maddox, Dick **36**
Maddox, George **36**
Maddox, James 61
Madsden, Chris **136**, **137**
Manning, Felix 'Doc' 173
Manning, Frank 172, 173
Manning, Jim 172, **173**, 173
Marais des Cygnes 32, 33
marshals 133, 134
Masterson, Bat **11**, **107**, **120**, 120, **121**, 121, 127, 128, 134, 157, 162–3, **165**, 186
Mather, Dave 'Mysterious Dave' 112, 134, **163**, 163–5, **164**
Maxwell, Pete **79**, 79
Meagher, Mike 126
Medicine Lodge **51**, 51
Mexicans 101–2
Mexico 96, 169
war 10, 22–3

Middleton, John 78, 82
Miles, General Nelson A. 65
Miller, Jacob B. 78
mining 14, **18**, **30**
Missouri 10, 36–7, 96, *and see* Kansas–Missouri border wars
Missouri Compromise 32
Missouri Pacific Railroad 96
Montana 26, 76, **133**
gold rush 27, 30
Moon, Jim 158–9
Moore, Eugenia **47**
Morco, John 146, 175
Morton, William 78, 79
Murphy, Lawrence G. 77, **78**, 83

N

'nesters' 88–9
New Haven Arms Company 106
New Mexico 47, 76, 163, *and see* Lincoln County
Newcomb, George 'Bitter Creek' **47**
Newton 56, 57, 103, 107, **110**, 111, 112, 125, 140, 142, 152
Nichols, Colonel George Ward 157, 174
Nichols, John **37**
Nickell, Kels P. 68
Nickell, Willie 65, 65, 68
Nixon, Cornelia **164**, 164
Nixon, Howard Tracy **164**
Nixon, Thomas C. 112, **134**, **164**, 164–5, 186
Northfield **44**, 44
Norton, Brocky Jack 146

O

O'Day, Tom 69
O'Folliard, Tom **82**
Oklahoma 32, 47, 51, 136
Oklahoma Territory **11**
O.K. Corral **120**, 120, **134**, 162, **179**, 179–85
Old Shell Store, 113, **114–15**
Olive, Isom Prentice 'Print' 143, **146**
Ollinger, Robert **83**, 83
Opera House saloon 164
Oriental saloon 180
Outlaw, Bass **53**, 53
Owens, Commodore Perry **76**, **86**, 87

P

Parker, Judge Isaac 46, **135**, **136**, 137
Paso del Norte **169**, 169
Patent Arms Manufacturing Company 19, 22
Pearl saloon **128**
Petillon, W. F. **121**
Phillips, Samuel F. 185
Pickett, Tom **84**
Pinkerton Detective Agency 41, 65
Pitkin, Governor 162, 163
Place, Etta, 72–3
Pleasant Valley 84, **85**, **86**
Plummer, Henry **30**, 30–31
Poe, John W. **79**, **83**
police 134–5, 137
Pottawatomie Creek 32, 33
Powell, Fred 65, 68
Power, Bill 47, 50
prostitutes 113, 117, **128**, 128–9, **129**

Q

Quantrill, William Clarke **15**, **36**, **37**, 37, 40, **44**

R

railroads 14, **100**
range wars
cattlemen and homesteaders 88–9
Johnson County 76
Lincoln County 76–83

Pleasant Valley 76, 84–7
Ray, Nick 69
Raynor, William P. 168–9
Red Legs **37**, 37
Reeves, Baz **136**, 136–7
Regulators **76**, 82, 137
feuds 92
Johnson County **89**, 89
Remington, Eliphalet 37
Remington, Frederic **13**
Remington New Model Army revolver **36**, 37, 167
Rennick, Robert 'Cowboy Bob' 168–9
revolvers 19–26, 33, **36**, 37, 106, 148
Rhodes, John **85**, 87
Richardson, Levi 166–7
rifles 33, 106–7, 148
Riley, James H. 77–8
roadagents 30–31, **31**, 157
Roberts, Andrew 'Buckshot Bill' 82
Roberts, Jim 87
Roberts, Mose 87
Robertson, Ben 51
Rough Riders 65, **137**
rustling 15, **84**, 84, 88–9, 162

S

St Joseph **33**, 44–5
St Louis 18, 36, 127, 128
saloons 112–13, 120–21, 128
Samuel, Reuben 40
San Antonio **101**, 147
San Francisco 18, 18, 19, 27
Santa Anna 19, 22
Saratoga saloon 112–13
Scarborough, George **63**, 53
Schieffelin, Al **179**, 179
Schieffelin, Ed **179**, 179
Schutz, Solomon 172
Sears, Red 27
Sedalia 96, 102
Selman, John **53**, 53
Seltzer, Olaf C.
'Execution of George Ives' **31**
'Robber's Rock' **30**
'The Vigilantes Oath Organization' **31**
Sharps, Christian 33
sheriffs 133–4, 137
Short, Luke **15**, **61**, **64**, 64, 120–21, **121**, **137**, 163
Silver City **61**, 61
Slade, Joseph Alfred 'Jack' 31, 133
slavery 32–3
Smalley, Ed **65**
Smith, Thomas J. **135**, **140**, 140, 141, 186
Smith, Sheriff William 111
Smith & Wesson 106, 148, 153
Sparrow, Joe **146**
Spence, Pete 180, 185
Spencer, Christopher Miner 106
Spicer, Wells 185
Springfield 36, **174**, 174
squatters' rights associations 132–3
'Squirrel-tooth' Alice **128**
Star saloon 113
Stevens, Lucille 128–9
Stillwell, Frank 180, 185
Stoudenmire, Dallas **169**, 169–73, 186
Sughrue, Michael **165**
Sughrue, Patrick **165**, 165
Sundance Kid, see Longabaugh, Harry
Sutton, Billy **92**, 92–3
Sutton, Michael **165**, 165
Sutton–Taylor feud 92–3

T

Taylor, Buck 92
Taylor, Charles 92
Taylor, Creed **92**
Taylor, Jim **77**, **92**, 93

Taylor, Philip **77**, **92**
Taylor, William T. 92
Tewkesbury, Ed 84, **85**, 87
Tewkesbury, Eva 87
Tewkesbury, Jim 86, 87
Tewkesbury, John **76**, **85**, **86**, 87
Texas 22, 22–3, 45, 53, 68, 76, 92–3, 101, 125, 135
cattle trails 96–100, **100**
Texas Rangers 19, 22, **23**, **53**, 53, 135, 135, 169, 172
Thomas, Heck **135**, **136**
Thompson, Ben 120, **135**, 146–7, **147**, 157–8
Thompson, Billy **101**, 120, **143**, 146–7, **147**, 158, 175
Tilghman, William 'Bill' **11**, 11, **106**, **134**, **136**, 164
Timberline **129**
Tombstone 120, 120, **134**, 148, **164**, **179**, 179–85
Topeka 32, 142
Tunstall, John 76, **77**–83
Tuolumne County **18**
Tutt, Davis K. 157, 174–8
Tuttle, Perry 111
Twain, Mark 31, 117

U

Union Army 36–7, 157
Union Pacific Railway 19, **73**, 127
Utter, Charley **159**

V

vigilantes 14, 18–19, 26–7, 30–31, 89, 132, **133**, 133, 137
Virginia City 18, **30**, 30, **16**, **186**

W

Wages, Gale H. 45
Waite, Fred 60
Walker, Captain Samuel 23
Walker, William **27**, 27
Wallace, General Lew 83
Watson, Ella 'Cattle Kate' **76**, **88**, 88–9
Webley 'Bulldog' pistols 148–9
Webster, Alonzo **120**
Wells Fargo 19, **149**, 149
Western Trail **100**
Wheeler, Ben 51, 60, **101**
White, Marshall 148
Whitney, Chauncey B. **101**, 142–3, **143**, 146–7, **147**, 175
Whitney, Eli 23, 26
Wichita **56**, 56, 100, **101** 107, **110**, 110, 113, 125, **127**, 127, 142, 152
Wichita–Newton Trail **100**
Widenmann, Robert 78
Wild Bunch 69, 69, **73**
Williams, Captain James 31
Williams, Captain John 23
Winchester, Oliver F. 106, **107**, 107
Winchester rifles **23**, 106–7
Wolcott, Major Frank 76,**89**, 89
Wyeth, N. C.
'The Admirable Outlaw' **10**
'The Gunfight' **148**
'The James Brothers in Missouri' **41**
'The Last Stand' **186**
'Wild Bill Hickok at Cards' **125**
Wyoming 69, 76, 88–9
Wyoming Stock Growers' Association 88

Y

Younger, Cole **15**, 41, **44**, 44
Younger, James 41, **44**, 44
Younger, John 41, **44**, 44
Younger, Robert 41, **44**, 44

PICTURE CREDITS

Handcuffs; deputy sheriff's badge made from back of fob watch.